PRUDENCE CRANDALL
A BIOGRAPHY

by

MARVIS OLIVE WELCH

Gift of
Marvis Welch

JASON PUBLISHERS
MANCHESTER, CONNECTICUT

B
Crandall

1237

First Edition

JASON PUBLISHERS
153 Eldridge Street
Manchester, CT 06040

Printed in the U.S.A.
Printers Inc, West Hartford, Connecticut

Dedicated to
my nieces and nephews
Nancy, Dorothy, Thomas and Dennis

FOREWORD

For several years I was responsible for promoting the ideas and ideals of civil rights. Seeking historical precedence in this connection I came upon the case of Prudence Crandall. It seemed to me that a woman who took a strong stand for the education of Black girls in 1833 would have done other interesting things after she was forced to close her school. She seemed worthy of further study.

There were discrepancies in the few articles about her so I decided to use only primary sources in my research. The search covered many months and many miles. Starting in Hope Valley, Rhode Island where she was born in 1803 I followed her into the five states where she lived to the Kansas prairie town where she died in 1890. Public documents supplied much information. The Connecticut State Library contains complete records of her trials which show the vigor with which she was prosecuted and defended by outstanding lawyers and judges.

Diaries and documents, legends and letters were provided by descendants of Prudence's brother Hezekiah. Several of these family members related anecdotes told to them by their grandparents who knew Prudence and in some cases lived with her when they were children.

A person with wide social, religious and political interests, Prudence was frustrated and restricted by the limits encountered by women. She was sufficiently versatile to remove from the comparative comfort of a settled New England town to the prairie frontier where she developed a successful farm with the help of a teenaged nephew. She was called a "royal queen among women" by her step daughter and "an old squash head" by her husband. Her opponents considered her "obstinate and unreasonable." One of her white male students lauded her as "the Mother of Liberty."

In preparing this book I have taken some liberties with traditional form. In using or quoting letters to, from or about her, I have retained the original spelling. Spelling patterns change. Some of the words we might identify as incorrect were acceptable according to an 1824 edition of the dictionary. Instead of line by line notes I have summarized sources. This provides information for those who may have a scholarly interest and does not interrupt the flow of the story for other readers.

I hope readers will find pleasure in getting to know Prudence Crandall from this book. There was much joy and satisfaction in researching and writing it.

ACKNOWLEDGMENTS

A great deal of material for this book was obtained from members of the Crandall family. I am very grateful to them for this and their continuing friendship.

Throughout the years I have found librarians to be consistently co-operative and congenial. The libraries I have used include the American Baptist Historical Society, Rochester (NY); Boston Public Library; Brooklyn (Ct) Library; Connecticut College Library, New London, Ct; The Connecticut Historical Society and the Connecticut State Library both in Hartford; the Cornell University Libraries, Ithaca, NY; Howard University Library, Washington, D.C.; Kansas State Library, Topeka; the Marine Historical Society, Mystic, Ct; the New Haven Colony Historical Society; the Quaker Archives in the libraries of the Moses Brown School and Brown University, Providence; Suffield (Ct) Public Library; Trinity College — Watkinson Collection; Windham (Ct) Public Library; and Yale University.

Individuals who have been helpful are too numerous to mention. Those who have given much time, effort and thought to the project deserve recognition. Anne L. Hess was my traveling companion and typed the first draft. Clare B. Weir provided valuable editorial suggestions and typing. I drew frequently on the expertise of Rheta A. Clark, educator and librarian. David White, Curator of the Museum of Connecticut History, generously shared his research findings with me. Mr. and Mrs. Charles R. Underhill and Mrs. Lewis White of Canterbury provided information about the town and the surrounding area. Mrs. Parizo typed the final copy. Lois Norcross helped with editorial and technical suggestions.

TABLE OF CONTENTS

ILLUSTRATIONS

PRUDENCE CRANDALL
from portrait in Uris Library, Cornell University

CHAPTER ONE
BEGINNINGS

IT was spring in 1813. Pardon Crandall stood at his gate talking with his neighbor Mr. Arnold. For a while they discussed the problems occasioned by the war. As they began to converse about a business matter, Pardon turned and told his little daughter Prudence who was standing nearby to go up to the house. To his surprise, and possibly her own, she said, "I won't!" Without a moment's hesitation, Pardon took firm hold of her ear and led her to the door. He called to his wife,

"Esther, take this child!"

Esther exclaimed, "Oh, Prudence, what hast thou done to provoke thy father?"

Her nine year old daughter replied, "I only wanted to hear father and Mr. Arnold talk. 'Kiah stays there. Why can't I?"

" 'Kiah is a lad and will soon be a man. He needs to know about business but that is not necessary for thee. Now, sit down and do a stint on thy sampler."

Prudence never forgot this incident. She recounted it many years later to her brother Hezekiah's granddaughters.

It was only a few weeks later that Prudence and her mother found out what Pardon and Mr. Arnold had planned. Pardon had decided to move his family to Canterbury in Connecticut where he had bought a farm in November of 1812. Mr. Arnold would rent their house in Hope Valley. This decision made Esther very unhappy.

For Esther, Hope Valley, a village in the town of Hopkinton, Rhode Island, was all the world she wanted. On the crest of a nearby hill stood the commodious house her father had built in 1778. To this house Hezekiah Carpenter had brought his young bride, his third wife, Prudence Johnson. Here Esther and her brother John were born. They grew up with the children of their half-brother, Daniel Carpenter. In the big house Esther was married to Pardon Crandall when she was 15 and he 21. All the excitement and joy of her wedding was a treasured memory. How proud she had been of her high-waisted black satin wedding dress and the bright red cloak and bonnet!

Her father was so dignified — tall and straight — in his knee pants and cutaway coat. Her mother wore a gray striped dress of soft silk. Although December 19th was a very cold day, relatives and friends had come from miles around. Pardon's parents, Christopher and Tacy Crandall, came from Westerly with his brothers Christopher and Asa and his sisters Prudence and Esther. Tacy's many relatives, Babcocks and Frinks, from Stonington were there. Crandalls from Newport and Carpenters from

Swansea were present to witness the ceremony performed by Elder Ellet Locks, a Baptist.

Pardon seemed very wise and mature to his young bride. He was respected in the community as an industrious, intelligent young man. Experienced in farming and in the work of iron foundries owned by his father and his father-in-law, he was well prepared to provide for a wife and family.

Through the marriage of Pardon and Esther, two old American families were drawn together. Alice Carpenter Southworth came to America to become the second wife of Governor William Bradford. Her brothers soon joined her. Pardon Crandall had heard many times the story of his ancestors. John Crandall came from England in 1635. With Roger Williams and other Baptists he was driven from Massachusetts Colony into the wilderness which became Rhode Island. Settling first in Providence then moving on to Newport, he had eventually participated in the purchase of Misquamicut from the Indians. A leader of his church and his community he made unpopular forays into Massachusetts and Connecticut to preach Baptist doctrine. He was one of a committee of men who went to England in 1663 to secure the charter from King Charles II, which granted the colony of Rhode Island political and religious freedom forever.

Joseph, one of John Crandall's five sons, from whom Pardon descended was married to Deborah Hubbard Burdick whose forebears included Thomas Hubbard, one of the martyrs burned at the stake in 1555 for refusing to recant his Protestant adherence on orders from Bloody Mary, Queen of Scots. The Crandall family was numerous and prosperous in and around Westerly through 115 years from 1663 to the time of Pardon's birth in 1778.

Esther's father was descended from William Carpenter who came from England on the Bevis in 1638. His family was among the early settlers in Rehoboth and Swansea in Massachusetts. Esther's father, Hezekiah, was born in Swansea in 1725 and moved to Hopkinton, Rhode Island as one of its first settlers in 1745. In Hopkinton, he built iron mills for making household utensils and farm equipment, using water power supplied by the Wood River. Here, in the Hope Valley section of Hopkinton, he built a substantial house for his family and in 1799 built a small house adjacent to his, for his daughter Esther. His declining years were cheered by her young children. Hezekiah died in 1809.

After 14 years in Hope Valley, Pardon had decided to take his family to Connecticut. Rich, level land was available for farming in Canterbury. A cotton mill, grist mills and mills for processing bog iron were in operation in this thriving town in which nearly 3000 people were living. Pardon and his family had espoused the Quaker faith within recent years and in Canterbury and nearby Plainfield there were a number of Quaker families. These facts and an indefinable restlessness caused Pardon to plan to leave Hope Valley as soon as possible after the birth of his fourth child.

The children faced the change with mixed feelings. Hezekiah, nearly 13, liked the idea of owning a better farm. He was capable of doing a man's work and, like his father, was energetic and ambitious.

Prudence was a dainty, thoughtful little girl, not quite ten years old. Excited at the thought of having a new home, she was sad to think of leaving her cousins and the other children with whom she had attended the Friends' school at Richmond. She was aware of her mother's unhappiness about moving, having overheard conversations between her mother and grandmother. She wondered why her mother did not protest against the move. She knew that her father made the decisions and rules for the family but leaving their home was such a big change it seemed that her mother's feelings were deserving of more consideration. She pondered over this as she rocked the cradle of her baby sister, Hannah Almyra. Hannah was just three weeks old, having been born on June 27th. Prudence fairly glowed with love for her, watching every move of the tiny hands, alarmed by the slightest whimper.

Grave young Reuben thought he would miss the banks of Brushy Brook and the Wood River where he gathered flowers and berries and watched the squirrels and chipmunks. His father told him of a wider river — the Quinebaug — near their new home.

On the last day in July the Crandalls moved to their new home. Early in the morning the wagons were loaded. Grandmother Carpenter and Uncle John and the neighbors gathered about to say good-bye. They would seldom see each other from now on since 30 miles was a day's journey and a conscientious farmer could not often afford a day away from his work.

Reuben rode in the oxcart driven by Hezekiah. This carried the larger furnishings. Pardon and Esther and their little daughters rode in the horse-drawn wagons. Up the steep hills of Voluntown the road wound through thick, dark woods. Neither Esther nor the younger children had ever been this far north before. Visits with their relatives had taken them occasionally to Westerly and Stonington. The children looked with mounting excitement at everything they passed. Esther was aware only that each turn of the wheels took her farther from her cherished home. Pardon concentrated on keeping the horse moving at a slow pace so that the oxcart would not be left too far behind.

By noon they had reached Preston where they stopped to eat their lunch of bread and cheese. While the horse and oxen were being fed and given a few minutes of rest, Prudence and Reuben explored the woods nearby.

After crossing the river at Jewett City, the road was comparatively level. On either side were long stone walls surrounding neat, prosperous looking farms. Pardon named the owners of some of the homes they passed. He knew several who were Quakers. Their reputation as farmers was well known. Merchants in Norwich advertised "Quaker seeds at Quaker prices" during the early spring.

Late in the afternoon the Crandalls reached their new home. Set on a rise several feet from the road was the large house with four chimneys. Shaded by great trees it looked very inviting to the hot travelers. Esther's spirits rose as she saw the elegant house. Bustling about were neighbors who were preparing a supper for the newcomers.

Mrs. Phinne, Mrs. Frost and Mrs. Ensworth had spread out pots of beans, loaves of bread, a large ham and cookies and cakes. As soon as the Crandalls arrived the women drew up from the well a bucket in which they had placed butter and milk. A cooled jug of cider was brought up from the cellar. As they shared their evening meal, the women told Esther and her young children about Canterbury — the six stores near the Green, the skill of Dr. Harris, the mills where cotton and silk, fabrics and hats and iron implements were made. Also, there was the daily stage coach and the social activities, many of which centered around the Congregational church.

The men set up the cord beds and carried the feather beds into the large chambers. The trestle table, its bench and several chairs were placed in the kitchen and Esther unwrapped her dishes and arranged her iron kettles and bread pans near the fireplace. Prudence and Reuben explored the eight large rooms, the cupboards near the fireplace, the barn and other outbuildings.

It was dark when the neighbors left. The Crandalls settled into the home in which some of them would spend the next twenty-five years.

On Sunday, Pardon took Hezekiah, Prudence and Reuben to the Quaker meeting house on Black Hill. Here they met Doctor Green who conducted the Friends' school. Here, too, they met the Kinnes, and Cornells who were to have important parts in their future. From the crest of Black Hill they could look across the Quinebaug and see the farms and shed-like mills of Canterbury. The road from the meeting house was shaded by rows of large maple trees. At the foot of the hill they turned onto the Windham turnpike and a few rods farther they turned left. The magnificent Congregational church, which had been built in 1805, dominated the Green. Across from it was the spacious Paine house.

Prudence and her brothers quietly took in all these points of interest as they passed. Pardon was deep in thought and discouraged questions and conversation from the children. Prudence made a full report of all she had seen to her mother as they prepared the evening meal, while the boys helped their father tend the cows.

Prudence had her daily duties. For an hour each day she did her stint — working her sampler with bright thread, forming the letters of the alphabet in tiny cross stitches on the scrim she had woven under the direction of her grandmother in Hopkinton. She helped her mother with many household tasks, learning to cook and to care for the kitchen implements. She watched over her baby sister. Whenever she was freed from these responsibilities, she joined Reuben in his explorations. They roamed through the fields and woods of their father's property or crossed the road and went down to the banks of the Quinebaug. The broad, clear river was shallow during August but had a reputation for ferocious flooding at times. Reuben, as usual, gathered and studied the flowers, leaves and seeds of every weed and bush. Prudence picked bouquets and made daisy garlands.

A few days after they were settled in their new home, Pardon took his family to Stephen Coit's store on the Green. The children were fascinated by the variety of articles displayed. There were the usual barrels of flour and stocks of spices. There were also glass lamps, candles, ink-stands, slates, quills and threads, yarns and piece goods. Shelves and counters, walls and corners were crowded with boxes and bottles. Stephen Coit was an energetic young man who kept busy weighing and measuring the goods, and methodically entering each item sold in a large leather-bound ledger.

In addition to the supplies Esther wanted for the house, Pardon bought Prudence and Reuben slates for their classwork at the Friends' school at Black Hill. Esther thoroughly enjoyed her first outing in Canterbury. The large, well-kept homes indicated that her neighbors were prosperous. Those they met in the store and passed on the road were friendly. The stage with several passengers came by, headed for Chauncey Bacon's Inn. They stopped briefly at the Post Office where Postmaster Gabe Bulkley greeted them cordially.

The Crandalls were soon content in their new surroundings. Pardon took an active part in town affairs as he had in Hopkinton where he had been a Justice of the Peace. Hezekiah worked on his father's farm and occasionally in Fenner's Mill on Mudhole Road. At school, Prudence and Reuben made friends of the children of the Cornell, Kinne and Mason families. As in all Quaker schools, their texts included the George Fox Primer and Anthony Benezet's speller. Esther was busy at home — cooking, sewing, spinning, weaving and doing the countless, endless everyday tasks. As a prudent homemaker she considered as precious, every bit of food and scrap of material. The farm was productive and Pardon planned and provided well for his family, but it was war time and the future was uncertain. Everything which was not required for immediate use was carefully preserved for another time. Little Hannah always fulfilled her family obligation by charming her sister, brothers and parents.

After the war with England ended, Canterbury folks prospered. Blockades were removed and trade with Europe and the Indies was resumed. Pardon bought additional farm property. He took the products of his farm, and lumber milled from his timber lots to Norwich for shipping to the West Indies.

From one of his trips to the wharves he returned with the announcement that he had become a part owner with Gilbert and Barrell in the brig, Hope, a ship built in Wells, Massachusetts in 1802. According to the certificate of registry, it was 68 feet and 11 inches long, 21 feet 4 inches wide and 8 feet 2 inches in depth. It had a tonnage of 102 87/95.

On June 13, 1815, the Crandall family rode to Norwich to see the ship and to watch as it was loaded. The cargo included black and white oak shooks, staves, and many head of cattle. Hezekiah helped the sailors load the freight. Pardon talked at length with David Mitchell, the ship's master. Reuben proudly helped drive the cows and calves onto the dock. They made noisy protest against this venture.

Several weeks later Pardon reported that Mr. Mitchell had sold his return cargo in New York for $11,018.51½. (To Mr. Gilbert's share was added the ½ cent!) The cargo consisted of coffee, sugar and molasses.

Prudence and her brothers traced the course of the Hope with great interest. Its cargo varied on both outgoing and return trips. At one time (the record shows) it carried pigs, corn, potatoes, cheese, gin, leather, staves, shooks, hoops, oats and a bay mare, oil, beef, bread and beans.

Going from Norwich to Guadaloup, Demarary, St. Eustatius or Martinique usually took about 30 days. Sometimes the Hope would stop at Charleston, or New York and dispose of part of the cargo. Provisioning the ship for these trips was quite an enterprise. One bill shows that John Cornell was paid $10.92 for the baking of 875 pounds of bread. (This was apparently just price for the labor expended in the baking process — surely it did not include ingredients.) The length of time of the round trips depended heavily on the weather and winds and how much time was required to dispose of one load of goods and secure items for the return to the states. On one voyage some 30 cows became sick and died on the high seas. A successful voyage usually meant extra sugar and molasses in the Crandall larder as well as great satisfaction for Pardon.

In September 1815 a hurricane struck eastern Connecticut. The Quaker school and meeting house on Black Hill were demolished. In other parts of the community roofs blew off outbuildings, large trees were uprooted and there were losses of crops and, in some places, livestock. The Crandall house escaped damage.

The Quaker families took up a subscription for the rebuilding of the school and meeting house. John Monroe, Sylvester Wicks and Deacon Howland gave 45 acres of land on Black Hill for this purpose. Until the school building was put up, the children met in the home of Dr. Green.

The months slipped by with little change in routine, for the most part, but every once in a while there would be something new and unusual to attract the attention of the Canterbury folks. The Crandall young people were greatly excited when they heard of the exhibit which was to take place on July 1, 1818. An item in the *Norwich Courier* announced: "The majestic animal Columbus — a male Elephant to be seen at Kinny's Hotel, Norwich Landing on Wednesday and Thursday and at Lathrop's Tavern, Norwichtown on Friday and Saturday.

"The Elephant is not only the largest and most sagacous animal in the world but from the peculiar manner in which it takes its food and drinks of every kind in its trunk, is acknowledged to be the greatest natural curiosity ever offered the public. He will draw a cork out of a bottle and drink its contents. The one now offered is a male and the only one ever exhibited in America. He is 7 years old and is upwards of 7 feet high, 10 feet around the body and 16 feet 8 inches from the end of his trunk to the end of his tail. His ears are 2 feet, 1 inch in length.
Admittance 25¢
To be at Canterbury on July 1st."

Pardon was somewhat reluctant to put out enough quarters to permit all the children to see this exhibit. Many hours of work went into the earning of four quarters but since this was an exhibition of one of nature's rare beasts he decided to permit the children to see it. They joined a large number of others — young and old to see this creature in the barn of Chauncey Bacon's hotel.

At about this time newspapers began to carry advertisements for a new product: cooking stoves. A variety of parlor stoves had been available for some time and some local families had Franklin stoves but now there were large stoves with flat tops on which five or six kettles could be placed at one time. Prudence and her mother looked with great interest at the ads and descriptions of Wilson's patent stoves and Stafford cooking stoves. They were delighted when Pardon came from Norwich one day and announced that he had purchased one. The one he chose was quite elegant and had a tank at one end for warm water. Esther was very pleased that Pardon bought this for her but for several days she was timid about using it.

The decision to have a cooking stove, like all decisions affecting the family, was made by Pardon. His authority was usually unquestioned, but once in a great while Esther would follow her own inclination. Pardon had an unalterable objection to seasonal thorough cleaning. He declared it unnecessary; said he "wouldn't have it!" Business affairs took him back to Hopkinton once or twice a year. As soon as he was well on his way, Esther, neighboring women, whom she had alerted, and Prudence would take out the feather beds and beat and air them, then scrub and dust the entire house. All would be back in order when Pardon returned and he never seemed to notice the shine of the furnishings or the gleam of satisfaction in Esther's eyes. Prudence agreed with her mother that such attacks on their living quarters were desirable. She resented her father's dictation in matters which seemingly might be left to Esther.

At the age of 16, Prudence applied for the privilege of "being reared a member of the religious society of the women's monthly meeting" of the Greenwich (R.I.) Friends. She was received as a minor member on August 30, 1819.

Friends in Rhode Island were proud that a new boarding school was being built in Providence. It was located three fourths of a mile from Brown University, on an elevated site. The building was a massive edifice of brick and stone, 52 feet wide, 54 feet long and four stories high. There were two wings 42 by 44 feet. Started as a school for boys, it was shortly open to girls.

Prudence was overjoyed when Pardon decided that she might go to this new school. Here she could take up Latin, natural and intellectual philosophy, moral philosophy, political economy and a course called "Evidence of Christianity." Among the textbooks in use was Whelpley's "Compend of History." This was a very formidable history of the world containing a chart showing what was happening in the world at the time of the prophets of Bibilical note. It also contained the information that "the United States would always be an agricultural country since it had no natural resources."

The rules of the school provided that "unsuitable apparel" would be set aside if sent to the school. "Good habits, plainness in speech and dress" must be observed. There were 135 students at the school. With one exception, they came from the New England states. Prudence's training in this school rounded out her preparation to be a teacher — her avowed ambition.

Upon graduation, she returned to Connecticut and taught at a school in Plainfield. She was so successful that she was well remembered by some of her pupils after more than fifty years.

These were pleasant, happy times for Prudence. She enjoyed visits with Hezekiah's growing family. She spent many hours studying and participated in community activities. She read extensively in Quaker books and tracts but she followed with interest the ideas and activities of other sects.

She listened to the discussion over the appointment of a Unitarian minister in the neighboring town of Brooklyn. The more orthodox Christians held that Rev. May could not be a Christian if he did not believe in the Holy Trinity. The dominance of the Congregational Church had suffered a severe blow in 1818 when the Constitution adopted by the state ruled out a state religion. Congregationalists felt an additional threat from the Baptists whose numbers were increasing in the wake of revivals. All of these developments Prudence watched with interest. On her visits home she had long discussions about religion with Reuben and her father.

Pardon bought a large new Bible and set himself the task of reading it from cover to cover. Members of the family were shocked when one evening he slammed his Bible shut, slashed its cover with a knife and shouted, "It's a damned lie!" Stunned to silence, no one quite dared question or challenge his statement. After he stalked from the room, Esther, trembling at such blasphemy, retrieved the Bible and carefully hid it in a chest. Reuben, whose interest in religion was as keen as his interest in science was greatly troubled about his father's state of grace for the rest of his life.

Reuben had been tutored by Dr. Andrew Harris in Canterbury in those subjects which he could not take up at the Quaker school. In 1824 he entered Yale and four years later received his degree as a doctor of medicine.

Hezekiah had worked for his father until he was 21. Then he had secured work at Fenner's cotton mill. In 1825 on April 14th, he had married Clarissa Cornell in a Quaker wedding. Friends and relatives of the bride and groom signed as witnesses to this event. The newlyweds had settled in Plainfield for a few years. In 1829, Hezekiah bought a farm and a small cotton mill in Canterbury. Hezekiah's family (including two daughters and a son) moved into their home on Mudhole Road.

In a section of Canterbury east of the river stood Daniel Packer's large woolen mill. This section became known as Packerville. When a Baptist church was built it became known as the Packerville Baptist Church. Rev. Levi Kneeland was installed as its first minister. Here Prudence attended a number of revival services and, after much soul searching, decided to affiliate with it. On July 3, 1830 she was baptized by immersion in the Quinebaug River. Prudence found this a profoundly moving experience for she felt that she had returned to the faith for which some of her forbears had endured severe trials. Reuben, who was living in New York State, carried on extensive correspondence with Prudence, questioning her minutely and exhorting her to have great care for the good of her soul.

CHAPTER TWO
CANTERBURY

THE period between 1815 and 1830 was a relatively prosperous time for New Englanders. Shipping and farming were lucrative. Manufacturing establishments were expanding and flourishing. Canterbury shared in the cultural and economic trends of the period. The village leaders took steps to shape up the town by controlling the wandering of domestic animals. In the Town Clerk's Record Book November 13, 1815, entry states:

> *Voted that Swine well wringed except boar swine over three months old will be permitted to go at large on all the Highways and Commons of the town the year ensuing within the limits as follows; viz on the Woodstock and Norwich turnpike road between the dwelling houses and roads near Job Rood's turning shop, on the Windham and Plainfield turnpike road between the road which crosses the same running from Samuel Bacons to Safford's mill on the Norwich road between the dwelling house of Dr. Walter Hough on the Buswell Road and on the Common or Green so called about the meeting house of the First Society of Canterbury. If any swine boar more than 3 months old should be found at large on any of the Commons in town or on the highway thereof the same shall be forfeited and shall thereafter belong unto the person who shall take up the same. If the swine last aforesaid should be of more value than $3 then the same shall not be forfeited but the same may be impounded and the owner thereof shall forfeit any pay to the person or persons who shall impound the same and the sum of $3 to be recovered by suit before any proper court. Voted that the Selectmen cause the foregoing vote to be printed as the law directs.*

In 1828 a Temperance Society was formed which included men and women from Canterbury and Plainfield. The names of Prudence Crandall and her sister-in-law, Clarissa Crandall are recorded as members. At one of the early meetings of the society it was announced that any male member could address the meetings but if any female member wished to communicate, she could do so by making her comments to the chairman who would speak for her. The Temperance Society rules implied that it would be unseemly for a woman to speak in public. The members included all the community leaders whose names appeared in other records including that of a deacon whose name also appears frequently in the ledger of a local store as a purchaser of rum.

In October 1828 a committee was appointed to study the question of domestic manufacture. The report of this committee is recorded on

April 6, 1829:

This committee was appointed in October to devise means for the production and growth of manufacture of such articles of necessity and convenience as shall advance the wealth of the town. It has become well established opinion founded upon the most unquestionable evidence that in the future our state and national prosperity must depend upon agriculture and manufacturing.

As these are protected and encouraged so will our State and Nation advance . . . It will not only become a matter of policy but also of necessity to unite the influence of these two branches of wealth and upon the principles of self preservation each should lend its aid to the other. In a small community like a town much may be done to encourage the mechanic and the manufacturer and advance the interest of the agriculturist. That mechanic who pays away his money for a single article which can be produced in his own shop may be deemed unwise. That farmer who goes abroad for his own bread stuff or pays away his cash for flax and wool to clothe his own family, loses sight of his own interest. A community is made up of individuals and interests and by the application of correct principles to their own conduct, all members would soon realize beneficial results. When we learn what advances are made in many parts of our own state by encouraging domestic industry we are called upon to survey our condition and enquire of ourselves whether the town of Canterbury is forward in this matter of improvement. The Committee learned with great satisfaction that in many towns in this vicinity a spirit of inquiry hath gone forth which hath been followed with permanent success.

To be behind our neighbors in prosperity is indeed a mortifying consideration and yet our destination will certainly be that condition unless our individual and collective energies are speedily called into action. The soil upon which we lived is capable of producing much more than we now obtain from it and the ingenuity of our fellow citizens is adequate to the business of supplying all our implements of husbandry. A reasonable encouragement to our mechanics and manufacturers would soon so far reward their skill that we should have no occasion to go abroad for the necessities and conveniences of life. Among the objects of cultivation and production the mulberry tree stands pre-empt. Our soil is well adapted to its growth and our climate not inauspicious to its culture. Should the farmer devote a small proportion of his time to the commencement of this work a few years would bring him a bountiful harvest.

Experience has shown that the mulberry tree does not impoverish the land upon which it grows. Hedges may be redeemed from waste and converted into profitable and productive lands. Sterile pastures may be converted into feeding lands for sheep and horses, which will not be forsaken for the richest meadows by animals which have the faculty of discrimination beyond that of man. The shade of the mulberry tree is supposed to impart both sweetness and nutriment to the grass within its influence. The labour required in the production of the silk is derived from those hands which cannot be employed to much advantage in the ordinary business of agriculture.

Among the articles which may be manufactured within our own town the committee takes the liberty to enumerate the following; wagons, plows, scythes, hoes, rakes, pitchforks, snaths, chairs, and cabinet work, buttons, wire scives, bricks, hats, augers, combs, tinware, corn broomes, cards, saddles, harness, spools and bobbins.

The Committee would remark that these essential articles and many more which might be named can all be produced within our own town . . . The only question for our consideration is, how shall this be accomplished?

The first step to be taken is for each and all of our citizens to manifest by their example their determination to encourage our own citizens by purchasing their domestic productions of the manufacturers and mechanics in our own town in preference to going abroad for the articles or encouraging foreigners to bring articles to us. These articles can be afforded as cheaply by our own artificers as by others and if there is a profit in the manufacture why not receive the benefit to ourselves."

David Buth, Chairman

Voted the treasurer shall pay $15 to the person who produces the greatest quantity of silk on a single farm.

During 1828 the town took a humanitarian step and under the chairmanship of Pardon Crandall, as overseer of the poor, built a poor house. Formerly the poor has been housed with the family offering to board them for the lowest fee. One elderly man was taken back to his former place of residence in New York State. The law allowed for whipping of vagrants or those who had no visible means of support unless they left town within a specified time.

The American Lyceum movement started at this time in Millbury, Massachusetts for the dissemination of information about the arts, history and public affairs. A lyceum group was formed in Canterbury and drew upon the same membership as that of the Temperance Society. One of the leaders in the social and political life of the town was an attorney named Andrew T. Judson. He was born a short distance away in Eastford and had lived in Vermont before settling in Canterbury. He served on various boards and committees, was town clerk, and was representative to the Legislature at various times. He replaced, as the leading attorney, Moses Cleaveland who died in 1806. Moses Cleaveland was the leader of the group of Connecticut natives who had gone to Ohio and laid the foundation for the city of Cleveland. When he was told that the Ohio settlement was to be named for him, he expressed the hope that it would become as flourishing a community as Canterbury.

People from Canterbury had a continuing interest in westward expansion. The Norwich Journal of October 26, 1831 carried the following article:

Emigration

"Those gentlemen wishing to emigrate to the West, having more particularly reference to the state of Illinois are invited to meet at the house of Capt. Chauncey Bacon, Innkeeper in Canterbury on Wednesday, the 16th. of November at 10 o'clock to take into consideration the expediency of uniting in an association for removing and settling colonywise.

It is designed that this invitation should extend through the counties of New London, Windham, Tolland and vicinity.

Any information relative to the country or mode of farming and removing a colony will be gratefully received by those that may meet."

Whether from this beginning or not, later developments show that people from Windham and New London counties did indeed settle in Illinois.

Several men in Canterbury were active in the Colonization Society which had its origin nationally in Washington in 1820. Its purpose was to settle in Africa Negroes, who were willing to go. Churches throughout the country cooperated with this movement by devoting to its use the collections taken nearest the Fourth of July. Many of the first members of the organization were sincerely convinced that their plan was best for the Negroes. Thousands of dollars were raised and in 1822 land for the colony was obtained in Liberia.

Canterbury was related to the rest of the country by its turnpikes and easy access to water transportation from Norwich. It was also related to national interests and concerns because of the intellectual caliber of its citizens.

People now turned their thoughts to increasing the opportunities for education for young people — even for girls. In fact as early as 1814 there was an advertisement in the *Norwich Courier* for Mrs. Value's new Boarding School in Hartford.

> *"Mrs. Value respectfully informs the public that she proposes opening a Boarding School for young ladies on the first Monday in January next when she will recommence teaching those branches of instruction which she formerly taught young ladies with success, viz orthography, reading prose and verse, writing, arithmetic, parsing English grammar, the elements of astronomy on the celestial globe, geography on the terrestrial globe, with a correct knowledge of the atlas and maps, history, Blaire lectures, composition, drawing, painting, plain sewing, needle work on muslin and embroidery — in addition to which Mr. Value will give a lesson every day (Sunday excepted) on polite manners, dancing, the French language and music. Terms for board and tuition $3 per week — it being understood that the young lady will provide herself with whatever will be necessary in the school (the globes, atlas and piano excepted) also her own wood and candles when she is not with the family."*

A similar school had been conducted for a year in Norwich by a Miss Hyde and Lydia Huntley Sigourney. In Hartford in 1822 a select school for young ladies was started by Catherine Beecher, daughter of the well-known Rev. Lyman Beecher.

In Plainfield there was a large and quite renowned academy for boys. This had been in operation since 1784. In 1825 it was moved to a fine new building on land given by Lydia Farlan. It stood on the brow of a hill east of the main street in town. One of the outstanding teachers at this school was Rinaldo Burleigh who graduated from Yale in the class of 1803.

Miss Pierce's school for young ladies in Plainfield was announced in 1820. This school offered board for those from out of the area.

All of these schools offered education beyond that available in the little district schools which were in session for a few months each year. Most of them were taught by men who were seldom well prepared and who took on teaching assignments to fill in their time when other work was not available. There was an increasing awareness of the need for improved education.

Those families which could afford to, gave serious attention to the education for their sons. Increased wealth, and resources to lessen the drudgery in the home, led many families to seek educational advantages and cultural opportunities for their daughters. Quakers, who had always considered women and girls to be quite as important as men, had led the way in educating them.

...ed Silks; rich
Feathers; Hats
Dresses, &c. &c.
82

S, &c.

Cast Steel Axes.
ack Strap Shov-
qual to "Ames"
lls.
anklin Gridirons.
ces.

st Steel Augur

its, together with

UTLERY.
sale and Retail,

ERT & SON.
3weow80

ANACKS,

oss, by
GGLESTON.
82

CO.
w-York, with a
le GOODS, all
low prices, and
r most kinds of

82

RS.
d two Pressmen,
ves by their in-
CANFIELD.

T,
se occupied by
Main-street.
CANFIELD.
82

MINARY.
d Female Semi-
d of November,

to act as Princi-
ng a part, if not
d in the instruc-
conding the ef-
Teachers who
ion; so that the
cation will, thus

Hartford, October 18. eowtf82

Embrocation

CHEMICAL EMBROCATION,

OR,

WHITWELL'S ORIGINAL OPODELDOC,

One Bottle of which is warranted to contain three times the strength of the HARD *kind.*

THIS article is considered by the first Physicians in the United States to rank higher than any other composition in existence for the following complaints, viz.: Bruises, Sprains, Gout, Rheumatism, Cramp, Numbness, Weakness or Stiffness of the Neck or Joints, Chilblains, Chapped Hands, Stings of Insects, Vegetable Poisons, &c. &c. It is applied both to man and beast.

☞ *N. B.—There are in the United States not less than fifty imitations of this article, (a pretty good evidence of the worth of the original,) but the public ought to be acquainted with the fact, that nine-tenths of these pretended imitations of this inimitable composition, sold under the name of "Liquid Opodeldoc," are little else than hard soap, and a small quantity of camphor, dissolved in whiskey or new rum.*

To encourage ignorant and bold pretenders, is to countenance imposture; to purchase of this class, time and experience will teach wisdom. Prudence, in all cases, is a desirable virtue; but the saving of a few cents in a phial of medicine, is pitiful economy, and may lead to worse consequences than the loss of the money.

The idea of prefering a physician because he was a cheap one, would be considered a mark of insanity. To prefer one medicine to another because it costs less, is equally adverse to sound judgment and common sense; *in both cases life and limb are at stake.* No person could use the same ingredients and afford the article at a less price. A knowledge of this composition, however, is known only to the Proprietor and to the physician whose certificate accompanies it.

WHITWELL'S BITTERS,

A most efficacious and wonderful cordial medicine, for dyspepsia, jaundice, sickness of the stomach, flatulence, want of appetite, &c. They give a tone to the solids, enrich the blood, and invigorate the whole system. No tavern should be without them. Price 12½ cents a paper. THE PURGATIVE POWDERS are highly important in all the above complaints, and should in most cases be used with the Bitters.

BOOTS and S...
do.
He has als...
1000 Lbs. ...
above, together w...
HARDWARE, n...
for the accommod...
Also, 160 Acres...
Columbia, Cuyai...
watered, and in th...
All of the abov...
credit, or farmers'...
October 4.

I...
1 Mahogany S...
1 " I...
1 Large Mirror...
1 Set China.
Also, a Cellar F...
Apparatus comple...

Hartford, Augu...

OS...
9 Bales, for sal...

August 9.

L...
FEMA...
Conducted by...
THE Winter T...
on the 23d...
structors are emp...
ing; and unremit...
tific, literary and...
the Principals *per...*
Tuition, five or...
the studies pursue...
Litchfield, Octo...

CAS...
RYE, COR...
I...
WHEAT, R...
rels or S...
and unbolted Mea...
part of the City, a...
at the subscriber's...
Bridge.

French Burr an...
and Bolting Clot...
ground PLASTE...
use.

Hartford, Febru...

Advertisement in the Connecticut Courant
October 18, 1831
Photograph by Gus Johnson

CHAPTER THREE
THE CANTERBURY SCHOOL

EARLY in the summer of 1831, Prudence was urged by seventeen substantial citizens of Canterbury to establish an academy there for young ladies. Rev. Dennis Platt, Rufus Adams, William Kinne, Andrew Judson, Dr. Andrew Harris, Daniel Packer, Daniel Frost, Jr., and Samuel Hough agreed to act as a Board of Visitors for the school. Some of them offered financial assistance for establishing the institution. They would enroll their daughters and use their contacts to secure other pupils.

Arrangements were made to secure the Paine House at the southwest corner of the intersection of the Hartford-Providence and Norwich-Woodstock Turnpikes. Situated on three-fourths of an acre, the house offered 10 large rooms in the main part and an ell in which there were seven small rooms. Each of the main rooms had a fireplace. The entrance hall was wide, with a handsome stair-case. This desirable property was purchased for $2000. Prudence gave a note for part of this money to Board Member Samuel Hough.

Throughout the early fall Prudence made preparations for her school. At the store of Stephen Coit she bought glass lamps and lamp oil, a fancy bellows and blue curtain paper. She also bought sewing supplies and medicines such as opodeldoc and camphor. Books chosen for the courses of study were the texts in use in the Friends' School in Providence. They included dictionaries by Worcester and Webster, Barber's *Elocutionist,* Brown's *English Grammar,* Parker's *Composition,* Smith's *Geography,* Robbin's *Outline of History,* Parley's *Common School History,* Whelpley's *Compend of History,* Burritt's *Geography of the Heavens,* Gray and Comstock's *Natural Philosophy,* Frost's *Class Book of Nature* and Dymond's *Moral Philosophy.*

Advertisements for the school were published in papers in Brooklyn, Norwich and other nearby towns. The *Brooklyn Advertiser* for November 9, 1831 carried the following announcement:

> *"Miss Crandall has lately opened a boarding school exclusively for females, at the village of Canterbury and will teach the following branches, viz, reading, writing, arithmetic, English grammar, geography, ancient and modern together with delineating maps, history, natural and moral philosophy, chemistry and astronomy.*
>
> *There will be no vacation during the year, therefore, scholars can enter or leave at any time without interruption.*
>
> *Books and stationery will be furnished at wholesale price if wanted.*

The terms of tuition for 12 weeks per term are as follows: "For English studies — $3.00. Board, including washing in the family of the instructress $1.50 per week.

Every scholar of the family is required to attend public worship, somewhere, on the Sabbath.

In connection with the school, Mr. Andrew Cutler, A.M., will deliver a course of chemical lectures during the coming winter, commencing on Tuesday evening, the 15th day of the present month."

"The Board of Visitors recommend to the public patronage of Miss Crandall's school and cheerfully add that she has already acquired a high reputation as an instructress and the assiduity and attention which she devotes to the health and morals of her pupils, renders her school a suitable place for education."

In early November the first girls arrived and throughout the month other students came. Prudence greeted them and helped each one to settle — four sharing the large rooms or singly in the little rooms. Eliza and Phoebe Hough were among the early arrivals. Frances Ensworth, Sarah Adams, Frances and Sarah Coit, Miss Avery, Miss Seth and Hannah Pearl from Hampton enrolled during the first week. The big house vibrated with life as the young ladies busied themselves in class groups or periods of respite and recreation.

Early in the morning they gathered in the bright south parlor for a period of devotion led by the dignified Miss Prudence. This was followed by a simple breakfast prepared by Marcia Davis who had come from Boston to help with the household tasks and to be near the family of her future husband, Charles Harris. During the morning hours and for part of the afternoon the students met with their teachers in the two north rooms in serious study of the several subjects they were expected to learn. Late in the afternoon, in groups of two or three, they went to Mr. Coit's store or the Post Office or, when the days were mild, for short walks along the bank of the Quinebaug.

On Tuesday evenings they heard Mr. Cutler deliver his chemical lectures and fequently some member of the clergy called to present a theological discourse. Other evenings were spent playing dominoes or other parlor games, reading riddles or resolving puzzles. Time passed quickly and pleasantly for the girls and their teachers.

There was great excitement on January 20th, when the Board of Visitors came to check out the progress of the students. Those girls whose fathers were members of the Board were especially nervous. The calm confidence of Miss Prudence reassured them as they wrote out the answers to mathematical questions and then were called upon to answer, orally, questions on history and geography. The nine grave gentlemen expressed genuine gratification with the accomplishments of the young ladies and the dignified demeanor of the teachers. Their approval was publicly expressed in an advertisement which appeared in the *Norwich Courier* on March 21, 1832.

"CANTERBURY
"Female Boarding School
"Prudence Crandall, Principal

"To the public she presents her grateful acknowledgements for the generous patronage hitherto received and respectfully solicits a continuance of same.

The location of the school possesses many natural advantages and is surrounded with good society.

Young ladies and little misses will be furnished with every accommodation to spend their time usefully and agreeably at this institution. The school is regularly organized and now open for the reception of scholars.

The course of studies pursued comprises Reading, Writing, English Grammar, Geography, History, Rhetoric, Natural and moral Philosophy, Anatomy, Music, Drawing and Painting together with the French language.

Terms of Tuition

For English Studies, the term of 12 weeks	*$3*
Drawing and Painting	*$4*
Music including piano	*$7*
French, taught by a gentleman	*$4*

Books and stationery furnished at the lowest prices. Board, including washing in the family of the instructress $1.50 per week.

The following gentlemen are appointed a Board of Visitors to whom reference may be made for further information.

Rufus Adams
Rev. Dennis Platt
Solomon Payne
Andrew Harris, M.D.
Deacon William Kinne
Daniel Frost
Daniel Packer
Samuel Hough
Andrew T. Judson

At a meeting of the Board of Visitors of the Canterbury Female

Boarding School on January 20, 1832.

Resolved unanimously: That the first quarterly examination of this school has given entire satisfaction to the Board of Visitors.

Resolved that the Chairman and Secretary sign these resolutions and present the same to Miss Crandall.

Dennis Platt, Chairman
Andrew T. Judson, Secretary

Canterbury March 10, 1832"

Prudence was serenely happy during these busy days. She enjoyed the lesson hours and the less formal times with the lovely, lively young ladies who were her pupils and found visits from their parents very satisfying. Her neighbors were congenial. A source of special pleasure were visits from her brother Hezekiah and his little ones: Mary, Esther and Obediah. Occasionally, on his way to Danielsonville, Hezekiah would bring his children to visit their aunts in order to give his frail wife Clarissa a day of rest with only the baby Reuben to care for.

The responsibilities of her school did not entirely satisfy Prudence's quest for knowledge. Always seeking "truth in science and religion," she sometimes left her charges under the care of Hannah Almyra while she went to meetings conducted by Baptist speakers in nearby churches. She hired the chaise from Mr. Coit and drove to Lebanon or Voluntown to hear Apollas Phelps or one of the other revivalists.

She set high value on the opinions of her brother Reuben and wrote to him concerning a number of questions which were of interest to her. His reply was not altogether satisfactory.

Dear Sister:

My mind has been very much exercised at times on your case and condition, and I hope sincerely for your own welfare, and that you use discretion in all your undertakings.

So far as regular religious activities are concerned, I will give my assent, provided no male is present who will or can officiate and in no other case as I believe it is strictly forbidden. I believe that female prayer meetings are in themselves, good, perhaps as good as any, so long as they maintain the honor and dignity of it, by secreting themselves, but as soon as the female rises or kneels down to pray, in public audiences, in the presence of her teacher, her protector, that moment she has started out from under the protection and instruction of the good apostle Paul, and set herself up as superior, by thus doing or she would never appear in this lofty place. The apostle, Paul, did not intend that woman should not exhort her neighbor or her brother, for he says: 'I command you to exhort one another', meaning undoubtedly, everywhere, thereabout in our daily walks and pursuits, for he again says, 'But let your woman keep silence in the churches, for it is a shame and abomination for woman to pray with her head uncovered'.

With respect to the saving grace or ordinance of baptism, I will give you a few weak ideas for I am nearly exhausted in writing. The Book says, 'If ye repent not, ye shall be damned'. This evidently shows that baptism is not saving or is not as essential as repentance for safety.'

On the subject of communion with other churches, I have said enough. I said enough when I was home, and I presume you think by this time I have said enough on any of these subjects. Perhaps I have, but I adjure you I have not done yet. When I get a little stronger you will hear from me again.

How comes on your school and state of religion? Do you, all hands run off three to four days to meeting? If you, the principal, or your assistants do, I shall have a very poor opinion of the principal and her assistants. I wish you would endeavor to make your school your dependence for your living, and no man can make a living in any business without he attends strictly to it. I wish you would adopt some system of reading in your school which will have a tendency to lay a foundation of after reading which is one of the beauties of a good education and a very essential requisite to make a finished and accomplished young lady. I should think it would be proper for Almyra to have an hour or two in the different parts of the day, aside from your regular school hours devoted to reading some amusing or well selected historical work, and make them take turns in reading aloud. It will have a powerful effect in qualifying a young lady to read well in public which is one of the greatest accomplishments she can possess. Another improvement I would suggest is to have some epistolary composition every week: this is too much neglected in common schools. It accustoms them to write without embarassment. Improvements in this thing are perceptible to parents more than anything else, hence, this will be a source of greatest satisfaction to them. There are many other improvements which have suggested themselves to me, but I have not time now, nor patience to make mention of them here. I hope your teachers will make good use of those books I left. Respects to the family with a sincere wish for their prosperity.

Yours respectfully,
Reuben Crandall

Prudence was offended by this, thinking it blatant affrontery. Had they not shared the same Quaker services and teachings? How could he hold to the conviction that women must be restrained even in religious matters? Heedless of his suggestions she continued to attend the meetings which interested her. On September 14, she hired a wagon from Mr. Coit and took several of her students to a meeting at the Packerville church. The girls were deeply impressed by the exhortations of the preacher and the intense emotional expressions of some members of the audience. They were subdued and thoughtful as they rode back to the school in the late afternoon.

The comfort and security of her own circumstances did not dull Prudence's concern and compassion for others. Her interest in Marcia, her colored helper, led her to a new awareness of the perplexities and problems faced by free Negroes. Brought up among Quakers whose teachings propounded the divine in all men, Prudence knew that slavery was an evil, but it seemed to be an evil far removed from Canterbury. It was disturbing to her to learn from Marcia that the attitudes of northerners resulted in great hardship for colored people. Marcia brought her a number of copies of the *Liberator,* an antislavery paper published in Boston by William L. Garrison which Charles Harris had loaned her. His father, William was the agent for the *Liberator* in Windham county.

The scathing articles against slave holding and slave trading stirred Prudence's mind and heart. The detailed accounts of cruelties inflicted on slaves filled her with horror. The articles on Colonization she found of particular interest since several Canterbury gentlemen, including Andrew Judson were active in this society. In an early issue there was a report of a meeting of "people of color" in Hartford at which sentiment against the program of Colonizationists was expressed. It read:

> *"At a large and respectable meeting of the colored inhabitants of the city of Hartford and its vicinity convened at the vestry room of the African church, on the 13th inst. (July 13, 1831) for the purpose of expressing their views in relation to the American Colonization Society, Mr. H. Foster was called to the chair and Mr. Paul Drayton appointed Secretary. The object of the meeting was then stated in a brief and pertinant manner, after which extracts from several speeches delivered by the founders of the colonization scheme, together with general sentiments extracted from the 'African Reporter' were laid before the meeting and the following resolutions were unanimously adopted:*
>
> *"Resolved: That it is the opinion of this meeting that the American Colonization Society is actuated by the same motives which influenced the mind of Pharaoh when he ordered the male*

children of the Israelites to be destroyed.

Resolved: That, though we be the last in calling a meeting we feel no less the pernicious influence of this Society than the rest of our brethren; and that we consider all their pretexts, whether under the cloak of religion or philanthropy, gratuitous and uncalled for. We would therefore, advise the Society, that as we have learned that there are $150,000 in its funds, it had better appropriate this sum in meliorating the condition of our brethren the slaves, in this their native land, and raising them from the degradation into which they are plunged.

"Resolved: That the thanks of the meeting be returned to Mssr. William L. Garrison, Isaac Knapp and every friend of emancipation for their benevolent exertions on our behalf.

"Resolved: That the proceedings of this meeting be signed by the Chairman and Secretary and sent to the 'Liberator' for publication.

Henry Foster, Chairman
Paul Drayton, Secretary"

It seemed very strange to Prudence that such an outstanding man as Mr. Judson would assume leadership in an organization which free colored men considered so abhorrent. She would show him this article and others dealing with the rights of "colored people." As a lawyer his viewpoint would be interesting. As the most outspoken leader of the Colonization Society in the Windham area, he would certainly be able to justify the plans of the organization. As one of the Board of Visitors of her school and a neighbor, she felt free to discuss these matters with him.

Opportunity for such a discussion never came but Prudence subsequently learned the opinions and feelings of Andrew T. Judson on this subject.

Frequently, when her work was done, Marcia would slip quietly into a classroom and listen to the lesson. She borrowed texts and other books and raised questions about a variety of subjects as she worked with Prudence and Hannah Almyra. Sarah Harris, the 17 year old sister of Marcia's betrothed, Charles Harris, visited her from time to time and realized how rewarding she found her association with the school. Sarah longed for more education than she had gained in the district school. She secured permission from her father, an industrious farmer, to seek admission to the school. Her request to be enrolled as a day student took Prudence by surprise.

After the house was quiet that night, Prudence sat in her room thinking about Sarah. She recalled the sympathy she had felt for the unknown "colored people" whose problems were so graphically described in the

Liberator. Here, on her own doortstep, was a young person asking for the very thing she was best prepared to give — education. This girl and her family attended the Congregational church. Sarah and her brother Charles had attended a district school. There had never been any hint or rumor to indicate that the family was less respectable than their neighbors. She could find no reasonable cause for hesitating to accept Sarah. She turned to her Bible as she often did, opening it at random, she read:

> *"So I returned and considered all the oppressions that are done under the sun: and behold the tears of such as were oppressed, and they had no comforter: and on the side of their oppressors there was power; but they had no comforter."*
>
> *(Ecclesiastes IV, 1.)*

Power indeed was on the side of the oppressors — the power of government and of wealth. She could be a "comforter" to one of the oppressed race!

Sarah arrived early each morning. She was well known to the girls who had been in school with her. For several days there was no indication that the presence of this new pupil made any change in the placid passing of the busy school day.

The following week several callers came to the school. This was not unusual in itself, but the purpose of these visits was different. First came Mrs. Peters, wife of an Episcopal minister. She chatted amiably for a while but before leaving she made it quite clear that she disapproved of the presence of Sarah Harris in the school. A more formal visit was made by Deacon Frost. He came as spokesman for the Board of Visitors. Gently he remonstrated with Miss Crandall, "in a most kind and affecting manner," labored to convince her of the impropriety and injustice of her action in accepting Sarah Harris.

Quietly Prudence reminded him that Sarah was a member and regular worshipper in church. She urged him to consider that there was no other school where Sarah could secure the training she desired to enable her to become a teacher. For every argument which Deacon Frost advanced, Prudence had a ready, positive answer. Bewildered and then angered by her audacity he withdrew to seek reinforcements from the Board of Visitors.

A committee of several members of the Board called. Seated in the spacious South Parlor, they talked of the excellent record of the school. They reminded Prudence of the importance in their various communities of the parents of the pupils. They hinted, delicately, that mixing of the races was unwise and might even lead to amalgamation.

Prudence calmly replied: "Moses had a black wife."

The gentlemen retreated, unable to meet this statement with further argument, unwilling to be bested in verbal encounter by a fractious female. They decided to let the women try to resolve the problem.

Within a few days, the mothers of several students called at the school. Assisted by Marcia, Prudence served tea before the fireplace. Neither the tea nor the fire could penetrate the chilly demeanor of her guests. With no regard for Marcia's feelings or perhaps with deliberate intent to affront her, they delivered an ultimatum to Prudence.

"Miss Harris must be dismissed. We will not have our girls in a school with a 'nigger'. If you do not send her away, we will withdraw our daughters and your school will sink."

"Then sink it must! I shall not dismiss her," came Prudence Crandall's clear reply.

Rumors flew, tensions grew in Canterbury. In church, at the store, wherever Prudence met her neighbors, they greeted her coldly, if at all. Her brother and her father reported that several families had assured them that they would withdraw their daughters from the school. Pardon cautioned Prudence not to be too stubborn.

Pleased with Sarah's progress, touched by her serious purpose and sincere gratitude for the opportunity to study, Prudence worried about the future of her school. To dismiss Sarah was out of the question, but the school needed at least 15 students or more to maintain it. Where would this number of students be found if the white girls withdrew? There was only one Sarah — but were there others like her? Who would know whether there were other colored girls in sufficient number to make a school practical? She decided to seek the advice of William Lloyd Garrison, publisher of the *Liberator*. Her letter to him was sent on January 18, 1833.

> *Mr. Garrison: I am to you, Sir, I know, an entire stranger and you are indeed so to me save through the medium of the public print. I am by no means fond of egotism, but the circumstances under which I labor forbid my asking a friend to write for me; therefore I will tell you who I am and for what purpose I write. I am, Sir, through the blessing of divine providence permitted to be the Principal of the Canterbury Female Boarding School. I received a considerable part of my education at the Friends' Boarding School in Providence. In 1831 I purchased a large dwelling house in the center of this village and opened the school above mentioned. Since I commenced, I have met all the encouragement I ever anticipated and now have a flourishing school.*
>
> *Now I will tell you why I write to you and the object is this: I wish to know your opinion respecting changing white scholars for colored ones. I have been for some months past determined, if*

possible, during the remaining part of my life to benefit the people of color. I do not dare tell any of my neighbors anything about the contemplated change in my school and I beg you, Sir, that you will not expose it to anyone, or it would ruin my present school. Will you be so kind as to write by the next mail and give me your opinion on the subject and if you consider it possible to obtain 20-25 young ladies of color to enter this school for the term of one year at the rate of $25 per quarter, including board, washing and tuition. I will come to Boston in a few days and make some arrangements about it. I do not suppose the number can be obtained from Boston alone; but from all the large cities in several states I thought they might be gathered.

I must once more beg you not to expose this matter until we see how the case will be determined.

Yours with greatest respect,
Prudence Crandall

Prudence announced to her associates and Board of Visitors that she planned to go to Boston to visit schools and see about equipment. She went by stage coach to Boston, staying at the Marlboro Hotel — a very respectable place. She immediately arranged to meet Mr. Garrison, sending him a note . . . .

Boston
January 29, 1833

Mr. Garrison: The lady who wrote you a short time since would inform you she is now in town and should be very thankful if you would call this evening at 6 o'clock.

Prudence Crandall

The next few days were exciting ones for Prudence. All those contacted were encouraging. Her enthusiasm for her new project increased as she met new friends. Her course of action is revealed in her letters and those exchanged by her supporters.

Feb. 12, 1833

Mr. Garrison: I can inform you that I had a pleasant passage home. Arrived here Saturday evening about 8 o'clock. Saw Mr. Packer on Monday. I told him the object of my visit to Boston. He said he thought the object praiseworthy, but he was very troubled about the result. He is fearful that I cannot be supplied with scholars at the close of one year and therefore he thinks I shall injure myself in the undertaking.

If you have not yet sent on to New York the information you intend, I would thank you if you would do so immediately, for I am expecting to take the next boat for New York and shall be in the city early on Friday morning. I have not the least acquaintance there but a friend of mine will give me an introductory letter to Mr. Miller, one of the colored ministers in the city.

The evening after I left Boston, I called on Mrs. Hammond who soon collected some of her friends, among whom were George Benson and a brother of his who appeared to possess hearts warmed by fellow feeling and awake to the cause of humanity. They engaged to do all for me in their power and I have no doubt they will. Saturday morning, I called on Mrs. Hammond again and she walked with me to the residences of three families of color with whom I was pleased. They seemed to feel much for the education of their children and I think I shall be able to obtain six scholars from Providence. When I return from New York, I think I shall be able to lay the subject before the public.

Reassured by conversations with Mr. Miller and others in New York and confident of the success of her plans she resolved to meet any problems which might arise with all the composure possible. Problems did arise. On February 26th, she wrote to Mr. Jocelyn, a new acquaintance in New Haven who was active in work with free colored people.

Mr. Jocelyn, Sir:

I can inform you that I arrived home last Friday evening . . . . soon called my family together and laid before them the object of my journey and endeavored to convince them of the propriety of the pursuit. My views, by them, were pretty cordially received. Saturday morning I called on several of the neighbors and to my astonishment they exhibited but little opposition. But since that time the people have become very alarmed for fear the reputation of their village will be injured.

Last evening they held a meeting to consult what shall be done to destroy the school I have now in contemplation. They apointed a committee (to wait on me at 9 o'clock this morning) comprised of four of the most powerful men in town. They called and had an interview with me — told me the meeting has resolved to do everything in their power to destroy my undertaking and that they could *do it and* should *do it and what will be the result of this commotion I cannot tell — knowing that the opinion of great men (such as Mr. Tappan) would stand against a swelling tide of opposition — I therefore made as free use of his name in laying the object before my friends and neighbors as I thought proper — I told them he was a friend of this benevolent object and that they did not doubt as they knew well his character. I was thankful for one expression that fell from his lips while on board the steamboat which he did not know but 'he should come with the scholars when they entered school.' I told this to the people and this seemed to allay their feelings very much. I presume his presence here would alleviate the feelings somewhat but that is a favour too great to be expected. I have written this day to Mr. Garrison and desired him to intercede with Mr. Buffum to visit me as he has not yet fulfilled his engagement. Your opinion and advice will be thankfully received on this occasion and I hope you will by no means with hold it but write to me immediately.*

Yours with greatest respect,
Prudence Crandall

Please write to me immediately.

Arthur Tappan was a wealthy textile merchant who had his business in New York. He had engaged in several beneficent activities in behalf of the free Blacks and was the target of bigoted vandals for this reason. Fearing for the safety of his family in New York, he moved them to New Haven. He commuted by boat from his home to New York. His friendship and financial aid was of much importance to Prudence in the ensuing years.

Arnold Buffum was a Quaker hat maker who had decided to devote his time and energies to the Abolitionist movement. He travelled about New England speaking and working in behalf of the cause.

Encouraged by her new friends and undaunted by the opposition of former friends and associates, Prudence moved ahead with her plans.

On March 2, 1833 an advertisement appeared in the *Liberator.*

Prudence Crandall, Principal of the Canterbury (Conn.) Female Boarding School returns her most sincere thanks to those who have patronized her school and would give information that on the first Monday of April next, her school will be open for the reception of young ladies and little misses of color. The branches taught are as follows: — Reading, Writing, arithmetic, English grammar, Geography, History, Natural and moral Philosophy, Chemistry, music on the Piano together with the French language.

The charge for board, washing and tuition is $25 per quarter.

Only the name of Daniel Packer remained on the list of sponsors from her former Board of Visitors. The others were names of outsiders, most of them recognized Abolitionists, some of them men of color. They were Arthur Tappan, Rev. Peter Williams, Rev. Theodore Raymond, Rev. George Bourne, Rev. Heyborn, James Forten, Arnold Buffum, George Benson, Theodore Wright, Rev. Samuel Cornish, Joseph Cassey, Rev. S.J. May, and William Lloyd Garrison.

CHAPTER FOUR
THE SECOND CANTERBURY SCHOOL

THE already angry residents of Canterbury were now aroused and enraged. They had been offended when Miss Crandall withdrew from their daughters' education. They were incensed that she now intended to turn her talents to teaching colored girls. She had refused to listen to reason when they had remonstrated with her about accepting one well known local "girl of color." Her present plan to flood the community with strange Negro girls backed by Abolitionists must be stopped. Whenever two or three people met, at the store or the post office or as they passed through the town, they stopped to talk over this dreadful development. The town fathers consulted together and counseled their followers. Certainly this woman would not stand against their concerted attack. The municipal authorities had squelched the plan for a manual labor school in New Haven the previous year. Surely Canterbury authorities would be just as competent in quieting the present furor. The contentious Crandall woman would learn the limits of their patience!

On March 4th, Arnold Buffum wrote to Mr. Garrison:

> *The good people of Canterbury, I learn have had three town meetings last week to devise ways and means to suppress Prudence Crandall's school and I am informed that the excitement is so great it would not be safe for me to appear there. George Benson, however, has ventured and gone there Saturday P.M. to see what can be done in the case. Miss C. was visited by a committee of men who told her that by putting her design into execution she would bring disgrace and ruin on them all! They professed to feel a real regard for the colored people and were perfectly willing they should be educated, provided it could be effected — some other place — "A sentiment," adds Mr. Benson, "you will say worthy of a true Colonizationist!"*

Mr. Garrison replied to George Benson on March 8th, 1833.

> *Although distracted with cares, I must seize my pen to express my admiration of your generous and prompt defense of Miss Crandall from her pitiful assailants. In view of their outrageous conduct, my indignation kindles intensely. What will be the result? If possible, Miss C. must be sustained at all hazards. If we suffer the school to be put down in Canterbury, other places will partake of panic and also prevent its introduction in their vicinity. We may as well, first as last, meet this proscriptive spirit and conquer it. We — i.e., all true friends of the Cause — must make this a common concern. The New Haven excitement has furnished a bad precedent, a*

second must not be given or I know not what we can do to raise up the colored population in a manner which their intellectual and moral necessities demand. In Boston we are all excited about the Canterbury affair. Colonizationists are rejoicing and Abolitionists are looking sternly.

The result of the meeting to be held in Canterbury tomorrow will be waited for by us with great anxiety. Our brother, May, deserves much credit for venturing to expostulate with the conspirators. If anyone can make them ashamed of their conduct he is the man, may the Lord give him courage, wisdom and success.

Rev. Samuel J. May recorded his contacts with Miss Crandall and his experiences at the town meeting of March 9th.

On Feb. 27th, I was informed of her generous, disinterested determination and heard that in consequence the whole town was in a flame of indignation and fanned by the influence of the prominent people of the village, her immediate neighbors and her late patrons. Without delay therefore, although a stranger, I addressed a letter to her assuring her of my sympathy and my readiness to help her all in my power. On the 4th of March her reply came, begging me to come to her so soon as my engagements would permit. Accompanied by my friend, Mr. George W. Benson, I went to Canterbury the afternoon of that day. On entering the village we were warned that we should be in personal danger if we appeared there as Miss C's friends; and when we arrived at her house we learnt that the excitement against her had become furious. She had been grossly insulted and threatened with various kinds of violence, if she persisted in her purpose and the most egregious falsehoods had been put in circulation respecting her intentions and the character of her expected pupils, and of the future supporters of the school. A town meeting was to be held on the 9th, to devise and adopt such measures as would effectually avert the nuisance or speedily abate it, if it should be brought into the village.

Though beat upon by such a storm we found Miss C. resolved and tranquil, the effect of her Quaker discipline appeared in every word she spoke and in every expression of her countenance. But, as she said, it would not do for her to go to the town meeting, and there was not a man in Canterbury who would dare, if he felt so disposed, to appear in her behalf. "Will you, Friend May, be my attorney?" "Certainly," I replied, "Come what will!" We then agreed that I should explain to the people how unexpectedly she had been led to take the step which had given so much offense and show them how she could not have consented to the demand made by her former patrons without wounding deeply the feelings of an excellent girl known to most of them, and adding to the mountain load of injuries and insults already heaped upon the colored people of our country. With this arranged we left her to await the ominous meeting of the town.

On the 9th of March I repaired again to Miss C's house, accompanied by my faithful friend, Mr. Benson. There to our surprise and joy we found Friend Arnold Buffum, a most worthy man, and able speaker and the principal lecturing agent of the New England Antislavery Society. Miss C. gave each of us a respectful letter of introduction in which she requested that we might be heard as her attorneys and promised to be bound by any agreement we might see fit to make with the citizens of Canterbury. Miss C. concurred that since her house was one of the most conspicuous in the village and not wholly paid for, if her opponents would take it off her hands, repaying what she paid for it and cease molesting her she would move to some retired part of the town.

Thus commissioned and introduced, Friend Buffum and I proceeded to the town meeting. It was held in the 'Meeting House' one of the old New England pattern, galleries on three sides with room above and below for a thousand persons, sitting and standing. We found it nearly filled to its utmost capacity, and with difficulty we passed up the side aisle into the wall pew next to the deacons' seat in which sat the moderator. Very soon the business commenced. After the 'Warning' had been read a series of Resolutions were laid before the meeting, in which were set forth the disgrace and damage that would be brought upon the town if a school for colored girls should be set up there, protesting emphatically against the impending evil and appointing of the civil authority and selectmen a committee to wait upon 'The person contemplating the establishment of said school . . . . point out to her the injurious effects, incalculable evils, resulting from such an establishment within the town, persuade her if possible to abandon the project.' The mover of resolutions, Rufus Adams, labored to enforce them by a speech in which he grossly misrepresented what Miss C. had done, her sentiments and purpose and threw out several mean and low insinuations against the motives of those who were encouraging her enterprise.

As soon as he sat down, Honorable Andrew T. Judson rose. This gentleman was a great man in town, a leading politician in the state and much talked of by the Democrats as soon to be Governor. His house on Canterbury Green stood next to Miss C's. The idea of having a 'school for nigger girls so near him was insupportable.' He vented himself in a strain of reckless hostility to his neighbor, her benevolent self-sacrificing undertaking and its patrons and declared his determination to thwart the enterprise. He twanged every chord that could stir the coarser passions of the human heart and with such success that his hearers seemed to be filled with the apprehension that a dire calamity was impending over them, that Miss C. was the author or instrument of it, that there were powerful conspirators engaged against them in the plot and that the people of Canterbury should be roused by every consideration of self preservation, as well as self-respect to prevent the accomplishment of the design, defying the wealth and influence of all who are abetting it.

When he ended his Philippic, Mr. Buffum and I silently presented to the moderator, Miss Crandall's letters requesting that we might be heard on her behalf. He handed them over to Mr. Judson who instantly broke forth with greater violence than before; accused us of insulting the town by coming there to interfere in its local concerns. Other gentlemen sprang to their feet in hot displeasure; poured out their tirade upon Miss Crandall and her accomplices and with fists doubled in our faces roughly admonished us that if we opened our lips THERE, they would inflict upon us the utmost penalty of the law if not a more immediate vengeance.

Thus forbidden to speak, we of course sat in silence and let the waves of invective and abuse dash over us. But we sat thus only until we heard the moderator say 'This meeting is adjourned.' Knowing that we would violate no law by speaking, I sprang to the seat on which I have been sitting and cried out 'Men of Canterbury, I have a word for you. Hear me!' More than half the crowd turned to listen. I went rapidly over my replies to the misstatements which had been made as to the purpose of Miss Crandall and her friends, the character of her expected students and the spirit in which the enterprise has been conceived and carried on. As soon as possible I gave place to Friend Buffum. But he had spoken in his impressive manner only five minutes before the trustee of the church to which the house belonged came in and ordered all out, that the doors might be shut. Here again the hand of the law constrained us. So we obeyed with the rest and having lingered a while on the Green to answer questions and explain to those who were willing to understand the matter, we departed to our homes.

Her friends did not go to Prudence's house. She had agreed that neither her father nor her emissaries would stop there after the meeting. It was considered inadvisable to draw the attention of the crowd to her home. The resolutions adopted at the meeting were formally presented to her in a few days. Sam Hough read them to her when he and three other men called on her.

Whereas it hath been publicly announced that a school is to be opened in this town on the first Monday in April next, using the Language of the advertisement, 'for young ladies and little misses of color' or in other words for the people of color, the obvious tendency of which would be to collect within the town of Canterbury, large numbers of persons from other states, whose character and habits might be various and unknown to us, thereby rendering insecure, the persons, properties and reputations of our citizens. Under such circumstances, our silence might be construed into an approbation of the project

Thereupon resolved — that the location of a school for the people of color at any place within the limits of this town for the admission of persons of foreign jurisdictions meets with our unqualified disapprobation and it is to be understood that the inhabitants of Canterbury protest against it in the most earnest manner.

Resolved — that a committee be now appointed, to be composed of the Civil Authority and Selectmen, who shall make known to the person contemplating the establishment of said school, the sentiments and objections entertained by this meeting, in reference to said school, pointing out to her, the injurious effects and incalculable evils resulting from such an establishment within this town and to persuade her to abolish the project.

Prudence listened attentively while the Resolutions were read to her. She expressed regret that her fellow townspeople disapproved of her intentions but she assured the gentlemen that she could not withdraw from the commitment she had made to the students who wished to enroll and to the sponsors of her school. Grimly her callers left to consider the next steps in their campaign against this troublesome woman.

Controversy continued between Prudence's advisors and her adversaries. As was expected of a lady, she stayed in the background, reading published accounts of the furor and receiving frequent visits from those who favored her position. Throughout the month of March she continued preparations for the new pupils who would arrive in April.

A few days after the town meeting, Rev. May answered a knock at his door and found Mr. Judson there, asking to have a few minutes of his time. Judson began the conversation in a conciliatory tone, admitting that he had been rather rough and rude in his treatment of Mr. May at the town meeting but stating he considered that Mr. May was unwise to promote Miss Crandall's school since it would undoubtedly have an undesirable effect on real estate values.

Rev. May replied, "If you, Sir, had permitted Mr. Buffum and myself to speak, you would have found that we had come there, not in contentious spirit, but that we were ready with Miss Crandall's consent to settle the difficulty of you and your neighbors peaceably. Miss Crandall was willing to move to a more retired part of the town."

Mr. Judson broke in "Mr. May, we are not merely opposed to the establishment of that school in Canterbury, we mean there shall not be such a school set up anywhere in our state. The colored people can never rise from their menial condition in our country; they ought not to be permitted to rise here. They are an inferior race of beings, and never can or ought to be recognized as the equals of the whites. Africa is the place for them. I am in favor of Colonization. Let the niggers and their descendents be sent back to their fatherland; and there improve themselves as much as they can and civilize and Christianize the natives if they can.

"You and your friend Garrison have undertaken what you cannot accomplish. The condition of the colored population can never be essentially improved on this continent. You are fanatical about them. You are violating the Constitution of our Republic which settled forever the status of the black man in this land. They belong to Africa. Let them be sent there or kept as they are here. The sooner you Abolitionists abandon your project the better for our country, the niggers and yourself."

Mr. May retorted, "Mr. Judson, there never will be fewer colored people here than there are now. Of the vast majority of them *this* is their native land as it is ours. It will be unjust, inhuman of us to drive them out or make them willing to go by our cruel treatment of them. If they should be willing to depart, it would not be practical to transport them across the ocean and settle them on the shores of Africa.

"The only question is whether we will recognize the rights God gave them as men and encourage and assist them to be as He has made them capable of being, or whether we will continue to deny them the privileges we enjoy, condemn them to degradation, enslave and imbrute them and so bring upon ourselves the condemnation of the Almighty Impartial Father of all men and the terrible visitation of the God of the oppressed.

"I trust you will ere long come to see that we must accord to these men their rights or incur justly the loss our our own. Education is one of the primal, fundamental rights of all the children of men. Connecticut is the last place where this should be denied. But as in the Providence of God, that right has been denied in a place so near me, I feel that I am summoned to its defense.

"If you or your neighbors quietly consented that Sarah Harris whom you knew to be a bright, good girl, should enjoy the privilege she so eagerly sought, this momentous conflict would not have arisen in your village. But as it has arisen we may as well meet it there as elsewhere."

"That nigger school will never be allowed in Canterbury or any town in this state," hissed the red-faced Judson.

"How can you prevent it legally? How but by lynch law, by violence which you surely will not countenance?" asked Mr. May.

"We can expel her pupils from abroad," answered Judson, "under the provisions of our pauper and vagrant laws."

"But we will guard them by giving your town ample bonds," was May's calm reply.

"Then we will get a law passed by the present legislature, forbidding the institution of such a school as Miss Crandall proposes in any part of Connecticut" was Judson's next threat.

"It would be an unconstitutional law and I will contend against it to the last. If you, sir, pursue the course you have now indicated, I will dispute every step you take, from the lowest court in Canterbury to the highest court in the United States," promised Mr. May.

"You talk big! It will cost more than you are aware of to do all you threaten. Where will you get the means to carry on such a contest at law?" queried Mr. Judson.

"Mr. Judson, I had not foreseen all that this conversation has opened to my view. True, I do not possess the pecuniary ability to do what you have made me promise. I have not consulted anyone. But I am sure that the lovers of impartial liberty, the friends of humanity, the enemies of slavery will justly appreciate the importance of sustaining Miss Crandall in her benevolent, pious undertaking that I shall receive from one quarter or another all the funds I may need to crush by legal means the attempt to balk the Canterbury school."

Mr. Judson slapped his hat on his head and rushed out to his chaise and turned back toward Canterbury. It was bad enough to be forced to give attention to the trouble started by an unreasonable woman, to have an upstart member of the clergy put up such a front was intolerable. He resolved to use every opportunity to give verbal and written expression to his opposition to the Abolitionists and their dupes.

After his caller had left Mr. May sat for a long while in troubled thought. He had tried only to help a neighbor to resolve her difficulty, but it now appeared that he was irrevocably committed to a part in a quarrel which would probably involve him in legal and legislative actions, new to him. At least he was not alone in this battle. Garrison would certainly use his fiery pen to support Miss Crandall. He smiled as he recalled the occasion on which he had rebuked Garrison for his sharp attacks on the slave holders. Garrison's answer was so vehement it was still fresh in his memory after more than two years —

"Do the slaves think my language too severe or misapplied? Do that husband and wife, that mother and daughter, who have just been separated for life by sale on the auction block, think my denunciations of the man who inflicts that wrong too severe?"

"But you are all on fire!"

"I have need to be all on fire for I have mountains of ice to melt."

The next issue of the *Liberator* contained the following item:

"Heathenism Outdone

"At a town meeting held in Canterbury on March 9th. Resolutions were adopted directing the civil authority and the Selectmen of the town to persuade Miss Crandall to desist in her plans to open a school for colored girls. Her emissaries, Rev. Samuel J. May and Arnold Buffum were rudely treated and prevented from speaking in her behalf.

We put the names of the principal disturbers in black — black as the infamy which will attach to them as long as there is any recollection of the wrongs of the colored race.

ANDREW T. JUDSON, RUFUS ADAMS, DR. ANDREW HARRIS, SAMUEL HOUGH, COMFORT HYDE.

To colonize those shameless enemies of their species in some desert country would be a relief and a blessing to society. This scandalous excitement is one of the genuine flowers of the colonization garden!

Prudence was aghast at Garrison's vehemence. She wrote to him on March 19th:

Permit me to entreat you to handle the people of Canterbury with all the mildness possible, as everything severe tends merely to heighten the flame of malignity among them. "Soft words turn away wrath, but grievous words stir up anger." Mr. May and many others of your warmhearted friends feel very much on this subject, and it is our opinion that you and the cause will gain many friends in this town and vicinity if you treat the matter with perfect mildness.

Mild commentary was not possible for Mr. Garrison. Both in speaking and writing about the Canterbury situation and Colonizationsists he used scathing, blistering language.

The other faction was not silent. An article signed by the Colonizationists appeared in the *Norwich Courier* on March 27th, 1833.

To the American Colonization Society:

To ameliorate the unfortunate condition of a portion of the human family in the progress of benevolence your Society has been devised and embraces many of our worthy and humane and patriotic citizens. The whole Christian community are united in sentiment and action to remove as fast as practicable to their native land, those who are bound in slavery. A territory has been ceded for their occupancy upon the shores of Africa and funds are now accumulating to meet all the expenses of their removal, where they may forever enjoy the blessings of education and freedom. It would seem that an institution so benevolent in its character, so well adapted to the condition of its beneficiaries and our safety, would find none to oppose it. But in this we are mistaken. Dissatisfied with this great plan of Christian charity — discontented with the prospect of good in store for them and us and hostile to that spirit of enlightened wisdom which animates the cause, a few individuals in our country have arrayed themselves against it and are casting in its way every obstacle within their reach. Mssrs. Buffum and Garrison are leaders in this opposition. They have set themselves up as dictators and the sum of misery to our country, should their project succeed, will be incalculable. A new association has been formed under the specious name of the "Anti-Slavery Society". In their public addresses and their papers their principles have been avowed — That the society, whose movements are under the guidance of these men, oppose the Colonization Society on the grounds that the Blacks ought not to be sent out of the country and should immediately be made free and remain within the United States, participating in all the affairs of government and on terms of entire equality, admitted within the bosom of society, and last of all in their wild career of reform, these gentlemen would justify intermarriage with the white people!!! Sentiments like these are somewhat alarming, and we have been led to an examination of their consequences by events which have recently transpired in Canterbury to which we need only recur, for the purpose of preventing the influence of statements, gross and exaggerated which are pressed upon the public by these men.

"Miss Prudence Crandall in 1831, having received the full aid of all our fellow citizens, engaged to establish a school for young

ladies in this place which has been continued down to the last month, when without consulting a single individual with whom she had made that arrangement, took a journey to Providence and Boston and soon after, unceremoniously announced her intentions to convert her female seminary into a school for blacks. Facts since communicated go to show that Arnold Buffum and William Lloyd Garrison both of whom she saw during her excursion, have had no small share in effecting this change. The Citizens of Canterbury assembled, and by a committee requested Miss Crandall to give up her project which she declined doing. A still larger meeting, by their committee urged additional reasons to dissuade her, but to no purpose. A Town meeting was then held on the 9th of March when the unanimous voice of the town was expressed in resolutions!

On the 14th of March these resolutions were communicated to Miss Crandall by the Civil Authority and the Selectmen who renewedly stated the various objections entertained by the town, and urged the impropriety of placing such an establishment in the town against their wishes. She was informed that the citizens of Canterbury were opposed to this school which was to be under the patronage of Arnold Buffum — his extravagant views were to be taught in the school — and in return that school was to become auxiliary in the work of immediate abolition as well as in opposing Colonization efforts. The Liberator was to be the mouthpiece of the school and Miss Crandall herself declared that 'Colonizing the people of color was a system of fraud from beginning to end.' When she justified her proceedings and principles on the ground that Moses married a 'colored woman', it was suggested she might as well advocate polygamy now, because it was lawful in the days of antiquity. In the language of the resolution we endeavored still to persuade her to abandon the project that she might not be the loser, in consequence of the original purchase of her house for the other school and not for this, responsible individuals offered and urged upon her, the sum she had paid for the house, upon condition that she would abandon the proposed school. This she declined. We might here rest our case in the hands of the public. We might ask the citizens of any town in New England wherever situated, would it be well for that town to admit the blacks from Slave States or other states to an unlimited extent? Once open the door and New England will become the Liberia of America . . . we appeal to The American Colonization Society to which our statement is addressed — we appeal to every Christian and every philanthropist — we appeal to the enlightened citizens of our native state and the friends of our country; and in making this appeal, we assure them all that they may rely upon the facts here stated and we ask them to apply to these facts those wholesome principles which we believe are universally cherished in New England and the issue, we will abide —

A.T. Judson, Rufus Adams, Asael Bacon, Chester Lyon, Walter Williams, Solomon Paine, Peter Morse, Comfort Hyde, Samuel Hough.

CIVIL AUTHORITY: Peter Morse, Asael Bacon, A.T. Judson, Ebenezer Sanger, Roswell Allen, (Selectman). Dated March 22, 1833.

Rev. May used the columns of the *Brooklyn Advertiser Press* to answer this message from the men of Canterbury.

Brooklyn, March 29, 1833
Andrew T. Judson, ESQ,

Sir; I left Canterbury, after the town meeting on the 9th ult. grieved that so large a number of persons could be so completely misled by the art and influence of a few individuals; and ashamed that in Connecticut (which claims to be the most enlightened and moral state in our Union) a community of free men could be found, who would thus yield themselves to be the instruments of such injustice and cruelty.

From your high official standing, Sir, both in the town and in the state it was to have been expected that you would have endeavored to allay the popular excitement, and to persuade your fellow-citizens to act advisedly. So far from it, however, you were the prominent actor on the occasion; and exerted yourself beyond measure to heat the imagination of your hearers, to enkindle their bitterest feelings against Miss Crandall and her friends and to hurry them on to an immediate decision — a decision which can reflect no honor upon the town, and which, if it cannot be reversed, may indirectly affect the happiness of millions in our land.

I therefore take the liberty thus publicly to plead with you and with your fellow citizens — nay — Sir, I have a right to claim from yourself and from the people of Canterbury and from the community at large, some attention to the defense I am about to offer of Miss Crandall's most benevolent project; of the part I have acted on her behalf; and of those gentlemen who with myself have encouraged her undertaking. I solemnly aver, that so far as I know anything about that young lady or her patrons or my own intentions, we have all been grossly misrepresented and traduced.

It was not until about the time of Miss Crandall's return from New York that I received the first intimation of design to open her school for the education of colored females. I expressed to my informant my heartfelt satisfaction that there was one so near me who would dare to brave the prejudices of the public so far as to devote herself to that great "labor of love." The young lady was then an entire stranger to me. I had heard however, of her good reputation as a teacher in Canterbury and Plainfield and better than that, of her great integrity of mind and benevolence of heart and energy of purpose; and therefore I determined to hold myself in readiness to aid her, if my assistance should be needed by her in any way.

A few days afterwards, i.e. on the 27th of February, I was informed that she had made her intention publicly known in your town and that the people were in consequence, filled with indignation at her, especially yourself and her immediate neighbors. Not having received from Miss Crandall any notice of her plans (though my deep interest in the melioration of the condition of our colored brethren must be well known in this vicinity) I at first concluded that she might prefer to avoid receiving any assistance from me, because perhaps of her strong objections to my religious opinions. On further reflections, however, it seemed my duty to offer her a helping hand. I therefore wrote her the following letter:

Feb. 27, 1833

"Miss Crandall:

"Although I am a stranger to you, I shall offer no apology for addressing you.

"The cause, which I hear you have espoused, is one which has long been deeply interesting to me. My situation and engagements have prevented my doing as much in behalf of our colored brethren, as I fain would have done. Last week I heard indirectly from Dr. Greene that you proposed to open a boarding school for colored girls. The intelligence rejoiced my heart, and I determined to do all in my power to assist you. You are probably well aware that my religious sentiments have rendered me obnoxious to the suspicion and ill-will of the clergy and a considerable proportion of the public in this vicinity. This may lessen very much my ability to serve you. But I wish you would command my services in any way in which you think I can be useful to you.

"Last evening, Chauncy Morse informed me that there was considerable excitement in Canterbury, in consequence of your proposal. This was to have been expected, so inveterate are the prejudices of people against the Blacks. But it is disgraceful to any community pretending to be Christian. I would enlarge upon this topic but I feel too deeply, to write in a proper temper.

"It has been intimated that there is to be a town meeting to prevent you from carrying your plan into operation. If there is, I shall endeavor to attend it. But how do they propose to prevent you? It has occurred to me that your conspicuous residence in the village might render your plans more objectionable. Perhaps your removal to a more retired situation would at once allay the violence of your opponents and be more favorable to your pupils, who would not be so exposed to insult as they might be where you are.

"I would be very happy to see you here or there — S.J. May

At the meeting, looking about us, I perceived many persons present from neighboring towns, who came there, as I have reason to believe with no very friendly regard towards the proposed school . . . . . In the gallery there were two or three decent looking colored men. Who they were I did not know, but supposed them to belong to your town. I saw nothing in their deportment at all improper, though if they had manifested great displeasure at some of your remarks, I should not have wondered. I am thus particular, because you have endeavored through the Norwich papers to make the public believe that the friends of Miss Crandall's school presented themselves to your 'perfectly orderly meeting' in a most formidable array, as if to awe your citizens into compliance with your wishes. Permit me to say, Sir, if you or some of your coadjutors had adopted the precaution of 'taking notes' at the time (for which precaution you seemed to be offended at the Providence young men) you probably would have given as correct account of the meeting as he has given in the Liberator, and not have committed so many mistakes in your communications to the Norwich papers as must be apparent to all who were witnesses of what you have therein attempted to describe.

On the first Monday in April the first scholar arrived by stage from Providence. This was Ann Eliza Hammond. Sarah Harris returned as a day student. The appearance of the first pupils gave emphasis to Prudence's determination to continue with her plans and added to the fury of her neighbors. Tales of their most recent actions were reported to

Mr. Jocelyn in a letter Prudence wrote on April 9th.

"Mr. Jocelyn:

"Dear Friend,

"In the midst of tribulation the gleaming hope that better days will yet be mine gives tranquility to my feelings while surrounded by those whose enmity and bitterness of feeling can hardly be contemplated. It is a fact that many inhabitants of Canterbury met last Friday evening at the Masonic Hall in this village and resolved that they would not sell anything to me or my family and that they would not in any way assist me. There was one man, Mr. Stephen Coit, that withdrew from the resolve and told them that if anyone wished to buy of him he would sell to them. This man and his wife I trust are Christians, and have previously been violently opposed to me.

"On Sabbath evening I had the pleasure of hearing Mr. William L. Garrison lecture at Brooklyn, Ct. I passed the night at the same house with him (the Benson home) and indeed it was a source of great joy.

"The next day he sent for the stage driver to come for him when the stage left for Hartford but to his astonishment he never came. Mr. George Benson soon procured a carriage and he overtook the stage after a ride of about three miles. Towards evening the news came that the Deputy Sheriff was in pursuit of him. The Sheriff went to Brooklyn in great haste and inquired for Garrison and if he had gone — he soon went to the hotel, took his horse and rode west. We have been informed that this morning the Sheriff returned but why we do not know and for what they were going to take Mr. Garrison we do not know but we presume for what he said in the Liberator.

"It was also hinted that they wished to carry him to the South. This indeed was the occasion for much sorrow. It was his intention to lecture in Hartford this evening to the people of color.

"His intention is to be in New Haven soon. I have but one boarder yet and one day scholar and I wish you to encourage those that are coming to come immediately. On account of the printer Mr. May's letter to A.T. Judson will not be out until Thursday of this week.

"It is supposed by a gentleman on whom I think I can rely, that there were five writs issued for Mr. Garrison yesterday. The truth of what I have stated I will write you by the next mail If I can possibly

obtain it. Please give my love to Mrs. Jocelyn and I remain with respect,

Yours,
Prudence Crandall"

Mr. Garrison's own account of his Brooklyn visit is contained in a letter which he wrote to his assistant Isaac Knapp.

April 11, 1833

"On Saturday, friend G.W. Benson took me to Brooklyn in a chaise, where I tarried until Monday under the hospitable roof of his parents. My excellent brother May was delighted to see me, and my pleasure was equally great in taking him by the hand. I did not expect to deliver an address in Brooklyn but could not easily avoid a compliance with the wishes of my friends. Accordingly, I occupied Mr. May's pulpit on Saturday evening, last.

"Miss Crandall having obtained information that I was to hold forth, came up from Canterbury with her sister (a very beautiful girl, by the way). She is a wonderful woman, as undaunted as if she had a whole world on her side. She has opened her school and is resolved to persevere. I wish Brother Johnson to state this fact, particularly in the next issue of the Liberator and urge all those who intend to send their children thither to do so without delay.

"The stage for Hartford on Monday morning neglected to call for me and half an hour had elapsed, after its departure before I was aware of the fact. As time was precious, I took a common wagon and followed in pursuit and at the end of the seventh mile overtook the stage. I was in a wretched plight, covered with mud and wet — for it rained heavily. I arrived in Hartford late that evening and the next morning thought of starting for New Haven; but at the urgent solicitations of the colored friends, I gave them an address in the evening in their church."

The letter continues from Philadelphia six days later:

"I saw Brother Jocelyn in New York. He showed me a letter which he received from Miss Crandall, in which she stated that I had not left Brooklyn more than half an hour before a sheriff from Canterbury drove up to the door of Mr. Benson at full speed, having five writs against me from A.T. Judson and Company and finding that I had gone, he pursued after me for several miles but had to give up the chase. No doubt the Colonization party will resort to some base measures to prevent my departure for England.

He made his way safely to England. By this time Mr. Garrison had made many enemies. Some of the Southern states had placed a price of

$10,000 on his head and he lived for many years in fear of being kidnapped and sent South. He also made many friends, especially among the colored people of the northern states. The *Liberator* carried a report of a meeting of People of Color of New York City which passed the following resolution:

> *"Resolved — That we highly approve the mission of Mr. Garrison to England, who from his very extensive knowledge of our condition in general and his particular intimacy with the best informed men of color in most of the States, with whose sentiment he is acquainted, render him eminently qualified truly to represent them......*
>
> *"Resolved that the establishment of schools for the education of colored youth receives our unqualified approbation, and will receive our undivided support. As it is reason that distinguished man from the brute creation; it is evident, that in proportion as reason is cultivated and improved, the distance is increased between man and brute or between cultivated and uncultivated men. The want of education among us is so manifest on the most cursory review, as to induce us most heartily to join in any proposed feasible plan for obtaining it. And it is hoped that the call on the British public for their kind offices in this regard, may equal the most sanguine expectations of the friends of the improvement of the people of color in this, the land of their nativity.*
>
> *"Whereas the above named mission in England will be attended with considerable expense —*
>
> *Resolved — That a collection taken up this evening in aid thereof and that a committee consisting of 9 persons be appointed to obtain subscriptions from those that may feel disposed to assist in this highly important business.*
>
> *Resolved — That the daily papers, friendly to the improvement and cause of the colored people, be furnished with a copy of these proceedings by the Secretary with a request that they be published.*

As he had threatened to do, Judson secured a warrant, warning that Ann Eliza Hammond must leave Canterbury or be arrested under the vagrancy law. Sheriff Roger Coit arrived and stated that it was his duty to read a writ to Ann Eliza Hammond in person. Prudence called her to the south parlor and stayed with her while the writ was read:

> *The Select Men of any town shall be, and they are hereby authorized, either by themselves, or by warrant from a Justice of the Peace in such town, directed to either Constable of such town, which warrant such justice is hereby authorized to give, to warn*

any person not an inhabitant of this State, to depart such town, and the person so warned, shall forfeit and pay to the Treasurer of such town one dollar and sixty-seven cents per week, for every week he or she shall continue in such town, after warning given as aforesaid, and when such person who shall be convicted of the breach of this act, in refusing to depart on warning as aforesaid, hath no estate to satisfy the fine , such person shall be whipped on the naked body not exceeding ten stripes, unless he or she depart the town within ten days next after the sentence is given and reside no more therein without leave of the Select Men.

Having done his duty, the unhappy Sheriff withdrew. The words in the statute, "whipped on the naked body" had of course had their dramatic effect on Prudence and Ann Eliza, but at the same time they could not fail to realize that this penalty could be imposed only if the fine of $1.67 per week were not paid. The fine itself was unjust because Ann Eliza was by no means a pauper. If Prudence paid it, thereby establishing a precedent, she might have to pay a like amount for every "foreign" student who came to her school, and this could easily prove an impossible burden. Ann Eliza declared she would be whipped if she must but she would not leave the school. Thinking of the sturdy granite whipping post in front of Westminister Church, Prudence shuddered. She sought advice from Mr. May. He offered bond to the Selectmen which they refused to accept. A few days later the Sheriff again appeared with a summons. It read:

To the Sheriff of the County of Windham, His Deputy, or either of the Constables of the Town of Canterbury, within said County, GREETINGS:

BY AUTHORITY OF THE STATE OF CONNECTICUT, You are hereby commanded to summon ELIZA ANN HAMMOND, of Providence, in the County of Providence, and State of Rhode Island and residing in said town of Canterbury, to appear before George Middleton, Esq. Justice of the Peace for the County of Windham presiding in the town of Plainfield in the County of Windham, next adjoining the town of Canterbury, which is the Plaintiff in this case, (there being no Justice of the Peace in said town of Canterbury, which is also the present place of the Defendant's abode, who can lawfully try this case) at the dwelling house of Chauncy Bacon, in said town of Canterbury, on the second day of May, 1833, at one o'clock in the afternoon, then and there to answer unto the town of Canterbury in said County, a public corporation of said County, who now sues and prosecutes this action, by PETER MORSE,

ROSWELLL ALLEN, EBENEZER SANGER, ASAHEL BACON, AND ANDREW T. JUDSON, Select Man of said town of Canterbury, in an action brought on one certain statute of Law of this State, entitled 'An Act for the admisssion and settlement of inhabitants in Towns,' where in among other things it is enacted as follows: to wit, Section 7th.

. . . (here the law was cited again in full, including the passage about whipping on the naked body) . . .

. . . and that in the 8th Section of the same act, among other things it is enacted as follows, viz: 'and the Select Men in the respective towns are hereby empowered to prosecute all breaches of this Act,' and now the said town of Canterbury, by their said Select Men further allege, that on the 12th day of April, 1833, One, ELIZA ANN HAMMOND, this defendant, who then was not, and never since hath been, and who is not now, an inhabitant of this State, but then was, ever since hath been, and now is an inhabitant of the State of Rhode Island, come to reside in said town of Canterbury, and on the 13th of April, 1833 did by a warrant from Rufus Adams, Esq. then and ever since a Justice of the Peace for Windham County in said Canterbury, directed to either Constable of said Canterbury, the Select Men of said Canterbury did warn the said Eliza Ann Hammond, to depart the town of Canterbury aforesaid, and notwithstanding said warning duly and lawfully served upon the said Eliza Ann Hammond, on the said 13th day of April, 1833, she the said Eliza Ann, against the provision of said statute, and against the peace, did continue in said town of Canterbury from said 13th day of April, the full period of one week, to wit: including the 14th, 15th, 16th, 17th, 18th, 19th and 20th days of April 1833, by means whereof the said Eliza Ann Hammond hath forfeited and become liable to pay to the Treasurer of Canterbury aforesaid, the sum of one dollar and sixty-seven cents, and a right of action hath accrued to the plaintiff to recover the same for the aforesaid, and the defendant hath never paid the same though often requested and demanded, and now to recover the said sum of $1.67, and cost of suit, this action is brought. Hereof fail not, but of this writ with doings hereon, lawful service and return the same. Dated at Canterbury, the 22nd day of April, 1833.

Signed, RUFUS ADAMS, Justice of the Peace.

Again a $1,000 bond was offered to cover Miss Hammond and other students and this time the bond was accepted. Ann Eliza was spared a dreadful experience but the newspapers did not spare the Canterbury braves in their report of this threat. It added to the widespread infamy which was published throughout the northern states and as far west as Indiana.

With only two boarding students and Sarah, Prudence began to fear that her school would indeed sink. In despair she wrote again to Mr. Jocelyn:

> *Canterbury, April 17, 1833*
>
> *My very Dear Friend*
>
> *Disappointment seems yet to be my lot. I have only two boarders and one day scholar — one girl is under warning to depart the town. Her accusation is that she is residing here against the peace of the State. A copy of the warning I gave to Mr. May to send where he chose and he immediately commenced writing to Mr. Tappan on the same sheet therefore I forebear sending a second copy not doubting you have read it ere this.*
>
> *I am informed that Miss Hammond is not to be carried home by the selectmen but I am to have a writ served upon me as soon as the law will allow it. Miss Hammond was warned on Saturday evening about 7 o'clock that the law obliges those who harbor foreigners to pay $1.67 per week. I presume that I shall be subjected to that penalty next Friday. Sabbath evening I went to see my dear, dear friend Mr. May. I asked him if in case of a writ should be served upon me whether I should pay the fine or stand trial and he said stand trial. I wish you would answer this question by the next mail after you receive this — it will not be in time for this week but it will be for the next. I think it best to pay the first fine when demanded but I shall not do without first consulting Mr. May. A written offer of bonds was presented to the selectmen by Mr. May to secure the town against any damage that shall be done by any of my pupils. I presume bonds will not be accepted by them. This is the day of trial — all who will dare venture to encounter the public feeling at all must expect to be branded with all the marks of disgrace that can be heaped upon them by their enemies.*
>
> *The thought that such opposition as has been raised in the minds of the people of Canterbury and the adjoining towns never once entered into my mind while contemplating the change I am now endeavoring to effect in my school. Very true I thought many*

now endeavoring to effect in my school. Very true I thought many of the high-minded, worldly men would oppose the plan but that no Christian would act so unwisely and conduct in a manner so outrageously was a thought distant from my view. I have put my hand to the plough and I will never no never look back — I trust that God will help me to keep this resolution for 'in Him only is safety for mine own arm never brought salvation.'

I have had in the Providence of God to pass through many trying seasons but place them all together they are very small compared with the present scene of adversity — yet in the midst of this affliction I am as happy as at any moment of my life — I never saw the time when I was the least apprehensive that adversity would harm me — but I can truly say I have many times been fearful that the blessings and mercies dispensed to me by the hand of God, my heart would become hardened in the ways of prosperity and I forget to thank the Giver while I enjoyed the gift.

If this school is crushed by inhuman laws, another I suppose cannot be obtained, certainly one for white scholars can never be taught by me. As for myself I think I shall fare well enough!! I have sufficient property in hand to pay my debts — to work I am not ashamed and to beg I do not fear the necessity.

April 20

Yesterday I called on Mr. May — found him very anxious to hear from you and Mr. Tappan. He says stand trial with the town if they sue me — it is his opinion they cannot collect the fine. Petitions to present to the General Assembly are circulating in various towns in this region of the country and I am informed by Mr. White that the petition of Canterbury is not like those that are circulating in other towns. I have not yet been able to obtain a copy of either but I think I shall soon. I have received a letter from that invaluable man, A. Tappan today — he thinks best to sustain the school where it is if it can be done without too great expense and if otherwise seek a place somewhere else. Mr. May yesterday received a letter from a friend of his telling him that in the town of Reading, Mass., the people are willing to have my school established. Do not mention this to anyone until we get further information from that town. Mr. Judson and his party think Mr. May's letters are so very flat that they are not worth much notice, certainly not an answer.

The boat leaves Norwich on Monday but I have not determined whether I shall take it for New York or not.

Yours with great regard,
Prudence Crandall

Mr. Jocelyn sent his ward, Harriet Rosetta Lamson to the school. The child of dissolute parents, she had been under his care for some time. She was 15 and it was arranged that she might do some household chores to help defray her expenses since Mr. Jocelyn's resources were limited.

Each week a few new students arrived. Mr. Isaac Glasco of Griswold, Connecticut brought his two daughters. He was a successful scythe and axe maker who owned a fine home and flourishing business. He also made special implements for the whaling industry. His wife and children were respected in the community and he enjoyed a fine reputation for reliability as a businessman. By the end of April there were 17 girls enrolled in the school ranging in age from 9 to 18 years. They came from Boston, New York, Philadelphia as well as Providence, New Haven and other Connecticut towns. They were awed by the elegance of their new home in Canterbury and awfully frightened by the crude behavior of the townspeople. Shy and quiet at first, they soon became outgoing and garrulous as they responded to the warmth and gentleness of their teachers and Marcia.

Prudence and the others shielded the girls as much as possible but it was difficult to anticipate the various forms which meanness could take — the carpet of cow manure spread over the great granite steps at the front door, eggs splattered on the door and numerous other annoyances were only part of the continuing harassment.

The school had many visitors. Prudence's father and brother Hezekiah came to bring them food and other supplies which they could not buy from most of the local merchants. All shopkeepers, except Stephen Coit, had refused to sell any goods to Prudence or anyone associated with her school. Rev. May called frequently and often shared a meal with the girls. Arnold Buffum stopped in whenever his anti-slavery work brought him into the neighborhood.

The friends of the school were kept busy trying to put out the flames of animosity which were fanned by their enemies. Rev. May's letter of April 6th confronted forthrightly the argument which was most frequently used.

> *He wrote: "It has often been charged upon those who advocate the abolition of slavery that they are aiming to amalgamate the blacks and whites. This string has been harped upon at the town meetings by all the opposers of Miss Crandall. It served to shock the prejudices of the people and dupe their judgment. The same charge is repeated in the Norwich papers . . . and I now call upon you and others who have brought this accusation to prove it, if you can. I know and am sure that such is not one of the intentions or wishes*

of the Anti-slavery society or an Abolitionists that I am acquainted with. Of course, we do not believe there are any barriers established by God between the two races. If there were any, the complexions of tens of thousands in our land show to our disgrace that those barriers are not impassable. Whether marriage shall or shall not take place between those of different colors, is a matter which time must be left to decide. We do not advocate them, we do not hope to see them, we only say that such connections would be incomparably more honorable to the whites as well as more consistent with the will of God and the virtue of the nation than that illicit intercourse which is now so common especially in the South." (Brooklyn Advertiser Press).

Others also wrote in sympathy for Miss Crandall and her charges. In the *Christian Secretary* of Hartford April 20th is the comment:

"Miss Crandall, who recently attempted the establishment of a school at Canterbury, is being compelled to relinquish it by the opposition of the inhabitants. If the unfortunate colored people receive such treatment in New England, we know not in what part of the Union they will find a refuge from oppression. If this be a fair specimen of the land of steady habits, Mr. Garrison and his associates had better suspend operations against the Colonization Society and lecture their neighbors on the subject of decency and common humanity."

Quoted from the Utica Baptist Repository.

Mr. Judson and his cohorts were fighting hard and they now had the whole state for their arena. Petitions signed in Canterbury were taken to the Legislature where with all the power of voice and verbosity he could muster he declared — with regard to the Canterbury school,"The establishment or rendezvous falsely denominated a school was designed by its projectors as the theatre, as the place to promulgate their disgusting doctrines of amalgamation and their pernicious sentiments of subverting the union. These pupils are to be congregated here from all quarters under the pretense of educating them but really to scatter fire brands, arrows and death among brethren of our own blood." The petitions were referred to a committee on "Inhabitants of Towns."

Pardon Crandall felt impelled to come to his daughter's defense. He sent to the Legislature the following statement.

"To The General Assembly:

I would inform you that some time past Prudence Crandall proposed and notified to open a school for young ladies and little misses of color in Canterbury. Instead of the leading men of Canterbury coming forward to encourage or assist to enlighten the ignorant or elevate the deprived people of color, they have called together a number of town meetings and passed resolutions to do all in their power to destroy this institution. Among others was one passed at the town meeting to appoint a committee of ten to draw a petition to the General Assembly now convened, to prevent people of color from assembling for the purpose of getting an education and also to correspond with other towns in the state to forestall public opinion for the same purpose which petition is now pending before the General Assembly. I entreat the members of the Assembly when acting on this petition to remember those self evident truths that all mankind are created free and equal, that they are endowed with inalienable rights of which no man nor any set of men have any right to deprive them. And my request is that you will not grant the prayer of any petition nor pass any act which will curtail or destroy any of the rights of free people of this state or other states whether they are white or black.

Canterbury, May 1, 1833
Pardon Crandall"

Prudence was justifiably proud of the wise words and sturdy support of her father. Her brother Reuben had remonstrated with her, urging her to change her mind and give up her school. Hezekiah was as helpful as he could be but he was less than enthusiastic about her actions since they were now embarassing to him and might well become an economic threat if the townspeople with whom he dealt in the manufacture and sale of cotton material became vengeful against the whole family. Her mother was worried about her safety and comfort and would have been greatly relieved if she had closed her school. But her father was consistently courageous and encouraging.

She had resisted for three months the temptation to give public utterance to her own views but she was finally persuaded to write a letter which was published in the *Windham County Advertiser* on May 7, 1833.

"Mr. Holbrook: Whatever reluctance I may feel to appear before the public, circumstance require that I should do so. After all that has been said in various newspapers, about me and my school and my friends it seems that I owe it to them and to myself to make a simple statement that you and others may know the object of my present school and also what first induced me to establish it; and to exonerate my friends and myself from several unreasonable censures and misrepresentations that are in circulation.

"A colored girl of respectability — a professor of religion — and daughter of honorable parents called on me sometime during the month of September last and said in a very earnest manner "Miss Crandall, I want to get a little more learning, if possible enough to

teach colored children and if you will admit me to your school, I shall forever be under greatest obligation to you. If you think it will be the means of injuring you, I will not insist on the favor.'

"I did not answer her immediately, as I thought if I gave her permission some of my scholars might be disturbed. In further conversation with her however I found she had great anxiety to improve in learning.

"Her repeated solicitations were more than my feelings could resist and I told her if I was injured on her account I would bear it — she might enter as one of my pupils. The girl had not been long under my instruction before I was informed by several persons that she must be removed or my school would be greatly injured.

"This was unpleasant news for me to hear but I continued her in my school. Previous to any excitement concerning her there fell in my way several publications that contained many facts relative to the people of color of which I was entirely ignorant. My feelings began to awaken. I saw that the prejudice of whites against color was deep and inveterate. In my humble opinion it was the strongest if not the only chain that bound those heavy burdens on the wretched slaves, which we ourselves are not willing to touch with one of our fingers. I felt in my heart to adopt the language of the Sacred Preacher when He said — "So I turned to consider all the oppressions that are done under the sun and behold the tears of such as were oppressed, and they had no comforter; and on the side of their oppressors there was power but they had no comforter. Therefore I praised the dead that are already dead more than the living which are yet alive.'

"I said in my heart, here are my convictions. What shall I do? Shall I be inactive and permit prejudice, 'The mother of abominations' to remain undisturbed? Or shall I venture to enlist in the ranks of those who with the Sword of Truth dare hold combat with prevailing iniquity? I contemplated for a while the manner in which I might best serve the people of color. As wealth was not mine, I saw no other means of benefitting them, than by imparting to those of my own sex that were anxious to learn, all the instruction I might be able to give, however small the amount. This I deem my duty, how to perform it, I knew not. With the friends of the people of color, called 'Abolitionsists' I was entirely unacquainted save by reputation.

"Having for some time wished to visit New York or some other places of schools and also to purchase for the benefit of my scholars, school apparatus, I came to the conclusion that I would

perform my long contemplated journey and visit the schools in Boston while at the same time the most prominent object of my tour was to visit William L. Garrison — to obtain his opinion respecting the propriety of establishing a school for colored females — and the prospect of success should I attempt it. Being an entire stranger in Boston previous to my journey, I took the liberty to enquire of several of my neighbors, if they had any friends in Boston to whom they would be willing to give me a line of introduction. Rev. Mr. Kneeland and Rev. Mr. Platt were the only persons I found who had any acquaintances in the place. These gentlemen very kindly gave me letters to distinguished clergymen in that city. Neither to these gentlemen, my neighbors nor my scholars did I make known all my business. And I felt perfectly justified in telling them I was going to visit schools, which I did and to purchase the before mentioned apparatus which was at that time my determination and the want of money was the only reason why I did not purchase.

"Now because I did not see fit to expose my business before I knew whether I could obtain a sufficient number of colored pupils to sustain my school and also did not purchase the apparatus, I am charged that too in a public manner of falsehood or at least wilful prevarication. False and scandalous reports about me and my friends are in constant circulation, some of which are dispersed by the papers far and near. In the piece signed "A friend of the Colonization Cause" that first appeared in the Norwich Republican, which you have copied into your paper, the author upon his own authority has declared that there are a few men in Boston and Providence who have laid the foundation of this school which is entirely false as I was wholly self moved in the plan, though I gratefully acknowledge their kind approbation. Furthermore, he asks 'and what do they intend to do with this institution?' After making several ungenerous and detestable replies the sentence is closed with this remark — 'In a word they hope to force the races (black and white) to amalgamate.' This is utterly false — the object, the sole object, at this school is to instruct the ignorant and fit and prepare teachers for the people of color that they may be elevated and their intellectual and moral wants supplied.

"You are surprised that the Rev. S. J. May is the warm friend and advocate of my school — He has pled my cause manfully and I trust he will reap a just reward.

"The truth of his remonstrances with A. T. Judson, Esq., and others, I presume that no one will attempt to deny in any material

point. After what he has published, it is unnecessary for me to enlarge, but simply to give this my public declaration, in favor of the correctness of all the statements he has made respecting myself and my school, many of which he made upon my authority.

Respectfully yours,
Prudence Crandall"

If she hoped through this letter to influence Windham County members of the Legislature she was overly optimistic. Petitions from Canterbury, Ashford and Hebron were submitted to the Legislature in support of the bill to outlaw her school. The Committee, chaired by Senator Pearl from Hampton, submitted an impressive report replete with historical references and hysterical inferences.

"The condition of the colored population throughout the United States and its influence on society ought to command the attention of every legislature. The slave trade commenced centuries ago and about 80,000,000 of the human race have been its victims. They have suffered death in various and cruel forms, or have been left to drag out a miserable existance in the most abject slavery. Nations and individuals have been engaged in the horrid traffic and our own country has participated deeply in its guilt but the trade is now forbidden by our federal government under the penalty of death, and nations are leagued together for its suppression. However effectual these measures may prove it will be long before we cease to suffer from evils entailed upon us by the slave trade.

"That every prudent and wise means for their mitigation should be anxiously sought and adopted is not less enjoined in regard to the welfare of society, than by the duties of humanity and justice.

"It is about half a century since the Legislature of this state commenced a system of gradual abolition of slavery, and the great object has been consummated, still the unhappy class of beings, whose race has been degraded by unjust bondage are among us and justly demand, at our hands all which is consistent with the common safety, and their own best interest, for the amelioration of their state and character.

"Our obligations as a State, acting in its sovereign capacity are limited to the people of our own territory. Our whole population of colored born within the last century are already restored to the blessings of freedom. The Constitution and laws of the State have secured to them all the rights and privileges of other citizens except that of the elective franchise and those of which it is essential. It is

not contemplated for the Legislature to judge the wisdom of that provision of the Constitution which denies the franchise to the people of color; but your committee are not advised that it has ever been a subject of complaint. In every other point the white and colored population of this State are entitled by law to equal rights and privileges. The latter, not less than the former are within all the provisions which relate to education. They are alike protected in their persons and properties and in the exercise of every occupation and profession. They also enjoy a special exemption from the poll tax and military duty. In regard to education of all those of that unfortunate class who belong to this State, the Legislature ought not to impede but so far as may be within their province and consistent with the best interests of the people to foster and sustain the benevolent efforts of individuals directed to that end. Here our duties terminate. The colored people of other states and other countries are under the laws and guardianship of their respective sovereignties and we are not entrusted with the powers of enquiring into the expediency or justice of their local regulations, except to acquire wisdom in regard to our own. Here are the boundaries of our Legislative rights and duties. We are under no obligations, moral or political to incur the incalculable evils of bringing into our own state colored emigrants from abroad. For this we have the example of other members of our confederacy by whom slavery is not tolerated. It is a fact confirmed by painful and long experience and one that results from the condition of the colored people in the midst of a white population in all states and countries that they are an appalling source of crime and pauperism. As this, in our own state proceeds from the degradation to which their ancestors have been wrongfully subjected, it imposes on us an imperious duty to advance their morals and usefulness and preserve them so far as possible from the evils which they have been obliged to inherit, but at the same time the duty is not less imperative to protect our own citizens against that host of colored emigrants which would rush in from every quarter when invited to our schools and colleges.

"The memorials which have been referred to your committee are signed by great numbers of respectable citizens who reside in different towns in this state. They have been occasioned by respected efforts made to establish literary institutes embracing their objects, the colored people from other states and countries.

"The citizens of those places, where the establishment of those seminaries has been attempted, have manifested toward them a united and very ardent opposition grounded, as your committee

believes, on most reasonable apprehensions of their effects especially on the places of their injurious locations.

"Although the introduction of colored persons for the purpose of education merely would seem to contemplate but a temporary residence, yet that class of people have seldom any settled establishment in their own state or inducements to return after the term of instruction has expired; and as their last association and attachments would be here; — a great portion of the whole number would make this state their permanent residence. The immense evils which such a mass of colored population would gather within this state when it has become their place of resort from other states and countries, would impose on our own people burdens which would admit no future remedy, and can be avoided only by timely prevention.

"The records of criminal courts, prisons and asylums for the poor where great numbers prevail among the white population, admonish us of the dangers to which we are exposed and evince the necessity in the present crisis, of effecting legislative interposition.

"Particular instances may occur in which the admission of a colored person belonging to any other state to the privilieges of a school might be justified from particular circumstances. The several towns in which schools are located, must be the first and greatest sufferers from too liberal an indulgence. It would seem safe and just to place the subject under the direction of their own civil authority and select-men with a view to these objects, your comittee respectfully report the accompanying bill for a public act. Respectfully submitted per order of the Committee.

Philip Pearl, Jr.
Chairman

Through this excess of labor the Act was brought forth. It was called "An Act in addition to an act entitled "An Act for the admission and settlement of Inhabitants of Towns." The text of it was:

Whereas, attempts have been made to establish literary institutions in this state for instruction of colored persons belonging to other states and countries, which would tend to the great increase of the colored population of the state and thereby to the injury of the people: therefore,

Section 1. Be it enacted by the Senate and House of Representative, in general assembly convened, that no person shall set up or establish in this state any school, academy, or literary institution whatsoever in this state, or harbor or board, for the purpose of *attending or being taught or instructed in such a school, academy or literary institute any colored person who is not an inhabitant of any town in this state without the consent, in writing, first obtained of a majority of the civil authority and also of the selectmen of the town in which such school, academy or literary institute is situated; and each and every person who shall knowingly do any act forbidden as aforesaid or shall be aiding or assisting therein, shall for the first offense forfeit and pay to the Treasurer of this state, a fine of one hundred dollars and for the second offense shall forfeit and pay a fine of $200 and so double for every offence of which he or she shall be convicted. And all informing officers are required to make due presentment of all breaches of this act.*

Provided, that nothing in this Act shall extend to any district school, established in any school society, under the laws of this state, or to any school established by any school society under the laws of this state, or to any incorporated academy or incorporated school for instruction in this State.

Sec. 2. Be it further enacted: That any colored person not an inhabitant of this state who shall reside in any town therein for the purpose of being instructed as aforesaid, may be removed in the manner prescribed in the sixth and seventh section of the act to which this is an addition.

Sec. 3 Be it further enacted, that any person not an inhabitant of this state, who shall reside in any town therein, for the purpose of being instructed as aforesaid shall be an admissable witness in all prosecutions under the first section of this act and may be compelled to give testimony therein, not withstanding any thing contained in this Act or the Act last aforesaid.

Sec. 4. Be it further enacted that so much of the seventh section of the Act to which this is an addition as may provide for the infliction of corporal punishment be and the same is hereby repealed.

(Section 6 & 7 referred to provided that any vagrant could be taken to the town boundary by the selectman and could be whipped through the town. Since most towns had similar acts the hapless one might be whipped through several towns!)

The statute was signed by Samuel Ingham, speaker of the House of Representatives, Ebenezer Stoddard, President of the Senate and Henry W. Edwards, Governor, on May 24, 1833.

The passage of this law brought a veritable day of jubilee to Canterbury. Andrew T. Judson was the hero. Men and boys congregated on the hill in back of Judson's house and fired 13 salvos from the town's cannon, jarring the house of the principal target of the law. They climbed to the gallery of the church and pulled the bell ropes continuously throughout the day. They snake danced around Miss Crandall's house shouting wildly.

Inside the house Prudence and Hannah Almyra did all they could to calm the fears of the poor bewildered girls. Rev. Kneeland and Rev. May came to offer comfort and, if need be, protect them.

The men of Canterbury found the joy of victory darkened by the attacks on them in some segments of the press. A particularly annoying poem appeared in one of the *Abolition Pamphlets.*

A New Ballad

I'll tell you a story, a story so merry
Concerning the people of Canterbury,
About their town meeting and speechifying
To send all the blacks from the country flying.

It is sad that a lady had dared to invite
Colored girls to her school, that she'd teach them to write
And, to the disgrace of the town and the nation
Intended to give them a good education.

When this news reached the ears of the Clerk of the town
He lengthened his visage, his eyes he cast down
Then swore by the shade of Jack Cade, no such school
The village should darken while he had the rule.

So the town's men were summoned. In haste they appear
In their hall, all aghast and all trembling with fear.
An orator rises, 'a note let me read
To declare to the universe some of our creed.

'Resolved, in this land to black souls are not given,
That from Africa alone is the black road to heaven!
And that we will resist teaching any such creatures
As rudely assailing a great law of natures.

Can anyone think, he cries, nature intended
By teaching, these blacks souls should
Be fitted to meet with us whites in debate
And aid us in making laws for our State?

Can Connecticut men e'er become such vile asses
As submit to this mixture of milk and molasses?
O save us, kind heaven, from these foul disgraces
And bless our descendents with unmixed white faces!!

When this manly resolve this bold speech had sustained
Long and loud were the plaudits the orator gained.
Next springs up the clerk, but how vain is all verse
His wisdom, his fancy, his wit to rehearse.

'I rise, fellow citizens, sad and dismayed
Our good town is ruined, our rights are betrayed!
If this school be established among us what then?
Black females are ladies and Negroes are men.

We must meet them at dances, at parties at prayers
Our houses and lands too soon would be theirs.
What right have these wooly heads hither to come
Let them go back to Africa — There is their home.

In vain did our forefathers cross the rough sea,
And leave us this land as the home of the free.
In vain did our ancestors bleed, in vain toil
If we suffer these Negroes to share in the soil.

Let us swear then together we never will yield
To the Negro a house or a school or a field,
But while Quinebaug flows through our town it shall never
Reflect a black face from its bosom forever!

He ceased and the townsmen with eager acclaim
Accept the resolve, which saves them from shame.
The calamity dire, the unending disgrace
Of treating like brethren the African race.

O patriot sages of Quinebaug river
Your wisdom shall brighten the world forever
And humanity, weeping o'er error and crime
Shall be cheered by your note to the last hour of time.

Rev. May read this with appropriate expression and great glee when he brought it to show to Prudence and the members of her school. In spite of the trying days, filled with apprehension and uncertainty, Prudence could still enjoy a bit of humor and this ballad brought her much amusement as she tried to visualize the reactions of the bombastic Mr. Judson.

The derisive ballad was mild when compared to some of the other comments carried by such journals as the *Emancipator*, an abolitionist paper published in New York. A letter signed "Justice" was printed in the June 22nd issue.

"Mr. Editor

"When the servants of the people, deputed to devise wholesome laws, for the regulation of the politic, violate their trust, infringe the rights of citizens and overlap the bounds of the constitution, it is the duty of every free-man to raise his voice against their unrighteous doings and condemn without fear or favor their unfaithfulness and misconduct. This I deem sufficient apology for troubling you with a few remarks in reference to a law lately passed by our wise Legislators in general assembly convened. You doubtless understand me as alluding to the law which makes it a penal offense to educate colored persons from neighboring states.

"With the school at Canterbury against which the law is directly and primarily pointed, I have nothing to do. It is nothing to me whether it stands or falls. Nothing whether some dozen or two colored persons succeed in obtaining there the education they seek or are forced to go elsewhere to procure it, or are forced to forego it entirely. I say it is nothing to me, for comparatively speaking it is so, my own share of the loss to the public from the failure or neglect of any one individual to cultivate his mind and qualify himself for usefulness, being but small. But, with the establishment of such a precedent as this law, if adjudged valid, does establish, I have *to do; every man who believes 'intelligence is the life of liberty' has to do; every man who regards the Constitution as the sacred Palladium of American freedom has to do.*

"What! shall the express provisions of the Constitution be violated; Shall the 'inalienable rights' of man be trampled on; shall the precedent be established, which in this land of equal rights *deprives one class of our population of certain valuable privileges which other classes enjoy, which imposes restraints on the acquisition of learning; which exludes from one avenue to improvement a portion of the free people of these free states and shall we who witness this perversion of right be unmoved and silent? We who boast of the enlightened condition of our beloved state, of the liberality which charaacterized its institutions, of the love of*

knowledge which pervades all ranks of its inhabitants, and the generous encouragement which learning receives from its laws?

"The Law of which I am speaking, I consider unconstitutional, unjust, inefficient for the avowed purpose of its passage, and disgraceful to the petitioners who prayed for it, to the legislators who passed, to the Governor who approved it, and finally to the people of Canterbury who with sound of bell and cannon celebrated its passage.

"1. That it palpably violates the Constitution who that can read, cannot plainly see? That instrument in express terms, secures to citizens of the several states, the rights and privileges of citizens in each state. Does this mean that every citizen of another state shall enjoy, in Connecticut all the privileges which he enjoys in his own state? Then does the law come at once in collision with the Constitution, for it takes from a portion of the citizens of other states privileges which they enjoy at home. Does it mean that the citizens of other states shall enjoy in Connecticut all the privileges which citizens of Connecticut enjoy at home? Then is the law as clearly unconstitutional as by the former construction; for it makes a distinction between the free blacks of Connecticut and the free blacks of other states, denying the latter privileges which are not denied to the former. For neither this nor any other law prohibits the instruction of the colored inhabitants of our own state in any school whatever, which they choose to attend, nor could a law be passed, I trust, which should extend so far. This law then directly violates an express provision of the constitution.

"2. It is unjust. The colored people have as good a right by nature as the whites, to whatever they can honestly acquire, be it wealth, be it useful learning, or be it elegant accomplishments. They have as good a right as whites to attend what school they please and where they please, and nothing in this law contradicts that right so far as the citizens of Connecticut are concerned. But the colored people of other states have the same rights by nature as the colored people of Connecticut. All colored people, as well as the whites, have a right to be judged by their character and not by their color; to be exempt from all ill effects of groundless prejudice. And any law which deprives them of any of these rights, any law which restricts their privilege in acquiring knowledge, where, and under whose instruction they please, which tends to strengthen and perpetuate the prejudices already existing against them, which judges them without regard to character and makes color a grounds for exclusion from the full privileges of citizenship is an

unjust law. That the law in question does this, I presume even its framers will not deny. It is therefore unjust.

"3. It is inefficient, for the avowed purpose of its passage. From the preamble of the act we learn that the supposed evil to be counteracted is the increase of the colored population. The avowed object of the law then, if any object it avows, is the prevention of increase. But as well might a handful of pebbles be thrown into the current of Niagra to check the rushing of its waters, as this law be imposed to stop the influx of a colored population. What does it exclude? Only those who come to acquire education and only part of those. All who wish to come in for the purpose of attending an incorporated academy or our public schools, have still full liberty to do so. All who would come to labor have still full liberty to do so. All who would come to rove about in idleness, to lounge in grog shops, to beg, to pilfer, to spread the contagion of vice have full liberty to do so. In a word, as many of the colored population of this or any other country who are ignorant and choose to remain so, as are vile, degraded and vicious and choose to remain so, may come whenever they please, and this law offers no opposition, though they come in numbers sufficient to darken the whole land. But if any manifest a wish to improve their condition, to rise from a state of ignorance and degradation and assume the rank of reasonable beings, then indeed does this — most wise, benevolent and salutary law interpose its restrictions to prevent so terrible an "injury to the people" of our hapless state.

"I have it on good authority, that the probable cause of the great unanimity with which the law was passed was information received a very short time before its passage that the legislature of Maryland had recently made appropriation of large sums of money for the purpose of carrying off the colored population of that state. It is reasonable to suppose, then, that the apprehension of great accessions from Maryland, to the number of our blacks, influenced the votes of some honorable gentlemen on the final question. Now, what proportion of the blacks of Maryland who may be transported to our borders (as being a cheaper way of dispersing of them than sending them to Liberia) it is probable will come here with a view of becoming members of a boarding school or private academy? Does any man in his senses believe there will be one in a hundred? I presume not. Nor is it likely the law will affect greater proportion of the colored emigrants from other states. What then is the efficiency of a law which touches not a hundredth part of the evil it is intended to prevent? Where this law closes one

avenue for the influx of a colored population it leaves a hundred open. Therefore, it is inefficient for the avowed purpose of its passage. I need not pause to allude to the impolicy (which must be apparent to every reflecting mind) of such a discriminating law, a law excluding that class of emigrants which would most probably furnish intelligent and virtuous citizens and leaving free ingress to those who are more likely to become nuisances to society.

"4. It is disgraceful to all concerned in its passage and approval. If ignorance of the fundamental principles of our government or a wilful and knowing disregard of them is disgraceful to those, who selected for their superior wisdom or greater acquaintance with public affairs, to form laws in accordance with those principles are doubly bound both to know and regard them; if, perpetuating a cruel prejudice against a much injured class of our fellow citizens; if perversion of legislative influence from the great purpose of consulting the public good, to the mean object of affording facilities to the persecutors of the feeble be disgraceful to grave legislators and enlightened men; if the imposition of knowledge, in a country whose whole system of government is based on the information and intelligence of the people, be disgraceful to professed republicans, to nominal friends and encouragers of learning and to pretended patriots; if palpable and glaring injustices, if rude and boisterous exultation at a supposed triumph, which if achieved, ought to mantle with the blush of shame the cheek of him who wins it; if these things be disgraceful to all participants in the injustice and the shameful triumph; then I ask, has not enough been shown to stamp the deep brand of foul disgrace on all who have aided in the passage of this law or joined in its clamorous celebration? As Yankees have a right to guess, I may hazard a conjecture that the avowed was not the real purpose of the law. Of course, an obscure, unlettered rustic like myself can not pretend to all the profundity which will fathom the depth of a Connecticut Legislator's wisdom or what acuteness which will penetrate his real designs in all his measures. But if I might be allowed to suggest what in my humble opinion would be an amendment to the Preamble, I would, with all due submission, venture to inquire whether it should not read in some such manner as this, 'Where as attempts have been made to establish a literary institution in the sovereign town of Canterbury within the limits of this State for the instruction of the colored persons belonging to other towns and states, which would tend to raise that class of people above the state of abject degradation in which they now lie and might

seriously endanger that superiority in intellectual attainments which the whites at present boast, and also a more immediate consequence might mortify the pride of A. T. Judson, candidate for Congress and Captain Richard Fenner, rum retailer on the Canterbury Green: Therefore to preserve from mortification these worthies and to render them due obedience as fathers of the party: to save the whites from the danger of competition in mental culture:

Be it enacted —!"

If the law was passed specifically to eliminate Miss Crandall's school it was indeed "inefficient" for this purpose. Advertisements again appeared in the *Liberator* and *Emancipator* offering her facilities to "Young Ladies and Little Misses of Color." This was a clear and flagrant indication that Miss Crandall had no intention of terminating the school, but was endeavoring to increase the enrollment. Andrew Judson was amazed at her audacity. After seeing a searing, sarcastic letter, this time in *The Courant*, he decided to press for the fullest enforcement of the law.

The Courant letter appeared on June 24th.

"Communication.

"Mssrs. Printers

"I was glad to learn from your late paper, that the Legislature of Connecticut at its late session passed a law that the people of color and their children, who might hereafter come into this state should not be instructed except at the pleasure of the Selectmen. And although the penalty may seem severe, it being $100 for the first act of teaching and $200 for the second and so on in the same ratio — and a like penalty for each opening of a school for a black child or for boarding one attending; yet when we consider the enormity of the offense and the necessity of proportioning punishment to criminality, all will agree that this law is right and just as it should be. The law does not prohibit colored people coming into the state — this you know would be against the Constitution of the United States, but it declares they should not be instructed. And why should they be instructed? They are not white and it is doubtful if they have souls or will exist in a future state. As well as I thought of the Legislature composed of true and fresh Republicans, I was afraid they would hardly come up to the important point; but they have done it and the new statute is an enduring monument of glory, at which our sister states and the old world too will be amazed. Before the committee reported the bill to the Legislature they consulted a learned phrenologist in the city of Hartford who brought into the room several skulls of the African race. They were fully satisfied from the phrenological developments that the blacks

do not belong to the human species. It is said that letters of thanks and congratulations already pouring in upon the leaders of the late legislature for taking this enlightened step — especially in these days of rash innovations in this country and sickish reforms in Europe. Some of these letters have been put into my hands and none of them are more warm and grateful than those from the State of Georgia, where, you know, laws of this sort have been passed cutting up the instruction of blacks by the roots — not even allowing them religious instruction. Since phrenologists have proved that blacks do not belong to the human family, why should they be instructed and why should they be indulged in the foolish whim of selecting schools for their children? No measures should be tolerated toward them whose tendency is only to rescue them from their appointed destiny. I wish I had been a member of the body which had thus dared in the face of the world to do so noble a deed it would be honor enough. Nero or Caligula could not have desired more . . .

"The planters of the South who you know are true lovers of liberty and would not deprive a fellow being of a single right, however degraded he might be, had begun to feel since the late insurrection in Virginia and especially since the English Parliament and the English Nation itself are so determined upon the wicked and romantic act of putting down slavery in their possessions, and as they pretend, the slave trade throughout the world, that Negro slavery in this country is threatened. But let us rejoice that Connecticut has taken her stand against these pestilential movements of liberty and these more hypothetical clamours about oppression.

"The new act is well drawn and is scrupulously right, for it is said that it was drawn up by the inspiration of a distinguished statesman from Canterbury not more celebrated as an elegant writer than as a lover of equal rights; and to make the new law more sure, the great lawyer it is said appeared before the Committee of the Legislature and instructed them to discharge their duty. This was unusual and made some talk but it is the just boast that our present rulers do nothing in the old way . . .

"The preamble I am sorry to say, does not exactly agree with the law itself. It sets forth as the occasion for this law that the black people come into the state but yet it contains no prohibitions as to their coming and only makes it criminal to teach them anything after they have come — but it was thought the people were not quite ripe for the real object of the law and the best was done that could be for the present . . .

"Now, Sir, I am glad that the clouds are breaking away, I have long been convinced that nothing is more false than the specious statement in the Declaration of our Independence 'that all men are created equal; that they are endowed by their Creator with certain inalienable rights; among them life, liberty and the pursuit of happiness,' and those other provisions insiduously got into the Declaration of Rights which stands at the head of the Constitution of this state, 'That all men are equal in rights' and that none are entitled to exclusive privileges from the community, this all flummery. Let us rejoice that the time has come when our political leaders have dared to abrogate these heretical and pestilential notions.

Canterbury"

How Andrew Judson writhed under the bite of this sarcasm. That it was signed "Canterbury" made him especially angry. He believed he knew the thoughts of his towns-people and that one should publicly assail his motives was exceedingly annoying. He called together his henchmen to determine what steps to take next.

CHAPTER FIVE
MISS CRANDALL AND THE LAW

ON June 27th, Prudence Crandall was arrested. The Sheriff's deputy George Cady presented her with a writ of arrest which read:

To Rufus Adams, Esq. a Justice of the Peace of Windham comes Nehemiah Ensworth, of the town of Canterbury, a grand juror of said town of Canterbury, duly chosen and sworn, and on his office oath, complaint makes and gives your worship to understand that at Canterbury in said County of Windham, on the 24th of June in the year of our Lord one thousand eight hundred and a thirty-three, with force and arms, in a certain school which before that time had been and since then was set up in Canterbury for the instruction and education of colored persons, not inhabitants of this state, Prudence Crandall of said Canterbury, wilfully and knowingly did instruct and teach and assist in instructing and teaching, certain colored persons, who at the time when so taught and instructed were not inhabitants of any town in this state — to wit Theodosher Delgrap, or Degrass, Amelia Elizabeth Wiles, Catherine Ann Welden, Ann Peterson, Mariah Robinson, G.C. Marshal, Ann Eliza Hammond, and others whose names to the complainant unknown, all which acts were done and committed by said Prudence Crandall, without the consent in writing first had and obtained, of a majority of the civil authority and also the selectmen of said town of Canterbury within which said school then was situated, against the peace of this state and contrary to the form and affect of the statute law of this state in such case made and provided.

The said Grand Juror, on his oath, further informs the Justice that at Canterbury in the County of Windham, on the 24th day of June 1833, with force and arms for the purpose of attending and being taught and instructed in a certain school which before then had been and then was set up in said town of Canterbury, for the instruction and education of colored persons who were not inhabitants of this State, Prudence Crandall of said Canterbury wilfully and knowingly did harbor and board and aid and assist in harboring and boarding certain colored persons, who when so harbored and boarded were not inhabitants of any town in this state against the peace of the state and contrary to the form and effect of the statute law of this state in such case made and provided.

"To the Sheriff of Canterbury, Windham County —
Greetings:

"By authority of the State of Connecticut you are hereby commanded forthwith to arrest the body of Prudence Crandall of said Canterbury and with her to appear before Rufus Adams, Esq., Justice of the Peace of said Canterbury of Windham at the dwelling house of Chauncey Bacon in said Canterbury or some other proper authority then and there to answer unto the matters contained in the foregoing complaint and be dealt with there on as the law doth require. Here of fail not but this writ with your doings know lawful service and return made.

Signed
R. Adams, Justice of the Peace

A similar writ was served on Hannah Almyra. The sisters were awed by the long writ and its terms of "with force and arms" and against the "peace of the state" which certainly did not seem to apply to their activities. They had no choice but to accompany the Sheriff's Deputy. Before leaving the house Prudence sent Marcia to fetch her father and have him hurry to Chauncey Bacon's. With all the courage and composure she could command, Prudence led Hannah Almyra to Mr. Cady's carriage for the short ride to Chauncey Bacon's.

It was apparent from the number of men and boys loitering on the sides of the road that news of the arrest had been spread about. Coarse comments and cat calls came from some of the onlookers. All the faces were familiar but none showed any sign of sympathy for the two women.

They found Justices Adams and Bacon waiting when they entered the main room of Mr. Bacon's Inn. Andrew Judson and Nehemiah Ensworth were there and several other men.

Deputy Sheriff Cady presented the prisoners and the clerk wrote out the required form.

"There by virtue of the within warrant, I have arrested the body of Prudence Crandall, the within named defendant, read the within complaint and warrant in her hearing and now have her here before Rufus Adams, Esq., Justice of the Peace.

Attest: George Cady, Sheriff's Deputy.

Travel to arrest	*.20*
Arrest	*.50*
Reading	*.12*
Travel to court	*.25*
Attending court	*.50*
Return warrant	*.05*
	1.62

Rufus Adams proceeded to read the complaint and when he had finished reading he asked Prudence how she would plead.

She clearly replied, "Not Guilty."

Justice Adams then read through each charge separately and after each statement asked if it were true.

"Do you maintain a school for the instruction of colored pupils?"

"Yes."

"Do you board these pupils?"

"Yes."

"Do you know that the Legislature recently passed a law against such schools?"

"Yes."

"Then you are guilty as charged and shall be bound over to the County Court which will sit in Brooklyn in August. Bonds must be furnished at $150 or you will be remanded to the County jail in Brooklyn."

The attention of the court was then turned to Hannah Almyra. The same procedure was followed but the court discharged her from custody since she was under 21 years of age.

During the course of the proceedings, Prudence's father and brother Hezekiah had arrived at Chauncey Bacon's. They knew that Prudence had anticipated the possiblity of arrest. Rev. May and other friends had conferred with her and reached an agreement that she would not provide bond but would permit herslf to be taken to jail. This would show the public the real extent to which her enemies would go and it would lend propaganda value to the efforts of her friends in the Anti-Slavery movement.

Judson had sent a messenger on horseback to inform Rev. May of the arrest, presuming that May would post bond for her since he was one of her most vocal supporters. The hearing had been finished but a few minutes when the messenger returned and whispered excitedly to Judson.

Judson's face reddened as he asked, "He won't provide bond? What did he say?"

The messenger replied, "He said there are enough gentlemen in Canterbury whose bond is as good as his. I asked him if he were not her friend and he said he is too good a friend to relieve her enemies of any embarrassment. I told him she would be put in jail and he said if her persecutors were unwise enough, then such an outrage would be committed."

Judson had a hurried conference with Justices Adams and Bacon. Rufus Adams then approached Prudence and asked if she could secure a bond. She assured them she could not. He then stated they would have to permit the Sheriff to take her to Brooklyn to which she replied, "I am ready."

At this moment she exhibited greater composure than anyone else in the courtroom. Pardon and Hezekiah were aware of her plans but reluctant to see her go to jail. Hannah Almyra was anxious about her and upset by the whole procedure. Judson and his allies realized that they had been outmaneuvered and would be severely criticized.

Sheriff Roger Coit was chagrined to find that he must take this lady to jail. He had known her for many years. His son Samuel had been one of her pupils when she taught in Plainfield. His father-in-law, Daniel Packer, was one of her staunch friends. He himself admired her courage and appreciated her fine qualities as a person. He delayed as long as possible, hoping that her brother or father or someone would come forward with the required bond. When it was apparent that delay was of no avail, they started on the long hot ride to Brooklyn. All along the way there were little groups of people standing in the dooryards to watch the red-faced sheriff and his prisoner go by. Prudence sat straight and steady throughout the trip. She felt calm and a bit bemused since she knew as the dumbfounded sheriff did not, that her friends had not deserted her. They drove to the home of Mr. Tyler, the jailor where they were warmly greeted and invited into the house by Mrs. Tyler. The jailor and Rev. May had been busy throughout the afternoon cleaning the room for Prudence. They brought a bed from the Benson home. Anna Benson had volunteered to stay in the jail with Prudence.

Rev. May gave Prudence a final chance to change her mind. She persisted in carrying out her intention of staying in jail over night, assuring him that she had no fears or misgivings about her decision.

As darkness began to settle, Anna and Prudence were led to the jail. It was a two story building. The walls were double blocks of native gray stone. On each floor were two rooms 17 by 12 feet with a room 8 by 8 feet in the center and a hallway. The rooms had seven-inch apertures on the outside walls and there was a six-inch opening in the door to each room through which inmates could be observed by anyone in the hall and through which they could receive their food.

Prudence and Anna were put into the small center room on the lower floor which was known as the debtors' room. The last occupant of this room had been a man named Watson who had been hanged for the murder of his wife. He had spent his last night in this room, with a special guard to prevent him from committing suicide and depriving the hundreds of spectators, who had come from miles around, the privilege of witnessing his demise.

Prudence and Anna slept little in the small hot room. They were greatly relieved when the morning came and Mr. Benson sent the bondsman fee which freed them. After a brief, refreshing visit and breakfast at the

Benson home, Prudence was taken back to Canterbury by Rev. May. Her sister and pupils were overjoyed to see her. The older students were distressed that she had endured such an experience for them but she cheered and reassured them and urged them back to their studies.

Some days later Rev. Kneeland visited the school. He stayed through the supper hour and was conducting a prayer service when eggs came hurtling through the open window. Marcia and some of the girls hurried to clean up the mess.

"Did you see who was out there? Who threw the eggs?" Rev. Kneeland asked of Prudence who had been seated near the window.

"It would do no good to know who threw them — the constables would not arrest anyone if we knew who did it," Prudence answered.

"But that leaves you without any protection," exclaimed the minister.

"We hope our prayers will bring us the protection that we need," Prudence said.

Rev. Kneeland drove back to Packerville, marvelling at the strong faith and constant courage of Prudence Crandall. Seeing her at work in her school and at service in his church convinced him that she was entirely sincere. Her teaching and guidance were obviously of great benefit to the girls. He looked forward to seeing their dark serious faces in his church each week.

Saturday brought a new and different attack. Pardon Crandall was visited at noon by Andrew Judson and Rufus Adams. They read the following letter to him:

> *"Mr. Crandall: If you go to your daughter's you are to be fined $100 for the first offense, $200 for the second and double it every time. Mrs. Crandall, if you go there you will be fined and your daughter Almyra will be fined and those gentlemen from Providence if they come here will be fined at the same rate and your daughter, the one that has established the school for colored females will be taken up the same as for stealing a horse or burglary. Her property will not be taken but she will be put in jail, not having the liberty of the yard. There is no mercy shown about it."*

"Is this a free country?" queried Pardon.

"When you sent your petition to the General Assembly, you did not injure me. It helped very much in getting the law through. When they received it, every man clenched his fist and the committee doubled the penalty. Furthermore they stated that 'If this law does not answer your purpose let us know and next year we will make one that will'," were Judson's parting statements.

He threw the letter onto the table and left the house, followed by Mr. Adams. Esther stood tearfully by while Pardon rushed to the barn, hitched up his horse, gathered up a basket of food and drove out of his sloping driveway at top speed. Overtaking Judson's carriage he pulled past it and then slowed down and drove defiantly to Prudence's house. He told her angrily of the latest development and waited for his enemies to carry out the threatened arrest. He waited in vain.

On Sunday, Daniel Packer sent his wagon and Pardon brought his carriage to take Prudence and pupils to the Baptist Church where Rev. Kneeland preached an inspiring sermon. On the return trip as the wagon neared the place for fording the Quinebaug the driver saw several big boys. He suggested that the girls alight. They quickly jumped from the wagon and gathered apprehensively around their teacher. The driver started to ford the river and was stopped by the boys who unhitched the wagon and overturned it in the shallow water. Pardon had caught up with the wagon but he did not dare leave his charges to assist the wagon driver. With his whip firmly in hand and plainly in sight, Pardon forded the river and drove his passengers to the school and then returned to pick up the stranded students. When all the girls were safely indoors, he secured the help of his son Hezekiah in drawing Mr. Packer's wagon from the river. They thought they had already witnessed the full scope of crude and cruel behavior but this latest episode was mean, dangerous and a profaning of the Sabbath.

Prudence decided the following Sunday to take her girls across the road to the Congregational Church. This brought forth the following letter from the "Society Committee."

"To Miss Prudence Crandall.

"When the Committee visited you last Feburary, stating their objections to your school, they understood from you, by your voluntary suggestion that you should never desire and never would put your colored scholars into the meeting house, that you would have preaching at your own house with black or white, and you also added, that the citizens of Canterbury need have no anxiety on that account, they might rest assured no such request would ever be made.

"It appears now that you have departed from this voluntary Declaration and put your colored scholars into pews ever occupied by white females of the parish. We ask you to inform us soon by whose license you have thus taken possession of the meeting house.

Solomon Payne
Andrew Harris
Isaac Knight

"Please inform Dr. Harris today."

"To Solomon Payne, & etc.

Canterbury, 29 July, 1833

"Gentlemen,

"I received a letter from you on the 27th, in which you ask me to inform you, by whose license I have taken possession of that part of the Meeting-house that was occupied by my scholars on the Sabbath previous. I can inform you that the license, whether lawful or unlawful, by which I permitted my family to enter the gallery of your church, was permission received from two of the Society's Committee, viz: Dr. Harris and Deacon Bacon.

"On Saturday the 6th of this month I sent a verbal request, by Samuel Hough, to the gentlemen whom I address, asking your permission to attend Divine worship with you on the Sabbath. I asked Captain Hough to inform you that I would purchase seats sufficient for my scholars if agreeable to you; if not, any part or portion of the meeting-house you might see fit for us to occupy would be acceptable, of this Mr. Hough said he informed you. Dr. Harris, in answer, said, we might occupy the seat in the gallery appropriated to colored persons. Mr. H. then remarked, that the seat would not be sufficient to seat the scholars. Deacon Bacon then replied that we might take the next pews until we had enough to be seated.

"Truly I said this to the committee that visited me in February last: — 'The scholars that come here shall not trouble you on the Sabbath; for we can have preaching either by colored or white ministers in our own house,' The Committee made me no reply at that time, if I am not mistaken, — and I think I am not.

"Upon mature consideration, (as regular preaching here was not readily obtained) I considered that I had done entirely wrong in depriving my scholars from attending religious worship in this village.

"These are my reasons for asking the privilege of entering your church; and all the license I have is given above.

Yours, with respect
P. Crandall

The following Sunday Prudence and her young ladies again went across the road to the church. This time the doors were barred by the grim deacons who forbade them to enter.

Rev. May summarized the disturbing, disagreeable developments of recent weeks in a letter to Arthur Tappan. He indicated that he would have to draw on the financial resources which Mr. Tappan had offered to make available. Being a man of action as well as of keen conscience, Mr. Tappan soon arrived in Brooklyn.

After a brief visit at Rev. May's the two men drove to Canterbury. Mr. Tappan urged that no expense be spared in providing the best attorneys possible to defend Prudence. Upon receiving the newspaper accounts about the school in Norwich and Windham papers and learning that they would no longer accept letters which refuted misleading information about Prudence and the school, he urged that a newspaper be started. Rev. May agreed to make arrangements for this. Through William Burleigh he was induced to seek Charles Burleigh, a law student in Plainfield, to help in editing the paper. An old printing press was found in Brooklyn and they started a four-page weekly called the *Unionist.*

Prudence was delighted to have Mr. Tappan as a visitor. After dinner she called the girls together in the south parlor for a "mental feast." The gentlemen who had been joined by Rev. Kneeland listened to a number of recitations. As a finale the four youngest girls — aged 10 and 11 — appeared in white dresses and sang "with great sweetness."

Four little children here you see
In modest dress appear.
Come listen to our song so sweet
And our complaints you'll hear.

'Tis here we came to learn to read
And write and cipher too.
But some in this enlightened land
Declare 'twill never do.

The morals of this favored town
Will be corrupted soon.
Therefore they strive with all their might
To drive us from our home.

Sometimes when we have walked the streets
Saluted we have been
By guns and drums and cow bells, too
And horns of polished tin.

With warnings, threats and words severe
They visit us at times
And gladly would they send us off
To Africa's burning climes.

Our teacher too they put in jail
Fast held by bars and locks!
Did ere such persecution reign
Since Paul was in the stocks?

But we forgive, forgive the men
That persecute us so
May God in mercy save their souls
From everlasting woe!

The men sat silent for a few moments after the little girls had withdrawn into the hall. Then they rose and very solemnly expressed to Prudence their appreciation of the girls' performance — especially the song which she had worked out with them. More than ever Mr. Tappan was convinced that the school should survive at any cost.

The next few weeks were comparatively uneventful. The girls stayed indoors most of the time, leaving the yard only to go to Packerville or Black Hill for Sunday services. Pardon and Hezekiah and a colored man named Olney from Norwich brought supplies to the school.

On August 23rd, Prudence and the girls who had been called as witnesses rode to Brooklyn with Pardon Crandall. Ann Eliza Hammond, Ann Peterson, Theodosia DeGrass, Elisa Glasko, Catherine Ann Weldon, Sarah Harris, Mary Harris, and Maria Robinson had all been served with legalistic subpoenas on the 16th. Mary Elizabeth Wiles had been issued a subpoena but it could not be served since she had left Canterbury to return home because of the illness of her mother. The six mile drive was hot and dusty and they were relieved when they arrived at the Benson home where they were to stay throughout the trial. Other witnesses were Hannah Almyra and Hezekiah Crandall, Rev. Levi Kneeland, Rufus Adams, Dr. Roland Green, George Roberts, Asael Bacon, Richard Fenner, Eliza Parkis, Jacob Gould, the deputy Sheriff George Cady and Miss Benson.

The session convened at 9 o'clock in the hot room packed with spectators. Judges Eaton, Griffin and Chase were present. Hon. Jonathon Welch was appointed State's attorney due to the illness of Chauncey Cleaveland, Andrew Judson and Isaac Buckley were his willing assistants. The Hon. Calvin Goddard, Wm. W. Ellsworth and Henry Strong appeared for the defense. They were three of the most respected attorneys of their day. Convinced of the merits of the case, they refused remuneration other than a $50 fee for all their services.

The jury was empanelled and sworn. The counsel for the defense objected to one juror from Canterbury on the grounds that he had signed petitions in respect to Miss Crandall's school, and taken active measures to put it down. The Court sustained the objection and the Juror was excused. They also objected to another of the Jurors on the grounds that he was a member of the Legislature which passed the law — was one of those who voted for it and had formed an opinion regarding its constitutionality. The Court decided that the Juror was competent to sit. (He asked to be excused because of illness.)

The charges against Prudence were two-fold. It was first charged "that the said Prudence Crandall, on the 24th day of June last, with force and arms" instructed colored girls and that she "wilfully and knowingly did harbor and board certain colored persons not inhabitants of the town without consent in writing of the Civil Authority or Selectmen."

In answering these charges Prudence pled "not guilty."

The prosecution then called the witnesses.

Asael Bacon said he called at Miss Crandall's home in the month of June, having heard that she had taken some scholars from abroad. Captain Sanger accompanied him — they were both selectmen of the town. Miss Crandall invited them into the house very politely. They asked about the scholars. She told them she had four from New York and one from Hartford. She called them in and introduced them — Theodosia DeGrass, Ann Peterson and Catherine Weldon were the names of three. Mr. Sanger concurred with Mr. Bacon's testimony.

George Cady then gave his testimony to the effect that he had conversed with Miss Crandall at her house when he went to serve summonses on witnesses last Friday. One named in his subpoena had been sent home on account of the sickness of her mother. Miss Crandall had said she did not see that there was any need of witnesses for she would admit that she conducted the school.

Ann Peterson was called to the witness stand next. Mr. Ellsworth objected to the witness since she could not testify without implicating herself. Mr. Welch read the clause in the statute, under which the prosecution was proceeding, in which it was enacted that pupils in a school kept contrary to the act might be compelled to testify. Mr. Ellsworth countered that he challenged the competency of the Legislature to compel a witness to testify or answer a question that might implicate him. He alluded to the State Constitution which he pointed out protected every person from criminating himself, by being compelled to give testimony. Not only was such compulsion to testify against fundamental principles but in this case the witness might be adjudged an aider and abettor and be subject to the penalties of the statute.

Mr. Judson hotly contended that the witness could not by her testimony implicate herself. The law was penal and must be construed strictly, even if she swore that she was instructed by Miss Crandall it would not charge her with any crime. He read at length from Starkie on evidence to show that the witness ought to be examined and was bound to answer questions as to what she knew of Miss Crandall's school. The Legislature had expressly determined that the pupils must be witnesses.

Mr. Ellsworth questioned whether the Legislature had the power to compel a witness to convict himself. He read from the opinion of Chief Justice Hosmer and the case of the People vs. Mather, on the subject of examining witnesses. By the principles decided in these cases which were the law of the land, he claimed that the witness was not compelled to answer any question in regard to her knowledge of the school.

The court ruled that the witness, under present circumstances, was not protected but must be examined. The examination was about to get underway when Mr. Ellsworth rose and stated to the court that the witness had been advised not to answer any questions about the school.

He stated, "I have no wish to embarrass the trial but a sense of duty compels me to advise the witness that she cannot be compelled to testify."

The counsel for the prosecution was instructed to proceed.

Mr. Welch asked, "When did you come to Canterbury?"

Ann Peterson declined to answer.

Mr. Welch raised other questions, "With whom do you board? Does Miss Crandall instruct you and other colored pupils?"

Frightened and confused, Ann still refused to answer, saying softly, "I might criminate myself."

The counsel for the prosecution then called Catherine Ann Weldon and Ann Eliza Hammond. They responded as Ann Peterson had.

Andrew Judson leaped to his feet and demanded that the girls be committed for contempt of court. Mr. Welch preferred to seek the testimony of other witnesses and reserved the right to cite them later.

Jacob Gould was sworn and stated he was acquainted with Ann Eliza Hammond. He had known her since she was a little child, living in Providence. He commented, "Her father, Thomas Hammond died in 1826. He left an estate of $1500-$2000, at present her mother lives in Providence."

Rev. Levi Kneeland was then called. He said he was not connected with Miss Crandall's school except as an advisor. Miss Crandall belonged to his church. When asked if he had seen the girls at Miss Crandall's school he declined to answer. He also refused to answer questions about if and when he had been at the school. When asked if he had eaten any meals at the school he replied he thought the court had no business to know this. The court decided he was bound to answer the questions, granted a motion to have him committed to jail and the Sheriif led him from the room.

Eliza Parkis took the stand. She admitted that she was acquainted with Ann Hammond. She knew her in Providence and had also seen her at Miss Crandall's. Mrs. Parkis stated that she was employed by Miss Crandall to wash and do other work because Miss Crandall did not like to keep the scholars away from their books to do housework. When she stayed over night she shared the room of Miss DeGrass. She never saw the girls in their classrooms but had seen them reading books in other parts of the house.

Dr. Roland Green was called — being a Quaker he did not take the usual oath but affirmed that he would tell the truth. He said he had often heard that Miss Crandall kept a school for colored girls in Canterbury. He had been to her house several times. He was called there as a physician when one of the girls was ill and no doctor could be obtained in Canterbury. He had heard some of the girls recite grammar and geography. Some of the girls had visited in his home.

It was late in the afternoon when the court adjourned, to resume in the morning. Prudence and her charges moved as quickly as possible through the crowd, shepherded by Pardon and Hezekiah, the Benson brothers, Rev. May and her attorneys. Even in this setting, some members of the crowd could not restrain their boos and jeers.

A pleasant welcome and generous supper awaited them at the Benson home. Although tired and worried, the girls soon relaxed and before the evening was over the whole company — family, students and guests were having such a pleasant time that Prudence suggested the name "Friendship Valley" for the Benson farm.

The trial resumed in the morning. Soon after the students had taken seats in the courtroom, Sheriff Roger Coit tapped Eliza Glasko, Theodosia DeGrass and Ann Eliza Hammond on the shoulder and handed them warrants.

The warrants were identical. That handed to Eliza Glasco reads as follows:

"Warrant of Eliza Glasko
Aug. 24, 1833

To the Sheriff of the County of Windham or his deputy, Greeting

"Whereas before the County Court holden at Brooklyn in and for the county of Windham on the second Tuesday of August in the year of our Lord 1833 Eliza Glasko of Griswold in New London County having been required to appear and give her evidence upon

examination of trial and information of the State of Conn. vs. Prudence Crandall of Canterbury in Windham County, now pending before said court and the said Eliza Glasko upon being so required did refuse to testify and declare her knowledge in the matter or case aforesaid and said court did there upon order that the said Eliza Glasko be committed to the common jail in Brooklyn in said Windham County there to remain at her own case until she shall give evidence as aforesaid as appears — whereof execution remains to be done —

"These are therefore by authority of the State of Connecticut to command you to arrest the body of Eliza Glasko and her commit to the keeper of said jail in said Brooklyn within the same, who is likewise hereby commanded to receive the said Eliza Glasko and her keep safely until she shall give evidence as aforesaid for which case this shall be your legal and sufficient warrant. Hereof you may in no wise fail but make the return with such your doings herein,

Attest Armin Bolles, Clerk
Brooklyn, Aug. 23, 1833

"Then the within warrant was put into my hands in the Court House at Brooklyn, Windham County. And by virtue thereof while the said Eliza was sitting in the seats for witness in said court house I proceeded to and did arrest her body and before I had any time to read this warrant or to take her into custody other than to touch her on the shoulder, the said Eliza immediately signified her willingness to testify and she did testify and I now return this warrant unexecuted.

Roger Coit, Sheriff

Travel to serve — 8 miles	*.40*
Arrest	*1.00*

Prudence and her attorneys had urged the girls to testify since it would be unpleasant for them if they refused and their testimony could not add to the general knowledge about the school. Prudence also thought that well spoken answers would tend to show courtroom spectators that the girls were intelligent, sensible people.

Eliza testified that she and the other girls were members of Miss Crandall's school. She reported that the school was generally opened and closed with prayer, the scriptures were read and explained daily. Some portions of the scripture were committed to memory as part of their education.

Rev. Kneeland was brought from the jail where he had spent the night. He, too, had agreed to testify. He stated that he had visited the school where he had prayed and conversed on religious subjects with the girls. He had eaten meals with Miss Crandall and her students and had heard them recite their lessons. When he tried to add that their recitations indicated an impressive level of intelligence his testimony was interrupted by Mr. Judson.

Hezekiah Crandall, being affirmed since he was a Quaker and would not take an oath, said his sister had a school for colored girls. He recognized Ann Hammond and Ann Peterson. He had never been at his sister's when classes were in session or heard the students recite. He visited his sister's house frequently and supposed the girls were boarded by his sister.

Mr. Judson made his summation for the prosecution. In measured tones and with obvious pleasure he read the act under which the trial was being conducted and then he launched into a lengthy speech in justification of the law and the trial.

(He read from an old edition of the statutes about the power of the legislature with respect to preventing disorders and the allocation of public monies for schools.) "This Act does not prevent any black from attending the district schools in the state or any higher schools. They have all the benefits of the school fund. The sole intention and provision of the act is that colored persons, from another jurisdiction should not be intruded into any town in the state, without permission from the selectmen and civil authority of the town in which they propose to reside. This is all and it is perfectly lawful. The whole tenor and affect of the law is to put a school for colored persons under the care and civil authority of the town. The legislature has exercised a controlling power over schools since 1717."

"Towns," he claimed, "have a right to say who shall be allowed to become inhabitants by residence in their limits and this law gives them no more power than is right and necessary. There are now 1500 schools in the state supported by a fund of $1,800,000 to which blacks may go. Small as this state is, smaller than single counties in some states, these facts are true and I am proud of it!

"Public policy absolutely demands this law should be maintained. It has been declared to be unconstitutional because it is exclusive in its operation in a particular class. Other laws of the state are liable to the same objections. Physicians and lawyers are subject to operation of exclusive laws. Tanners, taverners, surveyors and others must be licensed. Manufacturers are liable to be visited by the selectmen and civil authorities to see that the children employed in them are properly educated.

"The article of the Constitution of the United States with which this law is said to conflict is the 2nd section of the 4th article. This article refers to the rights and privileges of citizens, but the term 'citizens' does not include colored persons. If 'citizen' does not mean a white person only, then our state consitituion is a nollity for it allows 'free white males' alone to be electors. The privilege of being a free man is a higher privilege than the right to be educated. Why should a person be educated who could not be free?

"The first act in our own consititution would be nullifed by a decision that this law is unconstitutional — a citizen of another state can not maintain an action in our courts unless a substantial inhabitant of the state give bond for him. No one has doubted the constitutionality of this law and the law in question, with respect to constitutionality, could not be distinguished from it.

"In conclusion, let me allude merely to one other argument in support of this law, and that is the public safety. The southern states might emancipate their slaves and send them all to Connecticut instead of Liberia. The influx of that species of the population might be so great as to be overwhelming."

Overwhelmed by his own oratory, Mr. Judson continued for some minutes — pointing out the dangers which might ensue from the recent measures to end slavery taken by the British Parliament until he was interrupted by the Judge who said his discussion did not seem pertinent. Mr. Judson expressed the hope that his remarks had not been misunderstood. He had no wish to oppress anyone and heartily wished that all slaves might be emancipated immediately if this could be done without destroying our constitution and desolating our land. He hoped the jury would pay respect to his opinion of the law. He pointed out that the defendant was charged with boarding and educating these people and could be found guilty on one or both charges. It was not necessary to fix any exact date but if she had boarded and educated even one on any day it was a violation of the law. Proof had been given which was abundant and conclusive.

Mr. Ellsworth rose and made a number of preliminary remarks about his objection to involving the girls by having them testify. He stated that of course it was no secret that Miss Crandall kept a school for colored girls. He then set forth his basic arguments:

"It is up to the jury to determine whether my client, by conducting the school has committed a crime. You may find that she has violated an act of the State Legislature, but if you also find that she is protected by a higher power it will be your duty to acquit her. Each member of the jury must be satisfied in his own mind that a crime had been committed and the law under which this trial is held is constitutional. The real question you must settle is: Can the legislature of Connecticut pass a law prohibiting the citizens of other states from coming to this state to reside to pursue the acquisition of knowledge in a way open to the citizens of this state?

"My friend from Canterbury has claimed that colored persons are not citizens and that constitutional provisions for citizens do not apply to this class in our population. A person may become a citizen by naturalization, this does not touch on citizenship by birth. In the days of the Revolution colored men fought side by side with our fathers and shed their blood for this country. Their names are inscribed on the Pension Rolls. Where does the gentleman get the idea that the rights of man depend on color? A colored man can appeal to the laws for protection of his rights in every state, could he do this if he were not a citizen? I scout the idea that a man born here is not a citizen because his father was black while I am a citizen because mine was white."

Mr. Ellsworth continued in this vein, citing a variety of instances to prove that colored people were citizens and as such could come to Connecticut for an education. He was followed by Attorney Strong whose arguments were brief but convincing. Mr. Welch spoke briefly, supporting the accusation and arguments of Judson.

Finally Judge Eaton charged the jury that they must either find Miss Crandall guilty on the basis of evidence submitted to the court or they must find that the law was not consititutional and therefore she must be acquitted.

The testimony and arguments completed, the jury went into an adjoining room to deliberate. After several hours, the foreman of the jury reported that the jury could not agree on a verdict. The vote was seven to five but the deadlock was insoluble. Seven would find Prudence guilty — five held out for a not guilty verdict.

Prudence and her friends had hoped that she would be found innocent on the basis that the law was unconstitutional. Judson and her other opponents had hoped for a verdict of guilty and the closing of the school.

The expenses for the trial were extensive. Those chargeable to the defense were paid by Arthur Tappan.

Complaint and warrant to A. T. Judson	*1.59*
Summons to A. T. Judson	*.25*
Serving warrant to George Cady	*1.62*
Court fees to Rufus Adams	*.75*
Witness fees to Rufus Adams	*.25*
Copies to Rufus Adams	*1.50*
Service of summons to Cady	*1.00*

Witnesses:	
Pardon Crandall — twice	*.46*
Hezekiah Crandall — twice	*.46*
A. E. Wiles — twice	*.34*
Mariah Robinson — twice	*.34*
Sarah Harris — twice	*.34*
Mary Harris — twice	*.34*
George Cady	*1.75*
Jailer's bill for keep (Rev. Kneeland)	*.71*
Information — Court to J. A. Welch	*2.00*
Information — Court to J. A. Welch	*4.00*
Summons	*.25*
Printing copy for J. Bulkley	*2.22*
Court Jury — to Amin Bolles	*8.22*
Entry of copy	*.22*
Arraignment	*1.50*
3 attachments for witnesses	*1.77*
Service of first to George Cady	*.60*
Service of two others — Roger Coit	*2.50*
Services of copies for Witness Cady	*1.00*
Services of Summons # 1	*2.00*
Services of Summons # 2	*2.00*
Witnesses	
J. Gould from Rhode Island	*17.22*
Roland Green 7 miles	*1.10*
Hezekiah Crandall 6 miles	*1.10*
Almyra Crandall 6 miles	*1.04*
Aliza Glasko 6 miles	*1.04*
Ann Eliza Hammond 6 miles 2 days	*1.72*
Theodosia DeGrass 6 miles 2 days	*1.72*
Ann E. Weldon 6 miles 2 days	*1.72*
Levi Kneeland 9 miles	*1.22*
George Roberts	*.68*
Ebenezer Sanger 6 miles	*1.04*
Asall Bacon	*1.04*
Richard Fenner	*1.04*
Emily Parkis 4 miles	*.92*
Ann Peterson 6 miles 2 days	*1.72*
Mary Benson 1 mile	*.14*

D. Chase, Treasurer
State of Conn.

It is difficult to account for the accounting! Pardon Crandall was paid witness fees but no mileage expense. Almyra was paid both but having no conveyance rode with her father as did the students. Those who traveled six miles two days received only 68 cents more than those who traveled six miles once. Since Brooklyn is six miles from Canterbury center return mileage was evidently not provided.

Classes at the school resumed on Monday. The trial over, teachers and pupils concentrated on their daily tasks but they were not free from anxiety for very long. On September 26, 1833 Prudence was again arrested. This time a bond of $150 was posted by Richard Fenner and William Lister with the Justice Court. The trial was set for October 3rd at 9 a.m.

The Judge was David Daggett from New Haven who had played a leading role in blocking the establishment of a school for Negroes in New Haven in 1831.

Andrew T. Judson and Chauncey F. Cleavland conducted the prosecution. Henry Strong and Calvin Goddard represented Prudence. After a review of the facts and the testimony of witnesses, Mr. Judson opened the case. His statements were substantially the same as those made during the first trial. Mr. Strong spoke in defense of Prudence, challenging the constitutionality of the law, reaffirming Mr. Ellsworth's contention in the earlier trial that free colored people are citizens. Testimony and arguments of counsel took up all Thursday.

On Friday morning Judge Daggett made a very long charge to the jury. He expressed the proposition that the Court, that is the Judge, should state its opinion to the jury on all questions of law. He proclaimed at great length that colored persons were not citizens. He cited many areas in which they were not allowed to participate as white men did. He also claimed that the Connecticut law in question was constitutional.

If Judge Daggett perceived it to be his duty to secure a verdict of guilty he did it well. The jury returned such a verdict. Prudence's attornies appealed immediately.*

Undaunted, Prudence decided to continue her school pending the appeal. This was a most unpopular decision with her neighbors and other opponents.

The summer of 1833 had been a long hot one. It had been very dry and by fall the well in the cellar of Prudence's house had about run dry. This gave no great cause for alarm since there was a second well in the front yard. Soon after this well was known to be in use, Marcia was horrified to find that her bucket came up, not with clear cool water but full of manure from some barn. Recourse was had to the well of Richard Fenner whose

* See appendix

land bounded that of the school on the west. His well was near the road and was frequently used by passersby for water for their horses. The second time that one of the students sought a pail of water from this source, she was told by Fenner's servant that she must not use the well. Mr. Fenner had ordered that no one from the school might draw water there. Prudence then sought water from the well of Dr. Harris but was told that although the well had not failed, she was not to use it since the neighbors did not want her to have water. Thereafter until a new well could be provided she had to depend upon her father to haul water for her from his farm.

Frequent barrages of eggs came against the windows and doors. One evening during a time when ministers from Pawtucket were conducting a service in the front parlor a large rock, the size of an orange, came through the window. It rolled across the floor. As soon as it was determined that no one had been injured by it, Prudence picked it up and placed it on the mantel. It became a conversation piece and evidence for visitors of the kind of harassment to which the school was subjected.

Each unpleasant episode was widely publicized by the *Unionist* which was being regularly published by Charles Burleigh with the aid of Rev. May and the financial assistance of Arthur Tappan. Other papers picked up the news items and reprinted them so that the story of the Canterbury school was widely known. The *Christian Secretary* which was published in Hartford carried an editorial entitled "Mobocracy and the order of the Day."

> *It is the subject of fearful apprehension, that mobs and violence are becoming so frequent in the United States. The attack on Mormons in Missouri; the late mob collected in New York to prevent the formation of the Emancipation Society; the barbarity practiced toward Miss Crandall in Canterbury, defiling her well and then forbidding her to use other wells, and assaulting her apartments and breaking her windows with rotten eggs in time of public worship; the "firebrand" handbill tossed up in Boston calling upon the enemies of William Lloyd Garrison to mob, tar and feather him, and consequent assemblage about his office, these and other such like scenes of late occurred all indicate an approaching crisis in the country . . .*

The Emancipator, edited in New York City by Charles Denison formerly of Stonington, Connecticut, carried on a debate with the *Norwich Courier* about Prudence's decision to continue her school. The *Genius of Temperance*, another New York publication, entered the fray on the side of Prudence. While controversy intensified on the outside, inside the school there was relative calm. The students concentrated on their studies, knowing that if the appeal of the court case was adverse, they might lose the opportunity for an education. Isolated from the general community, they enjoyed the visits of a few friends. William L. Garrison was an especially welcome visitor. He had recently returned from England. He reported to his readers that "the school is in the full tide of successful experiment." He also reported on seeing the "stone which was thrown through the window by some unknown republican of Canterbury — the shattered panes of glass — the window curtain stained by a volley of rotten eggs and last but not least a moral non-descript, though physically a human being named Andrew T. Judson!"

In another issue of the *Liberator* Garrison related his experience with Canterbury squires.

> *Acknowledgement: Just before midnight on Sabbath evening last, in Brooklyn, Connecticut the Deputy Sheriff of Windham County on behalf of those high minded patriots, those practical Christians, Andrew T. Judson, Rufus Adams, Solomon Paine, Captain Richard Fenner, Doctor Harris, presented me with five indictments for a panegyric upon their virtuous and magnanimous actions, in relation to Miss Crandall's nigger school in Canterbury, inserted in the Liberator of March 16, 1833. I shall readily comply with their polite and urgent invitation to appear at the Windham County Court House on second Tuesday of December to show cause. As they have generously given me precept upon precept, I shall give them line upon line here (in the Liberator) a little, and there (in the court room) a great deal.*

Garrison had to be content with what he could give in the lines of the *Liberator*, since the case never came to court.

In November the members of the school family were very busy preparing for the wedding of Marcia Davis to Charles Harris and of Sarah Harris to George Fairweather. The wedding was planned for the 26th, Thanksgiving Day. The pastor of the Westminster Church, two miles west of the center of Canterbury, had agreed to perform the ceremonies. Hannah Almyra was making the wedding dress for Marcia and Sarah's mother was making hers. All the girls were sewing on pretty white undergarments. The plans called for dinner at noon time for the families of the brides and grooms with all the school friends to gather at the church at 3 o'clock for the wedding. Marcia was to continue to help at the school since she and Charles would live with his family, but Sarah was going to Rhode Island with her husband and would see her friends and family seldom.

Another romance was developing which was of interest to Prudence. Garrison paid frequent visits to the Brooklyn home of the Bensons and it soon became known that it was Helen Benson who drew him there. They were to be married in the Spring.

There was no let up in the problems of the school. The *Norwich Courier* had expressed disapproval of the continuation of the project after the Daggett decision and claimed that it was only forebearance on the part of her neighbors which enabled Prudence to continue the Institution. The *Windham County Advertiser* printed an inflammatory editorial on December 19, 1833.

> *TO ALL WHOM IT MAY CONCERN From what we learn we have great reason to believe that a determination has been formed to BREAK UP the negro school in Canterbury by some means or other in less than two months . . . The peaceable and undisturbed manner, however, in which the Instructress has of late been permitted to go on with her school, in violation of the law which the people of this state have deliberately enacted, could hardly have been expected by her. And we have no hesitation in saying that but few towns in this or any other state would have shown so much forebearance towards such an establishment, as have the people of Canterbury. We were not aware until we were so informed by our correspondent last week, that the number of scholars now in attendance at the Abolition school was so great. We know that great efforts have been made by its abettors, since the decision of Chief Justice Daggett, to fill up the benches of the school-house, and to increase the grievances and insults of our citizens, but we did not know until recently that those efforts had succeeded to the amount of more than thirty wenches, who are sent from all quarters of the globe!*

On the 27th of January the house was set on fire in the early afternoon. Fortunately the fire had not made much progress before it was discovered. Prudence and the girls, with some help from neighbors, put the fire out before any significant damage was done. It was gratifying to Prudence to learn that some of her neighbors would help her in time of crisis. A colored friend of the school, Mr. Olney of Norwich, who had brought wood to the school on the day of the fire was arrested and charged with arson. At his trial in March he was acquitted. Rumors were circulated that Prudence had started the fire herself to stir up sympathy!

Her friends had other ideas. Garrison commented in the *Liberator* of February 8th:

Suspicious Occurrence

We hear by the last Unionist that Miss Crandall's house was discovered to be on fire on Tuesday afternoon, 27ult under circumstances as led to the belief that it was the work of an incendiary. Fortunately it was extinguished without much difficulty. A short time since the Advertiser a worthless and illiterate print (the pliant tool of Andrew T. Judson) intimated that effectual measures would be taken to break up Miss Crandall's school in the course of a month. Base and desperate as her persecutors have shown themselves to be — lost to decency, honor and intelligence — still we dare not believe that they were accessories to a deed so truly diabolical. It is beyond the turpitude of those whose infamy shall thicken upon them with the increase of days and years.

Attacks were fairly well balanced by adulation. The *Liberator* reprinted from the *Genius of Universal Emancipation* a poem by ELA who is not otherwise identified.

To Prudence Crandall

Heaven bless Thee, noble lady, in thy purpose good and high
Give knowledge to the thirsting mind, light to the asking eye;
Unseal the intellectual page, for those from whom dark pride
With tyrant and unholy bonds, would fain its treasure hide.

Still bear thou up unyielding 'gainst persecution's shock,
Gentle as a woman's self, yet firm and moveless as a rock;
A thousand spirits yield to thee their gushing sympathies
And blessing of a thousand hearts around thy pathway lies.

Not to be outdone by the unkown ELA, Garrison published an Acrostic in the *Liberator* of March 22, 1834.

An Acrostic

Addressed to her who is the ornament of her sex.

Proudly shall History upon its page
Record in living characters thy name
Unequalled woman in this servile age!
Dauntless, though wrapt in Persecution's flame!
E'en as a star shall thy example shine
Nor time's profoundest depths obscure its light,
Cheering posterity's extended line,
Effulgent, fresh and lovely to the sight.

Courageously persue thy purpose high,
Reclaim from ignorance the darkened mind!
An outcast race around thee prostrate lie
Naked and hungry, captive, sick and blind,
Dare still to be their guide, instructress, friend
And bright shall be the crown of thy reward.
Let brutal men in wrath with thee contend
Loved — honored thou shall be and they abhorred.

Prudence accepted accolades with good grace. Her students were elated that she was thus honored.

CHAPTER SIX
NEW VENTURES

CALVIN Philleo, a recent widower with three children, a Baptist minister from Pawtucket, Rhode Island, attended the trial of Prudence in August. He paid frequent visits, subsequently, to her school until he departed for a pastorate in Ithaca, New York. He was said to be a forceful preacher, having a fine voice both for speaking and singing. He had been associated with churches in the eastern New York area, having been called to the ministry from his former occupation of blacksmith. The Baptist denomination sponsored revival meetings during the 1820's and became very active in Connecticut. Calvin accepted a pastorate in Suffield, Connecticut where he served for several years. It is said that his sermons caused strong men to fall on their knees and beseech the Lord for mercy. From Suffield he went to Pawtucket. Here his wife died, leaving him with three children. The older daughter, Emmaline, soon married. Elizabeth was in her early teens and Calvin Jr. was nine when Prudence first met them.

When friends of Prudence learned of his interest in her, they were disturbed because of a variety of rumors about him. Correspondence between William Garrison and his fiancee, Helen Benson, reveals the sequence of events in this period of Prudence's life.

2/11/1834 — Helen Benson to Wm. L. Garrison. Written from Providence where Helen's brother, George, lived.

> *You, have doubtless heard ere this that Prudence Crandall has again had her patience and fortitude put to a severe trial; her house has been fired, and not a shadow of a doubt remains of its being the work of an incendiary, the deed is wickedly laid to her charge by the Canteburians. (sic) Thus has her peace and quiet again been disturbed, and the little respite she enjoyed from persecution and which her friends hailed as the harbinger of happier days been sadly broken in upon, and her cheering prospects put to flight by the dark designs of her enemies. "Woe unto him by whom such offence cometh."*
>
> *I suppose in March you will again visit Friendship Vale that little spot of earth which P. Crandall in the fullness of a grateful heart denominates the asylum of the oppressed; do you think it worthy the title?*

* * * * *

> *P.S. Since writing the above I have rec'd a letter from home which mentioned P. Crandall was engaged to a baptist (sic) minister by the name of Calvin Philleo of Ithaca, N.Y.*

2/18/34 — Wm. L. Garrison to Helen Benson.

O, the persecuted, the dauntless, the heroic Prudence Crandall! What severe trials now are hers! What ecstatic joys shall be hers hereafter! She has my sympathy, my admiration, my prayers. I trust the firing of her house will yet prove to have been accidental.

You ask, whether she has rightly designated your lovely dwelling in Brooklyn, as "THE ASYLUM OF THE OPPRESSED." With my whole soul I respond — Yes!

3/8/34 — Wm. L. Garrison to Helen Benson. Writing from Roxbury, Garrison tells of his trip from Brooklyn to Providence, in which Mrs. Samuel May was with him.

My ride from Brooklyn to Providence afforded me some amusement. At one of our halting places, we took in a person who evidently rejected the doctrine of total abstinence, for he found it extremely difficult to speak coherently. I presume he did not know me; but he immediately began to ask me what I thought of the "nigger school" in Canterbury, stating that he "did not believe in it." Much to the amusement of the good lady who came from Brooklyn, and who sat by my side, I put a few satirical shafts into him which made him feel very uncomfortable, as he could not pull them out again. The poor fellow was horrified at the thought of intermarriages between the whites and blacks — it seemed to haunt him like a guilty consicience. Mrs. M. gave him a capital thrust saying that, if she had to choose either for a husband, she would greatly prefer a virtuous and sober colored man to an intemperate white man!

At another tavern, two young and dissipated pedestrians joined our company, and again the "nigger school" was brought up for condemnation by the same anti-temperance man. They, however, were for letting the school "go ahead," if any persons were willing to back it up; but as for the whites and blacks marrying together, that would never answer. One of them declared that if he had a sister who should marry a nigger, he would put a ball into his (the nigger's) heart in a moment. . . . But enough of their nonsense — I have referred to them simply to show what type of creatures cluster around the Colonization Society and oppose the education of our colored population.

* * * * *

I feel extremely anxious to learn the result of Mr. Olney's trial. Will you write soon?

March 13, 1834
Brooklyn Letter to William L. Garrison from Helen Benson

* * * * *

You say you are anxious to hear of the fate of Olney; he came off conqueror I can assure you. His trial continued until six o'clock Saturday night. It rained all day, but when the jury carried in the verdict not guilty, the clouds dispersed and the very heavens smiled propitiously. So Olney came immediately down here, with a smiling countenance, which bespake a peace within. He was warmly congratulated by twenty, or more of his friends, who gave him a hearty shake of the hand. I did not feel much anxiety on his account, for I thought a Divine Providence would overrule and not permit the innocent to suffer for the guilty. I will not enter into a minute account of their proceedings for Miss Crandall told me it was her intention to write you the early part of the week, therefore, she will give you the desired information, and what I should say, would be only a repetition.

P. Crandall asked me if I ever heard of Mr. Philio (sic) in Providence. I replied yes. She then questioned me so closely as to what I heard, that I was absolutely obliged to tell her. I felt rather a weight off my mind by so doing tho' I do not think anything I said, made the least difference to her; for "love" you know, "heightens every virtue," and I found in her estimation he was almost a perfect being. I do hope these reports will prove false. She read me a letter from a Baptist minister, who is intimately acquainted with Mr. Philio (sic) and who resides near, giving him a most excellent character. Said I, do you know that person by reputation who wrote this letter? Her reply was, no! but his name is on the list of ministers. I then said, so is Mr. P's and do ascertain if possible, what kind of character he sustains, and if he can be relied upon. She received all I said very kindly, and observed, tho' she had given him her heart, and a decided preference, still she had so perfect a control of herself, she could at any moment withdraw her affections. Wonderful woman! not one of a thousand, could have said as much. She imparted this to me in confidence, but I concluded from what she said, she would have no objections to your knowing it.

3/19/34 — Wm. L. Garrison to Helen Benson

The acquittal of Olney relieves my mind of much anxiety. As he was taken up simply for being in Miss Crandall's house at the time of the fire, suppose we have Andrew T. Judson arrested, as he lives in the dwelling next to her own.

You did well to deal frankly with Miss C., in relation to her marriage.

3/25/34 — William L. Garrison to Helen Benson

The Managers of our Society have voted to request Miss Crandall to have her portrait taken in Boston by one of our most distinguished artists. I shall apprise her of the fact in a few days. It is done at my suggestion.

4/1/34 — Wm. L. Garrison to Helen Benson

This afternoon I sent a letter by mail to our respected friend Prudence Crandall, urging her to come to this city, immediately if practicable, in order to have her portrait taken, according to a vote of the Managers of the New-England Anti-Slavery Society. — It had scarcely been gone two hours, before she arrived in Boston! — Of course, I hastened to greet her, and was glad, to find her in excellent health and good spirits. "Did you stop at our dear friend Benson's?" said I, somewhat eagerly. "O, yes — certainly!" was the reply, "and kindly and cordially was I received — the family are all well." "But have you not letters for me?" I inquired despondingly. "Yes — here are two."

Prudence will probably be detained in this city at least one week. When she returns, you may expect another letter from me.

4/5/34 — Wm. L. Garrison to Helen Benson

Our mutual friend Miss Prudence is enabled to return sooner than was anticipated and therefore she will leave today, at one o'clock, for Providence . . .

I am happy to say that the artist has been very successful in taking the portrait of Miss Crandall; but the story of her persecution will outlive the canvass. One thing she must guard against — namely, being exalted in her mind by the abundant panegyric of her friends. Certainly, she deserves the sympathy, the affection, and the praise of all those who feel for the suffering and the dumb — for what disgrace and opposition she has voluntarily encountered! What indignities have been cast upon her! What perils have beset her path! And then, how steadfast has been her purpose! How untiring her perseverance! How calm and gentle her deportment! How resolute her courage! Still, (and I am aware that these remarks are strictly applicable to me as to her) she must be careful lest she be "exalted above measure." We should meekly bend like the reed to the breath of eulogy, but be lofty and unyielding as the oak when the tempest of an unrighteous persecution is raging around us. How contemptible, how foolish, how disgusting is personal egotism!

These remarks have not been elicited in consequence of the appearance of anything vain, either in the language or conduct of our dear friend; for I am charmed with the simplicity and meekness of her manners; — but a situation like hers calls for sleepless vigilance.

Perhaps I may be interrogated by someone — "If praise be thus dangerous, why do you speak and print so highly in her behalf?" I answer, first because she is a meritorious woman — secondly, the excessive abuse of her enemies requires the ardent approbation of her friends — and, thirdly, in vindicating her conduct, we advance the cause of the entire colored population of the United States.

She will tell you, I presume, that her visit to this city has proved a very agreeable one to herself and to her white and colored friends. There are hundreds yearning to see her, who cannot get an opportunity. When an engraved copy of her portrait is struck off, I will send it to you . . .

The family with whom I board will leave "Freedom's Cottage" on the 20th of May, and move to "Mount Pleasant." I shall either hire the cottage myself, or return to the city. If Prudence had had time, she would have come out and spent a few hours here. The probability now is, that I shall take the cottage.

4/7/34 — Wm. L. Garrison to Helen Benson.

What a burden you have removed from my breast! — Your delightful favor of April 3rd and 4th is before me, and joyful am I to learn that my letters have all safely arrived in "Friendship's Valley." As our dear friend Prudence has delayed going until this morning, I must devote a few moments in heaping my thanks and blessings upon you. Excuse that which is hasty, and overlook that which is imperfect . . .

Am happy to inform you that Prudence has wholly given up Mr. Phillio.

"Friendship Vale," April 9, 1834

Dear Lloyd:

Prudence has arrived; how happy she looked and how kindly she spoke of you, as she greeted me. She knows all, thought I, nor was I mistaken, for her expressive countenance spoke volumes, and in a moment she handed me your dear letters, with two little books, for which accept my thanks. I ran by myself to read them; the contents were truly delightful! How much pleasure they afforded me.

Prudence had much news to impart to me, and so many things to say of you, and about you, that I almost fancied I had caught a glimpse of you myself. She was exceedingly gratified with the attention you paid her; and her heart seemed almost too full for utterance. She manifested so much interest in my happiness, I thought I might with propriety make mention of Mr. Philio. She replied it is done with, tho' I have not a single proof of the many numerous reports that are alleged against him. I thought her affections were strongly placed on him, and I did pity her. She says, only think Helen, I am expecting him every day. I replied, I am sorry for you, but we must think it is for the best; time will probably disclose the truth. She observed, I am resigned to it. She showed me many presents from England, and presented me with a seal, which I consider very valuable, and shall treasure it for the sake of the giver . . .

Our dear friend Prudence informed me, what a glorious time you had singing one evening with some of the coloured friends. How I should have admired to have been with you . . .

Prudence enjoyed her second trip to Boston. This time she was not an unknown schoolmarm but an acclaimed heroine. She was entertained in the homes of Abolitionists, meeting in person several of the people whom she had come to consider her friends because of their letters to her and comments they had made publicly about her school. Rev. May and Mr. Garrison had suggested that she have her portrait painted since it would be useful to have at meetings of the Anti-slavery associations. A young artist, Francis Alexander, who had come from Windham, Connecticut was engaged to do the portrait. He had studied in Boston "under the influence of Gilbert Stuart" and later studied in Europe and painted several famous people including Charles Dickens.

After Prudence returned from her trip to Boston she continued to receive gifts and adulation. Some were from abroad. Captain Stuart, a devout Abolitionist, returned from a voyage to Great Britain laden with presents. The most elaborate was a large, leather bound, two volume Bible. On the flyleaf was the inscription:

PRUDENCE CRANDALL
CANTERBURY
U.S.

Presented to Miss Crandall by the Ladies of Edinburgh as a mark of the respect with which they regard the Christian courage of her conduct toward their colored Sisters in the United States and from a conviction that such consistent love and strength could only be derived from the Divine Author of the Sacred Volume. John 21 verse 15 "He saith unto him Feed my Lambs." Psalms 40 Verses 1 & 2 "I waited patiently for the Lord and He inclined unto me and heard my cry. He brought me up also out of an horrible pit; Out of the miry clay, and set my feet upon a rock, and established my goings."

Edinburgh 5th March 1834

There were also two lovely Staffordshire plates decorated with appropriate symbolism and Prudence's name. Other gifts included a book entitled "Life of Miss Graham" from Lydia and Mary Moline; a pin cushion from A. & E. Blair of Wilbert Street, Bath; a "working" from "dear little girls," students of Rebecca Waterhouse of Liverpool; a pin cushion and pen wiper from Jane and Caroline Blair of Bothwick Hiss. There were also many letters lauding Prudence for her courage. One was from May Anne Erskine, Secretary of the Ladies of Edinburgh Emancipation Society. All of these gifts and other attentions were carefully noted in the *Liberator.*

On the home front, one of Prudence's most vocal enemies met a come-up-pance. The *Liberator* noted on April 19th:

Political Overthrow of Andrew T. Judson

The result of the recent election in Connecticut shows that she has become politically and consequently in this instant morally regenerated. The triumph is indeed a noble one! It is but just to presume that the infamous black laws which were enacted by the last Legislature of the State will be repealed by the new.

But especially it is matter of congratulation that even the town of Canterbury has altered its political and therefore its moral character. It has voted down the notorious Andrew T. Judson and refused to send him as its representative to the Legislature. How contemptible and yet deplorable is the condition of that wretched and guilty man — scorned and detested he is, not only by humane and good throughout the country but also throughout England, forsaken and cast down by his own townsmen. The curses of an injured race resting upon his head — and the indignation of a righteous God burning upon his soul! It is difficult as it would be unpardonable, to speak in terms of moderation respecting the dastardly conduct of this tyrannical persecutor of a helpless woman, and still more helpless race. See what a single year has effected! Twelve months ago this discarded and crestfallen non-descript towered high in his pride of place and exalted himself above all that is called good. His evil power was potent and his arrogance insufferable. Behold the change! His name is now a proverb — a byword and a hissing — and the blackest African is white as snow by the side of his infamy! A year ago, his amiable victim, Miss Crandall was derided and condemned unmercifully. Now she stands upon a pinnacle of honor higher than the pyramids and is receiving enthusiastic plaudits of millions. Her fame is rising and brightening like the sun going up from beneath a cloudy horizon to an ethereal zenith.

Garrison's hope was badly founded — the Legislature did not repeal the Black Law. In later years Judson went on to higher posts.

On the local level harassment continued. William Burleigh was pelted with rotten eggs one night and the girls were derided whenever they stepped out of the house. The *Unionist* printed an article about the students:

Miss Crandall's School

One of the children now in the school is the daughter of a poor woman in the city of N.Y. who obtains a living by her daily labor. Of course she is unable to give her children an education, and this child is supported by another woman who once was a slave and purchased her freedom by her own exertions. Another of Miss Crandall's scholars is the daughter of a father who was himself a slave.

Where can we find such a thirst for knowledge among our white population? — Where can we find a man, nay where can we find a woman who has risen from a state of the lowest degradation by her own unaided exertions, under the weight of all the prejudices which are crushing her in the dust, against the seemingly irresistible tide of public opinion which is ever setting against her —

I say where can we find a person with a white skin who has risen from such a situation and taught himself the real worth of man, the real dignity of the human mind and exalting and enobling power of education to such an extent that, although by no means in affluent circumstances he is willing to spend a portion of his little all to support at school the child of an indigent neighbor?

There were now 22 pupils in the school. Some had been there almost a year and their progress justified their teachers' faith in them. Disappointed that the Legislature had not repealed the law, Prudence put her hope for the future of her school in the decision of the Supreme Court of Errors which would be meeting during the summer. Her plans with regards to Calvin Philleo had changed and she was again considering marriage.

Firm as she was in her determination to maintain her school, Prudence could evidently vacillate when it came to Mr. Philleo. The misgivings of her friends were discussed in continuing correspondence between Helen Benson and William L. Garrison.

5/22/1834 — Helen Benson to Wm. L. Garrison Thursday a.m.

"Prudence came here Sunday evening and passed the night with us. She seemed very happy in her mind. Said she was expecting Philio every day. William H. Burleigh has gone to assist her in keeping the school. It is her intention to visit coloured families, and impress upon them the importance of imbibing correct principles, and setting a good example to their children. I think she may be the means of diffusing a good deal of light and information in that way, and hope she may be enabled now to mingle more among the baptist, (sic) who I believe are making up on the subject. She certainly is a valuable women. (sic) I know not where you would find another female who has the subject more at heart, and who was striving so hard to enlist others in the good cause. She really makes me blush, I feel as if I did not think of the poor slaves half enough, when I see her . . ."

5/30/34 — Wm. L. Garrison to Helen Benson.

". . .Our dear friend Capt. Stuart, it seems, has not had the pleasure of visiting either Brooklyn or Canterbury. Say to Prudence that he hopes to be enabled to visit her shortly. He has left in my charge a variety of elegant and valuable presents to her and her pupils from the ladies of Birmingham, Liverpool. & c. which I shall

transmit almost immediately. You will be amused and pleased to see them..."

6/2/34 — Helen Benson to Wm. L. Garrison.

"Dr. Green has returned from the south. I have not seen him. His son called on me Saturday & (assured?) his father came on in the boat with Mr. Philio, and that he thought him very disagreeable, and took a very great dislike to him, his son seemed to regret he was going to be married to Prudence. . ."

6/6/34 — Wm. L. Garrison to Helen Benson.

"In your next, I shall expect to hear the particulars of Mr. Philleo's visit to Canterbury. I am troubled in spirit lest our dear friend Prudence marry ill. The step which she is about to take will seal her earthly destiny, either for good or evil. Let her seriously weigh the consequences. Is not the thought of her allied to a worthless person insupportable? To marry, or not to marry, is a most serious question for man or woman to consider, and ought not to be settled hastily. Tell Prudence that she has my fervent prayers and best wishes for her happiness. Also convey my compliments to Miss Almira . . ."

Helen Benson to Wm. L. Garrison

Friendship Valley June the 9, 1834
Monday Afternoon:

"Last Saturday, Prudence with Mr. Philio came to our house the former staid over the Sabbath with us. The latter only took tea and then left for the village; so I saw him only for a few hours. I must say, I was rather agreeably disappointed in his appearance; he was a much meeker looking man than I anticipated — tho' there is nothing prepossessing in his manners, I think it probable I should have been quite favorably impressed towards him, had I not previously had so many intimations of his ill behavior, that I could not in his presence divest my mind of prejudice. Prudence was extremely anxious to have her friends think well of him, and I wanted to say something to her in his favor as far as I could with truth on my side, so I told her what little acquaintance I had with him I was not disposed to censure him, nor believe anything that he could satisfactorily clear up. She then stated all the storys to me she had heard about him, from her friends and exactly as he stated them to

her, and she was perfectly satisfied with his explanations. But to my mind his acknowledgement in part made me believe more than ever that he was guilty of the many charges that had been laid against him. When I see you I will tell you all about it. I was as polite as I could be to him, invited him to tarry with us the night but he declined to my joy, for I dislike to feel so towards any person and be obliged to treat them with so much politeness. Mother went to hear him preach Sunday. She was exceedingly gratified with the sermon. I would have gone to have heard him could I in conscience have set under his preaching believing the reports true in circulation about him. He could make Prudence believe black was white if he chose — I tell you, as I have before; love is blind, blind to all faults and failings in the image it adores. I love Prudence dearly it would have done my heart good could I have congratulated her in her happy choice. But how could I do so. She observed to me yesterday she thought heaven had bestowed on her the choicest blessing by sending her Philio. It may be so. We will hope for the best. I begin to think myself something of a predestinarian. If Prudence does feel perfectly satisfied she is unhappy, I know, to think her friends have formed such an opinion of Mr. P. I was fearful she would think me indifferent as to her future happiness, — but could I only have approved of her choice, I should have been one of the first to wish her joy. I rather think from what she said it was her intention to be married as soon as practicable, for her to leave her school. She was very much disappointed to think Mr. May was absent as she was desirous I suspect to give Mr. P. an introduction to him. Sarah has just informed me of a fact I was not aware of before, that Prudence told her Mr. Philio said the school should be sustained, and from what she concluded he would remove to Canterbury rather than the school should go down. Suppose when Mr. May returns, she will conclude what to do. Tell Mr. May when you see him his wife and children are well; she observed yesterday some one enquired after her husband & she started for she had almost forgotten she had one. I intend to stay all night with her to night. I shall then deliver your message to her . . ."

6/14/34 — Wm. L. Garrison to Helen Benson. This was in response to Helen's letter of June 9 where she said of Rev. Philleo that she had heard "many intimations of his ill behavior" and that she was prejudiced against him, but that Prudence was blind in her love for him.

"I have read your sketch of Mr. Philio's visit to B. with considerable care, and feel as much perplexed in relation to the real character of

the man, as you do. If he is an innocent man, he is certainly an injured man; and he had better be both than a bad man. Let us hope for the best. I think if Prudence marries him, she will act wisely in giving up her school . . . "
" . . . If Prudence cherishes half the attachment for Mr. P which I bear toward you, you need not wonder that she clings to him so dutifully . . . "

6/21/34 — William L. Garrison to Helen Benson.
"Rev. Mr. Philleo is now in this city, and called upon me last evening and to-day. He leaves Monday morning. He certainly appears to be a good man, and I hope that 'He is a man more sinned against than sinning.' "

Helen Benson to Wm. L. Garrison

"Friendship Valley" June the 18, 1834
"Mr. Philio leaves Canterbury to day from what I can learn they have been very happy together. Prudence says Mr. Tappan advised Mr. P. to go on with the school and he seems very willing to sustain it. Should he have any thing to do with it, I hope they will go out of the village of Canterbury for I do believe there will be no end to contention as long as they remain there. Prudence told me that Mr. Philio did advertise for a wife, & at the same time he was engaged to a lady who afterwards refused him, because of the various reports about him. She also stated that he called at a milliner's shop to see a lady for the first time, and if she was agreeable he intended to offer himself the next time he saw her — called some where & ascertained she had a husband; so sent her a note saying he should not fulfil his engagement to call again. Prudence thought nothing about the stories and it is not strange when we consider that he offered himself to her, the first call he ever made her: He will not let you look him in the face but holds his head down a good deal, seldom (gives) you chance to look at his eyes which strongly indicates guilt. Perhaps I do wrong . . .
I heard last evening Prudence Crandall was at Mr. Mays yesterday afternoon. Mr. P. has not yet left. She was in great tribulation on account of the reports about Mr. P. and come over to see her sympathiser in all her sorrows. She said her school was to continue & she some expects to be married next month. Poor girl I pity her."

ANDREW T. JUDSON
Photo by C.R. Underhill, Courtesy of Florence Clark

CHAPTER SEVEN
THE FINAL TRIAL

GARRISON spent some time at his future father-in-law's home in Brooklyn in July and wrote to his brother-in-law about some of his experiences and observations.

Brooklyn, *To George W. Benson*
July 10, 1834 *Providence, R. I.*

This afternoon, we think of making a visit to Rowland Green. Yesterday his son spent an hour with us and I was pleased with his deportment and conversation. As I have not yet visited Prudence, we shall journey to Plainfield via Canterbury. The Canterburians recently killed a cat, cut her throat and hung her by the neck to Prudence's gate. We may say that the victim Requies-cat in peace — and to the perpetrators of the murderous deed, "you have added another black act to the long cat-alogue of your offences." The Cat-astrophe will be duly chronicled, not dog-matically but categorically.

Summer days in Canterbury now were fairly quiet. All concerned with the school were awaiting the judgment of the Court. Such was not the case elsewhere. Riots and the burning of Negro churches and homes had broken out in New York and Philadelphia. Lewis Tappan's home was entered by a mob which threw the furnishings into the street and burned them. Arthur Tappan armed the clerks in his store and when rocks were thrown there, the clerks fired into the air to show their attackers that they would not hesitate to protect themselves and the property. Thirty-one houses and two churches were burned before the rioters had been brought under control. The violence spread to New Jersey and to Norwich, Connecticut where an Abolitionist minister was driven from his pulpit and local Negroes were attacked. This was the climate which prevailed when the Supreme Court considered the case.

The five judges held the review of the case in chambers in Hartford on July 18th. It was not considered necessary to call the principals. The attorneys for both sides presented briefs — long, long briefs.

Attorneys Ellsworth and Goddard presented statements substantially the same as they used in the previous trials. They contended that Negroes were citizens and entitled to the same rights and considerations accorded others. They pointed out that Negroes served in the armed forces, had access to the courts, were occupied in licensed capacities, and conducted businesses. Although they could not vote in Connecticut, they could and did vote in all of the other New England states, New York, New Jersey,

Delaware, Maryland and even in such southern states as North Carolina and Tennessee. They stressed that females could not vote anywhere but no one questioned their citizenship.

Attorney Judson, representing the prosecution gave a loquacious harangue on the constitutionality of the Connecticut statute. He dwelt at length on the many evil results which would befall communities if schools such as Miss Crandall's were permitted to flourish.

The Justices were now confronted with a delicate decision. They could not in good conscience or logically call the law constitutional. On the other hand, they were reluctant to reverse the decision of the revered Judge Daggett who was soon to retire. The long delayed report states:

> *The Court reversed the decision below, but did not decide either of the points presented by counsel. The ground of the reversal was, the insufficiency of information, it omitting to allege that the school was not set up with the license of the civil authority and selectmen.* *

By the end of July, the decision of the Judges was made public. Prudence was greatly relieved. She assumed that her troubles were over.

Rev. Philleo had returned and they planned to be married in August. He felt especially fortunate to have won such a cultured, dedicated young woman for his second wife. Her splendid home and successful school were real assets.

Prudence was overjoyed to have the affection of a stalwart, well-known clergyman. She yearned to take care of his frail young son. Being thirty, she considered her marriage an unexpected blessing rather than a highly romantic development.

Her young students viewed the matter differently. To them the marriage was a wondrous event. They expected that their beloved teacher would be protected by this handsome man. They busied themselves with making small gifts for her.

We learn more of the events of the following days from the correspondence between Helen Benson and Wm. L. Garrison.

7/19/1834 — Helen Benson to Wm. L. Garrison.

> *I have been down in Mr. May's study this morning and had a chat with him. He told me two baptist Ministers were in his study yesterday of whom he enquired if they had any acquaintence with Mr. Philio. They replied yes and gave him a most excellent character they believed him to be a good man — but very eccentric*

**See appendix*

as every body knows who has ever heard of him, Mr. May said he wished it was not so but there was no help for it.

Rev. Kneeland was very ill. The minister of the Congregational church had agreed to perform the ceremony but at the last minute backed out in response to protests from some of his deacons.

8/13/34 — Helen Benson to Wm. L. Garrison.

Last evening B. looked gloriously after a severe thunder shower.

I think it probable ere this you have seen the bride, Mrs. Philio, as I understand she has gone to Boston. She came to B. yesterday, and was married by Mr. Tillotson. Her minister, as the story goes refusing to marry them. To think she should beat us. It was sudden I expect for not one of us knew it.

After a brief ceremony, Prudence and Calvin set out by carriage for Boston. Arriving at the Goodwin home, near Providence, Rhode Island, Prudence met her step-daughter Emmaline, the wife of John Goodwin. She was a young woman in her early twenties with a boy, little John, who was not quite two and tiny Elizabeth who was one month old. This was their first meeting and Prudence gave her the bridal bouquet which had withstood the heat fairly well. The two women formed an enduring attachment for each other. From Emmaline, Prudence learned a great deal about Calvin. She was enthralled with the young children and happy with her newly acquired family.

8/18/34 — Wm. L. Garrison to Helen Benson.

It seems, then, that Prudence Crandall is no more! — This will be handed to you by Mrs. Philleo, who has taken her place, and who resembles her in all things precisely.

On Thursday morning last, on my regular excursion to the cottage, who should I see approaching me but the Rev. Philleo with Miss Prudence Crandall — no, no, Mrs. Philleo on one arm, and Miss Philleo on the other! — What — thought I — is it possible that the deed has been done? that the twain have become one? that the Gordian knot has been tied? that the hymeneal yoke has been put on? that the maiden has been transformed into a wife, and the widower into a husband?

It was even so!

And so, my dear, they have got the start of us by almost a month.

Our salutations being ended, they let me into the secret of their union, and told me that they were compelled to come to Brooklyn to be married, as the Canterbury parson was afraid to make them husband and wife. It was not the fear of God, but of Andrew T. Judson, that deterred him.

They left Brooklyn somewhat hastily for this city, as they had some expectation that new writs should be issued by the court then sitting.

I could not congratulate them upon their union, but I could and did wish them much happiness. The bride looked smilingly — the bridegroom manifested a complacent spirit — and the young miss betrayed symptoms of hilarity.

"To-morrow," said I, "you must go and see my cottage in the woods." "Agreed," said they — and so we parted.

As I left them, I felt disposed to say with Peter Pindar —

"O Matrimony! thou are like
To Jeremiah's figs:
The good were very good — the bad
Too sour to give the pigs."

But I will not apply this either relatively, invidiously, or prophetically, to the new couple. Joy and peace and prosperity be with them through life! I cannot wish them any thing less — it would be folly to wish them anything more.

In the morning, on Friday, they visited the cottage, and expressed themselves highly gratified at its appearance and location. Mrs. P. thought it could not fail to please you. It is true, every thing now is in its prime, and therefore one can hardly form a true opinion of its suitableness.

Yesterday afternoon, and in the evening, Mr. Philleo preached to our colored brethren in their meeting-house. Both sermons were very good, and apparently very sincere. I am more and more puzzled to determine accurately his real character. He may be an eccentric man — a covetous man — and, occasionally, an erring man, in trivial matters; but I can not think he is habitually a bad man.

This morning they leave for Canterbury. When I commenced this letter, I intended to send it by Mrs. P; but as they may be detained by the way unexpectedly, I have concluded to send it by the mail, that you may be sure to receive it on Wednesday.

CHAPTER EIGHT
END OF THE SCHOOL

ON Saturday Prudence and her husband and his children, Calvin and Elizabeth, returned to Canterbury. As they settled down for a comfortable life of teaching and preaching, the future seemed to hold very pleasent prospects.

Their peaceful plans were short-lived. When her opponents realized that the court had failed to convict Prudence, they decided to settle the matter in their own way. At about midnight on September 9th, the family and students were wakened by an unearthly din. Crashing glass and wood, accompanied by the howling and yelling of men, fairly shook the house. The terrified girls gathered in a hysterical huddle around their teacher who reassured them as best she could while her husband went from room to room looking out of windows to determine what the next move might be. He blamed himself for not having secured a gun with which to protect his family. The mob, hilarious over their mischief, withdrew. The dark figures moved off in all directions.

Calvin went downstairs to find that several of the window sashes and all the windows were ruined. Some of the bars which had been used were dropped in the yard. No one slept again that night. They watched in fear that the vandals might return.

When the girls gathered in the lower room in the morning, Prudence pointed out that it would be impossible to have lessons that day. Instead, they all helped sweep up the shattered glass. Calvin rode off to Brooklyn to consult with Rev. May who returned with him early in the afternoon. Pardon and Hezekiah came to view the wreckage. The four men conferred briefly, agreeing that the damage was too extensive and the danger too great to permit the school to continue. Prudence was persuaded that for the physical safety of her girls she must send them to their homes. Disheartened and defeated, she finally agreed — but her courage failed — she could not face her pupils to tell them this bitter news so Rev. May took on the sad task.

The story of the final hours of the school was told by one of the students in the *Liberator*.

"The Separation

"It was one of the pleasant sunny mornings in September when I took leave of my teacher and schoolmates. Never, no, never while memory retains a seat in my breast shall I forget that trying hour. On the night preceding my departure, while all within was as silent as a chamber of death, we were suddenly aroused by a tremendous noise. When, to our surprise we found that a band of cruel

men had rendered our dwelling almost untenantable. The next morning, we were informed by our teacher that the school would be suspended for the day. In the afternoon our friend requested that we all be called together. He, with feelings apparently of deep regret, told us we had better go to our homes. With regret, I prepared to leave that pleasant yet persecuted dwelling and also my dear school-mates, in whose society I had spent so many hours; thankful to my Heavenly Parent, that our lot was no worse; yet not without many tears did I return to my distant and solitary home.

There is something in parting from those we love from which nature recoils; and when I thought of the distance that would be between us and contemplated the uncertainty of things, I could but acknowledge the probability of never meeting again in company of my school-mates.

I have found among them simple manners and intelligent minds; and there, if any where, love was without dissimulation. My teacher was ever kind: with her I saw religion not merely adopted as an empty form but a living all-pervading principle of action. She lived like those who seek a better country; nor was her family devotion as a cold pile of hypocracy, on which the fire of God never descends. No it was a place of communion with Heaven.

Another item in the *Liberator* gave the final announcement.

Miss Crandall's School Abandoned

Human nature has its bounds and the requirements of duty have theirs. By the following advertisements which we copy from the Brooklyn Unionist it appears another cowardly attack has been made on Miss Crandall's (now Mrs. Philleo) dwelling, by some midnight ruffians in Canterbury and that it has been deemed advisable to abandon the school in that heathenish village and to let Andrew T. Judson and his associates with the whole State of Connecticut have all the infamy and guilt which attach to the suppression of so praiseworthy an institution.

The first advertisement read: $50 Reward!! During the night of Tuesday, September 9 about 12 o'clock, the house of the subscriber in Canterbury was assaulted by a number of lawless persons with heavy clubs and iron bars — five window sashes were destroyed and more than 90 panes of glass lashed to pieces and the family greatly alarmed.

The above named reward is hereby offered to any one, who will give information that will lead to the detection of the perpetrators of the outrage or any one of them.

Canterbury, Sept. 11, 1834 — Calvin Philleo

The second advertisement told still more:

For sale — the house in Canterbury occupied by Prudence Crandall, now the wife of the subscriber. The impunity with which repeated assaults have been made upon these premises, has awakened the apprehension that the property and perhaps the lives of those connected with the school, are insecure. I have therefore thought it proper and do hereby advertise the house and appurtenances thereof for sale.

For further particulars inquire of the subscriber or of Pardon Crandall of Canterbury or Samuel J. May of Brooklyn.

Calvin Philleo

As a married woman Prudence no longer had control of her property. The business and professional woman had become a wife who had lost control of her earned possessions.

Prudence and her family moved into her father's home. Her house was quickly repaired and rented to William Kinne.

On November 15, Prudence and Calvin sold her house to James Aspinwall. The deed provided that the Kinne family could continue to live there until April, 1835. The sale price was $2000, the sum which Prudence had paid for it in 1831.

Prudence helped her mother with the household affairs. Both women were anxious about the frail Elizabeth and Calvin. The four Philleos attended the Packerville Church. Calvin frequently conducted the services since the church was without a pastor, Rev. Kneeland having died in August.

In the community, hostility against Prudence was intense and unrelenting. She went about very little, except to visit Hezekiah's family. Her sister-in-law, Clarissa, was a very pleasant woman, patient with her lively family of five small children, clever and thrifty in managing her household. A conscientious Quaker, Clarissa had encouraged Prudence to maintain her school when other members of the family questioned the wisdom of her stubborn stand.

CHAPTER NINE
OUT OF CANTERBURY

WITH the coming of spring 1835, Calvin became restless. He resented not being called to the Baptist pastorate and he was chagrined at continuing hostility toward his wife. He finally decided to move to Boonville, N. Y. where he owned a small farm which he had purchased in 1833. Prudence was reluctant to go so far from her family, but she was eager to get away from the town where she had endured such unpleasant experiences, where she was still treated with impudence.

In May, they left for Boonville. They traveled by stage, steamboat and canal boat. The trip was arduous but the scenery was breath-takingly beautiful. Trees leafed in soft shades of green contrasted with the deeper hues of cedars and spruces, flowering bushes and trees were white, pink and yellow. The Berkshire hills showed silvery crowns of granite, glistening with quartz. In the valleys, the farmers were plowing and the rich browns of the fertile soil gave promise of luxuriant crops.

Crossing Connecticut by stage, they stopped briefly in Suffield then on to Amenia, New York where some of the Wheeler family still lived. There the children had a visit with their mother's relatives. They then traveled up the river from Poughkeepsie to Albany by steamer where they boarded a canal boat which took them to Utica. Prudence and the children were fascinated with the activity on the boat and along the banks of the canal. Calvin, who had traveled the course several times, spent his time conversing with other passengers, expounding at great length his theories on masonry and anti-masonry — he was against both. He also discussed slavery and temperance and such other topics as might hold an audience.

Arriving in Boonville, they stayed a few days at the Hulbert House — a large, three storied hotel built of native gray stone. Six massive columns stretched the full height of the front of the building, supporting a peaked gable which extended out several feet, giving cover to the board walk. The entry and some of the public rooms seemed dark and cavernous. In the dining room were tables made of heavy planks. Benches and settles were of sturdy construction. At the end of the long room was a tremendous fireplace. Great beams crossed the ceiling. Light was provided by oil lamps in iron wall brackets. Upstairs, the rooms were plain but light and comfortable.

Situated at the busy intersection of the main streets, the hotel was near the wharves of the Black River. Barrels of rum and molasses, sugar and other imports were handled on this wharf. Wagons were loaded and unloaded by rough, rugged men. Boats and barges passed on the river.

Along the banks of the river and at other points in the town there were asheries, tanneries, iron works, a saw mill and a grist mill. All were working at peak capacity. Boards, hides and iron products were stacked on the wharf for shipping to Albany.

Calvin had purchased a 20 acre farm from John Dewey. He and Prudence spent two days making the small house ready and purchasing furnishings to supplement the few items they had brought from Connecticut.

By comparison with the homes she had known in Connecticut, this house was cramped and unattractive. However, it was centrally located next to the public burying ground, facing the main road. Prudence and young Calvin planted a kitchen garden and a few flowers. Calvin sought out his acquaintances from ecclesiastical circles to secure preaching engagements. He had been very active in this region before going to Connecticut. As general agent, he had settled a difference between two factions in neighboring Steuben — convincing them of the folly of building two meeting houses, inducing them to use one of the structures for an academy. Now he called on the deacons of several churches to let them know that he was again located in their neighborhood. He and his family attended church in Boonville except when he was engaged to preach nearby.

As the months wore on Prudence found more and more of her time was needed for nursing Elizabeth, whose health seemed to be failing alarmingly. Frequently flushed and feverish, she lost weight and lacked energy. Prudence prepared soft foods for her and spent many hours comforting her. Daily, the family prayers were petitions for God's blessing on her. The local doctor could offer little aid so Calvin wrote to his brother Bonaparte who was pracaticing medicine in Newport, New York. He came for a visit of several days but knew of no remedy for Elizabeth's condition which he identified as consumption. He suggested rest and a continuation of care, urging that Elizabeth prepare herself for the next world.

Prudence enjoyed the visit of her brother-in-law, who was active in the anti-slavery movement and in temperance work. He was fascinated with the story his sister-in-law told him of her experience with her school. He too had encountered intense animosity because of his out-spoken support for immediate emancipation. Like his brother Calvin, he was a big man, vociferous in expressing his opinions and impatient with ideas he opposed. He at least called his opinions his own while Calvin always claimed a divine concurrence for his.

Although less than a year had passed, Prudence sometimes wondered if she had made a wise decision in marrying. Her husband was a veritable dictator in his home. He asserted all his legal authority with regard to money. Since the property of a married woman belonged legally to her husband, he had taken all of the money Prudence had at the time of their marriage and as a result of the sale of her house. Having been independent in such matters for several years, it was difficult for Prudence to feel that she must ask for every penny and account for each expenditure. Even more trying was her feeling that her husband was too severe with young Calvin. This quiet boy liked to read and often to write but his father insisted that he spend a goodly part of each day on chores, which Prudence considered to be beyond his strength. Even on days when he complained of feeling ill, his father insisted that he get up early. Prudence learned that she could not prevail through persuasion so she seldom argued. She used the periods when Calvin was away to give his son a chance to rest and relax. She really rebelled when Calvin questioned her intellect and withheld from her books which she wished to read. She was deeply interested in philosophy and religion. Her husband tried to limit her reading to Baptist publications. From time to time, Rev. May or some other friend would send her a book or paper dealing with Unitarianism or some sermons of Methodist or Congregational divines. These she would carefully store away until she could plan on an uninterrupted hour for reading. Calvin's long diatribes and perpetual prayers which had been inspiring at revivals were rather repetitious and even boring in daily doses.

Prudence was hopeful that her young sister Hannah Almyra would have a happier marriage. She had written glowing letters about John Rand whom she planned to marry in August. They would live in New York City.

All the news from home was not so joyous. Prudence was informed that her brother Reuben had been arrested and jailed in Washington, D.C. He had gone there to give botanical lectures and to gather specimens. One evening a young man named Jeffers who lived in his rooming house stopped in to chat with him. Spotting copies of the *Liberator* he asked if he might borrow one. Reuben readily gave it to him. The young man left and was soon displaying the paper to a group of men in a nearby store. Within a matter of minutes Reuben was arrested, charged with circulating seditious literature.

Prudence felt sorry for her brother. She felt even more sorry for her mother whom she knew would be greatly distressed. Reuben had never been very sturdy and his health had always been a matter of considerable concern to his mother. Although he had not made Canterbury his home since graduating from Yale, he had paid frequent, lengthy visits to his family.

Prudence longed to be with her parents during this worrisome time, but even a brief visit was not possible. Elizabeth needed constant care. Calvin's affairs seemed to require that he be away from home a great deal and there were no funds for the expensive trip east. She kept busy with her immediate duties but her thoughts were turned wistfully to the more intersting days when she was ministering to eager young minds.

The departure of Prudence from Canterbury did not end the controversy which her activities had started. Married to Helen Benson from Brooklyn, Garrison was a frequent visitor in the area. Charles Burleigh and Arthur Tappan had formed a firm friendship for each other and with Samuel May in their joint operation of the *Unionist*. Arnold Buffum and Theodore Weld of Hampton met from time to time at the Benson home and accepted invitations to speak in meetings in the Packerville church and at the home of Dr. Green. Cutting references to Canterbury were still carried in anti-slavery and religious publications.

More than a year after Prudence closed her school the village fathers considered it necessary to justify their actions. A November issue of the *Liberator* printed the resolution which was adopted at a Canterbury town meeting on Oct. 5, 1835.

"Canterbury Again.

"To justify themselves to future generations the following resolution was adopted by the town vote:

"Resolved: that the government of the United States, the nation with all its institutions, of right belong to the white men who possess them; they were purchased by the valor and blood of their fathers and must never be surrendered.

Resolved: that our appeal to the Legislature of our own state in a case of such peculiar mischief was not only due to ourselves but to the obligations devolving upon us under the Constitution. To have been silent would have been participating in the wrongs intended. The manner that protection was afforded by the Legislature is a sure guarranty that in future should the imposing attempt be repeated here or elsewhere in our state, that attempt would be met with protection to our fellow citizens as it has been afforded to us. In the open defiance of the laws of state and in the abusive manner we have been assailed because we sought that protection, we see displayed the temper and motive which hitherto have characterized; this organized foe of our common country.

Resolved: that the effects produced by such efforts upon the peace of the Union are exactly those which every reflecting mind must have anticipated when it beheld the spirit of oppression and imposition with which this combined force erected their standard of rebellion upon our soil; and when their Counsel in a Court of Justice in their behalf declared as a matter of right establishment upon Canterbury in defiance of the law, we saw more than ever the necessity of the appeal we had made, and now we rejoice that the appeal was not in vain."

Isaac Clark, Town Clerk."

As Prudence read this she wondered what consolation the townfolk could possibly draw from it. Certainly they had not accomplished their objective by any "appeal" but only by appalling vandalism. It was not through the Legislature or the Court that they had defeated her but by brute force. At least it was a source of some gratification to know that they were still sensitive to the criticism which was directed at them. Her bitter feelings were not so much because of her personal loss as because the students were thwarted in their desire for learning. It seemed particularly ironic that Col. Judson who had gained state-wide fame by his infamous behavior had been elected to Congress.

Letters from her family dealt largely with their concern for Reuben. None of his friends in Washington dared visit him for fear that they would be arrested as conspirators. His father was torn between his desire to try to see Reuben and the probability of being detained on some trumped up charge. Reuben's mail was censored and letters sent to him were opened before being given to him. Pardon wrote in one letter . . .

"I have to lament the loss of our rights. Our whole land is sick; our Constitution, the Supreme Law of the land, is violated by our rulers, the officers of the state, high and low. The rights of the people to be secure in their person, property, papers and effects are now destroyed by mobs and people, peaceably assembled to do their own business and to petition the government for the redress of grievances, have been disturbed by officers, and judges of the court with mobs at their heels, not withstanding they destroy the rights of man . . .

A goodly number of our people have petitioned Congress for the abolition of slavery in the District of Columbia. Their petition has been received by Congress with contempt and the cry is, that Congress has nothing to do with slavery. Suppose the Sable Sons of

Africa should send an ambassador to the United States to demand the release of their sons and descendants that are in slavery, would not our government be bound to receive such ambassadors; or suppose they should come into an alliance with France or any other allied powers of Europe, and they should demand release of their slaves, Congress of the United States Government is the only power that can do anything with it, for no state has any right to receive any ambassadors, make any treaties with any foreign power. At a time like this when the freedom of speech and the right of people to peaceable assembly is invaded it seems the duty of all of us to think and speak out for it. And particularly our militia should be held in readiness to support the law and to put down mobs and riots and to suppress insurrection and rebel invasion and support the indpendence as declared by our fathers in the memorable Declaration of Independence. We all ought to know that a thousand can enjoy a thousand times more happiness as one, and that the road to happiness should be open to all, and that by industry, frugality and good economy every member of this republic may enjoy happiness.

"But to return to your case, we are sure you have committed no crime, and your confinement is an unjustifiable outrage upon law and constitutional rights. Why does not your counsel commence a suit in the U. S. Court against the persons that have confined you in prison of false accusations? Set it a going, and not remain there in prison, and not make any effort to lawfully extricate yourself and also demand remuneration for your false imprisonment . . . "

Reuben's reply was sent to Prudence by her father. It gave more information than she had heard before. Dated Jan. 29, 1836, the letter read:

Washington Jail
January 29, 1836

"My dear Father:

I received your kind letter in due time and should have answered before, were it not that I wanted to put you in possession of proceedings of the Court and the probability of my getting bail. The debate in Congress on the Abolition question has kept up the prejudice against me so much that it was thought unsafe to go to trial at this term; that it would be no worse next term than now, and perhaps much less; besides, if prejudice should subside, I *should be able to obtain witnesses from New York that would be essential to my release. It would have been impossible for them to come here at this term, just expired. My counsel moved the court that I should be admitted to bail, and that the court should fix the amount. Mr. Francis Scott Key, the states attorney opposed my being admitted to bail. He said that I was an abolition emissary; That the abolition society, being rich, would pay any sum rather than have the prisoner punished, and under such circumstances it would be contrary to the law to admit bail, and that if the court determined to admit bail, it should be consumate with the offense charged. The court said they would take time to consider it. And in a few days agreed on $2000 bail. Mr. Key moved the court to raise the bail to $15,000, saying that I was certainly an emissary and that he could prove it. And by making this and other false declarations to the court, they were induced to raise the bail to $5000.*

Mr. Key takes very unwarrantable grounds against me for nothing only to bully people into the belief that he is with them in this affair hook and line. He is very distrustful of people as well as they of him. He has once been a preacher of the gospel, and then turned politician and lawyer. He has been called, heretofore, the Black's lawyer, as he took their cases for them when they sue for their freedom, and in this way, has a great many enemies. By his former conduct, the people are distrustful of his honesty of motive. But what is more than all, he has acknowledged to some of his confidential friends that there is no evidence against me, that can convict. This, he has told to a friend of mine, who has informed me a long time ago. He is only biting his own nose. The people begin to understand it, and will more so, as their prejudices will admit.

I am in good health now, and want for nothing, inasmuch as I am obliged to stay here. I don't think of getting out on $5000, notwithstanding it would be very agreeable. I am the same as dead to the world, as far as my usefullness is concerned.

You say you have it in contemplation to come and see me. However much I should be gratified for you to do so, I do not think it would be wise for you to do so. There is nothing you can do for me here. If I could get out I would come and see you. It would be advantageous for me to get out on account of getting witnesses for more complete testimony. The next court is the last of March. Probably in April, so sometime, I shall have my trial. If anything transpires different, I will let you know immediately.

Please remember me to all our neighbors. I should be delighted to be there amongst you if it were possible.

Your affectionate and obedient son,

Reuben Crandall

In April, Reuben's case was tried. The trial took ten days. Chief Justice Cranch shared the bench with Justice Thurston and Justice Morsell. Francis Scott Key was the prosecuting attorney assisted by J. M. Carlisle. Attorneys R. S. Coxe and J. H. Bradley appeared for the defense.

The prosecution built its case primarily on excerpts from the issue of the *Liberator* which was presented as evidence of Reuben's mischievous intent to "excite insurrection among slaves and the free colored population."

The passages cited were:

1. *The defendant published a libel containing these words 'Then we are not to meddle with the subject of slavery in any manner; neither by appeals to patriotism, by exhortation to humanity, by application of truth to the conscience. No, even to propose in Congress that the seat of our republican government may be purified from this crying abomination under penalty of dissolution of the Union...*
2. *A letter from Arthur Tappan replying to a letter of Rev. R. R. Gurley, Secretary of the Colonization Society contained the startling statement 'We will not insult your understanding, Sir, with any labored attempt to prove to you that the descendents of African parents, born in this country have as good a right to a residence in it as the descendents of English, German, Danish, Scotch or Irish parents. You will not attempt to prove that every native colored person you meet in the streets has not the same right to remain in his native land that you and we have. Assuming this to be true we hold it self evident that they have as good a right to deport us to Europe under the pretext that there we shall be prosperous and happy, as we have to deport them to Africa on a similar plea..."*

The third item was the bitterest libel! It was in a report of a visit to a sugar plantation by Henry Whitby who wrote that he saw such vicious treatment of slaves that he felt impelled to report to the attorney in the area. The attorney is quoted as saying "The plantation work could not be carried on without the cart whip!"

The chief witness for the prosecution was Mr. Jeffers who had secured the *Liberator* from Reuben. He said that he had remonstrated with Mr. Crandall.

"I told Crandall there would be terrible things happening if the slaves should be freed. We shall have our throats cut and the next thing would be amalgamation."

Justice Thurston gravely questioned "Would the amalgamation occur after our throats are cut?"

One of the witnesses called for the defense was Congressman Andrew T. Judson. His testimony was as follows:

"I have known Dr. Crandall from boyhood. I am a representative from the district in which he has lived. His father lives in the town where I live. He studied with my family physician, Dr. Harris, and I have been acquainted with his reputation. No young man stood better in society. He maintained a perfectly fair reputation in all respects."...

Mr. Key made an impassioned plea asking the jury to find Dr. Crandall guilty of circulating seditious literature which must be considered an act of treason. He urged the death penalty be imposed.

The jury returned a verdict of "Not Guilty."

Prudence read some of these facts in the *Liberator.* Other details were reported to her by her family. Reuben returned home with a persistent cough and other evidence that his nine months in jail had taken a toll of his strength.

The account in the *Liberator* bore the usual vehemence of Mr. Garrison.

"Acquittal of Dr. Crandall —

"The trial of this excellent but suffering man before the District Court in Washington City, for circulating Abolition documents, which occupied the time of the court for 10 days resulted in his acquittal. The District attorney, Francis Scott Key, seems to have cherished deep malignity of purpose toward Dr. Camdall and to have spared no effort to procure his conviction. Mr. Key is a leading manager of the American Colonization Society. Failing to prove that Dr. Crandall had circulated anti-salvery publications he offered to prove that the prisoner was a manager of the American Anti-slavery Society! What a horrible crime, if true! And how richly would Dr. Crandall deserve to be gibbeted, could the charge have been sustained!

Imprisoned eight months — the tyranny of Nero was no worse than this. The case of Dr. Crandall ought to rouse up the people of the free states as one man, to demand redress for the violated liberty of this person...N.B. There were two vital charges. He is the brother of Prudence Crandall. She attempted to educate certain colored females at Canterbury, not believing in the fundamental doctrine of the Colonization Society, that the colored race cannot be elevated in this country."

Prudence smiled to think that Garrison and Andrew Judson were on the same side in a controversy! Judson was in the news again in a few weeks. The *Norwich Courier* which had idolized him when he was persecuting her seemed to have a different view of him now that he was being mentioned for a Federal Judgship. Pardon sent her a clipping from the June 6th issue which started:

"District Judge

"It is rumored that the Hon. Andrew T. Judson has been nominated as Judge of the District Court of Connecticut. Should the rumor prove true we have another instance of democratic republican rotation in office. Mr. Judson has been either in or a candidate for office ever since he was of age and he joins any party that will gratify his ambition. While the old federal party existed he was a federalist of the bluest sort and furious was the bombast he poured out upon Madison and the war. Afterward he became a tolerationist and obtained office under the Nile's "political trinity." Then he joined the republicans and supported Adams and Clay for the sake of self — Subsequently he put on the democratic republican federal coat and thereby crept into Congress. Failing in his aspirations after a seat in the Senate, he intrigued for the bench and if he reaches it will have a snug berth, almost a sinecure with a salary of about $1500 for life. By the side of Judge Thompson, with whom he will be associated in the Circuit Court, he will look and sing small."

Other news from Connecticut included an item by Mr. Jocelyn.

Obituary of Harriet Rosetta Lamson — age 18.

"It was a happy Providence which led Miss Prudence Crandall to my house, about the time she established her school, and offered us an opportunity of sending her (Harriet) to her school where she made rapid improvement in important studies although much of her time was devoted to domestic assistance in the family on account of which, her expenses of board were defrayed, being at that time myself unable to defray them without that arrangement.

"An extract from one of her letters to me bringing into view the mercy of God toward her and others is particularly interesting. The letter is dated in Canterbury, 5/20/34 in which she alludes to the fact, that, at that juncture, the people had ceased most of their persecutions but they did not allow the scholars to attend the Congregational Church in the village. She observes 'We go to Packerville. They have had a protracted meeting which continued eight

days. God's Spirit was there, convincing and converting; and many, who, a short time since were dead in trespasses and sins, are now rejoicing in the love of Christ. I went 5 days and it was a solemn scene to see the aged sire and his grandchild coming to the mercy seat. Here were verified the words of holy writ — "out of the mouths of babes" — Last Saturday night was a happy moment for me for I trust that God forgave my sins and the last Sabbath was the happiest I have ever spent . . ."

I look back to the scenes of Canterbury in the history of persecution of the school and their devoted teacher, and its friends with no less abhorrance than before but with more pain when I think of the future state of all impenitent persecutors of the poor, and of the melancholy conditions of a church whose members to a great extent could sacrifice on the alter of prejudice, the law of love and unite with wicked men in measures which must ever be held in abhorrence by all humane and honorable minds.

"She never uttered to my knowledge one unkind word toward the people of Canterbury and in one of her letters she states that she is sorry for one of the principal persecutors of the school. May the children of God, who were in any degree led astray by the wicked and their own prejudices at Canterbury to unite in the persecution of the school weep in repentence and praise God for His great mercy to this lamb of His flock."

CHAPTER TEN
BACK TO CANTERBURY

EARLY in 1837, Prudence faced a new and frightening problem. Calvin became very ill with an ailment diagnosed as "over-work of the brain." A period of intense fever was followed by several weeks of listlessness. When he regained his strength, he was subject to seizures during which he sometimes had momentary loss of memory or interruptions of his thoughts. Occasionally the seizures were more severe and he would lose consciousness and fall. All that year he was afraid to accept any speaking engagements. His physical symptoms were serious but his attitude toward his problem made it even more difficult to bear. He believed that his affliction was a manifestation of God's displeasure with him. He alternately fussed and prayed over this — seeking his wife's counsel in trying to analyze his guilt but rejecting her suggestions or advice on this or any matter. Prudence felt great compassion for him and gave him the best possible care. She did not believe that God wreaked vengeance on his children. She feared that his constant introspective fretting was contributing to his illness rather than alleviating it.

In July, Prudence received a pathetic letter from Reuben. He had returned to his parents' home since he was not well. Hannah Almyra was already there and she was very ill. Reuben urged Prudence to come to Canterbury if she would see her sister alive, but Prudence could see no way to leave her home where Elizabeth was ill and her husband still at an uncertain stage of recuperation. She wrote comforting letters to her family and sought balm for her own harrowed heart in the faith which had strengthened her in other trials.

Hannah Almyra died in August. Reuben felt somewhat improved but decided to seek a warmer climate. He selected Jamaica and a letter to his folks was sent on to Prudence.

Jamaica, Nov. 18, 1837

"Dear Mother and Father:

I sit down today to address a few lines to you. I left New York on the 1st, as you have been informed by Dr. Rand. We had a quiet Passage of Thirteen Days, encountering no storms. I was not sea sick at all, while almost every other passenger on board was sick. A part of the way we encountered a tremendous sea, owing to a recent gale which took place in that vicinity. My health continued good 'till we met the heavy sea, (which lasted several days) compelling me to take to my berth, and there lie. Further, my bread all spoiled and I was compelled to eat such bread and other things as I could get. All very good of their kind, but none fit for me.

We had a cow on board to give us milk, which did very well 'till we got into warm regions, and then the milk soured soon after being milked. I got a diarrhea the last day or two of the voyage, and it has not entirely left me yet, although I am much better.

I am staying now for a few days in Kingston, the principal seaport of the island. The woman's name that keeps the house, is Kelly, a colored woman. She has a large house, principally of transient boarders.

Monday. I don't know how the climate is going to agree with me. It is very hot and sometimes very oppressive and prostrating. The climate of all the West Indies is decidedly too warm for northern consumptives. If I had known, experimentally or otherwise, this fact I should have gone to some southern part of the U.S. in preference.

The physician who attends me is a very skillful man, and gives me every attention a physician can. He advises me to keep to sea in this lattitude. He thinks that sea voyages in warm climates will benefit me more than being on land. If I do that, it will necessarily cost me more than staying where I am. In case I adopt the doctor's advice, I shall sail for Cuba or Turk's Island, or some other island where I shall be constantly falling in with American vessels. I may run over to the American shores — St. Augustine, St. Marico or some other place. The change of diet and climate as I said before is very great, not so much on sea as on land. What the result will be Heaven only knows. I have done the best I could and acted from the best information I could obtain. That I can find different climates in the island, is true, but on inquiry they are damp and totally unfit for complaints like mine. The climate in the highlands is changeable and many times is piercing cold.

My love to Hezekiah's family, to Dr. Green's and all other inquiring friends. I hope I may see them and you, all again. All things work for good to them that love and fear God.

Dear Father and Mother, I must bid you adieu for the present and will write the first opportunity that again occurs.

P.S. The packet sails next Saturday, that takes this letter, Dec. 1st. The above vessel had been detained and will be 'till the middle of this month, probably on account of refusing to take the first pilot that boarded.

I like the climate here, better than I did. I am pretty feeble in muscular strength, owing to not having carriage exercises. I am going next week to get a horse to see if I can ride horseback to advantage. If so, I shall buy me a pony. There are many passing ponies brought from the Spanish mariners and sold for $50 or $60. Good American horses are extremely dear.

I wish father or Hezekiah would send me some winter pears and Dr. Baldwin's winter sweet apples, enough to make up a barrel full of apples and pears: Send it by steam boat to New York and request them to take it to the vessel in a boat to prevent jamming. I miss my sweet apples and pears very much. They have no sweet apples here: they have only winter fruit. Apples are worth now 6¢ to 8¢ a lb. and will continue to be that price 'till after Christmas and New Years.

The ship "John W. Cator" will be the first packet out from New York. John must write when she sails. You must send the barrel some days beforehand that it may be stowed away in the hold. Hezekiah must pack it up with cotton waste to prevent jamming the apples and pears.

I have no dispepsia bread. They have no flour as they raise no wheat here. The bakers don't know how to make Indian bread. They make their Indian meal almost as fine as flour. My living is goat's milk and graham crackers. The crackers are toasted and are quite eatable. I shall have some flour and a few pounds of Indian meal sent me. Mr. Rand will attend to all that. I put cat-nip into my milk and water. It makes a pleasant tea. I will write the next packet. This packet is bound for Philadelphia.

Reuben Crandall"

In January 1838 Reuben Crandall died. He was with friends who arranged his funeral, settled his financial affairs and wrote letters to his parents.

A letter from Prudence's father indicated changes to come in her father's plans.

February 23, 1838

Dear Daughter Prudence Philleo, I write to inform you of the Death of your Dear Brother Reuben he died the 17th of January in full assurance of his blessed immortality letters say he had his senses to the last and had great anxiety for the repentence of his friends and their return to the Lord.

Hezekiah is some unwell has been Raising some blood and rest of the family is as well as could be Expected considering all things.

I have settled with Mr. Philleo on your account you know that I had given my note to Doctor Harris for 300 dollars and to Comfort S. Hide for one hundred dollars out of which you sent me fifty dollars on the three hundred and fifty and interest on the same and Hezekiah's account to the amount of forty or fifty dollars for the payment of which I have agreed to take five building lots in the City of Brooklyn, New York the rest of your account it is agreed shall be an advancement to you and so to be settled by my Executors or administrators.

Now for my concerns I have swaped away my farms in Canterbury for six hundred acres of land in the state of Illinois. I shall Settle my affairs as soon as I can and go into the wilderness to seek any assylom or hiding place from the turmoils and contentions of this world and find a place to lay my weary and decreped bones. I don't know as I shall accomplish my undertaking for I have everything against me. Your Grandmother is in deep trouble and your mother often in Floods of tears. Whether I shall be obliged to give up the interprise or not is now uncertain. I have Sot the time to go on the first of April whether your mother will live through this trying scene is quite uncertain. I have put my hand to the plough and I hate to look back. It has been sickly in this neighborhood for a time past. there has been a number of deaths, Alpheus Moss's wife is dead and he is sick unto death Capt. Sethe Clark is dead and his funeral is to be attended tomorrow. I have nothing more particular to write and I shall yield the pen to your mother.

Pardon Crandall

My dear I would give the gold of ofer if had it if thee was here and could go the journey with us we must go to New York and then to Philadelphia and then to Pits Burgh and then down the Ohio river and then up the Mississippi and then into the Illinois river and land at Rockwell twelve miles from our land there is 3 hundred people lives round Troy Grove our nearest nabour is one half mile the'r name is Root they went from Windham County I am so nervous I can scarsley hold the pen in my hand He cannot go this spring but he will go as son as he can get ready grandmother will go to live with thy Uncle John

We all send our love to thee Due rite ameadatly something or other thy affectnate

Mother
Esther Crandal

Canterbury Ct
Febry 23 *Paid 18 ¾*

Prudence Philleo
Boonville Oneyda County
New York

Prudence felt it imperative to return to Canterbury before her family left there permanently. Calvin had taken to roaming about again. He had arrived in Canterbury, stopping at Hezekiah's house. Prudence was chagrined to learn that he had sought money from her father at such a time.

When Calvin returned to Boonville, she insisted that they sell their home. Having a good offer for the property, Calvin agreed and in April they returned to Canterbury.

It was a joyous reunion for Prudence and her mother. Pardon had gone out to Illinois to prepare for moving his family there. Hezekiah's health had improved. Clarissa was nearing the time of birth of her sixth child. Esther and Prudence shared the household duties, caring for Esther's mother and Elizabeth.

The Greens, the Packers and a few of Prudence's friends were still in the community. Samuel May had left for a parish in Syracuse. Young Calvin renewed old friendships. He had not made many friends in Boonville, Although he had lived in Canterbury briefly, he considered this his home. Here he felt as though he were part of a family. He was a few years older than Hezekiah's son Obediah but they were nearly the same size and played happily together. He liked to be with Hezekiah who was an easy going man, patient with the questions and foibles of children.

At this time the General Assembly repealed the infamous "Black Law" under which Prudence had been arrested five years before. Francis Gillette in Hartford was one of the leaders to move to repeal this Act which he considered made Connecticut the target of well deserved criticism from other enlightened states.

Phillip Pearl of Hampton who wrote the law had been converted to the Anti-slavery movement by Theodore Weld another Hampton resident. Now Mr. Pearl worked for the repeal of the law saying, "I could weep tears of blood for the part I took in this matter. I now regard it as utterly abominable. The truth is my prejudices against that poor persecuted class of people were so violent as to blind me to the dictates of common humanity and justice."

How Prudence wished this attitude had prevailed in 1833! How different her life might have been if she could have continued her school and be still in possession of her lovely home on the green.

Word from Illinois indicated that Pardon had driven a well and had a small house built. He described rich soil and flat prairie land well worth the $1.25 per acre. He also said he had been ill but had recovered and would return in June. Esther dreaded the thought of setting out for a home so far away. She was particularly reluctant to leave her aged mother although she knew her brother John and his wife would take good care of her. Esther and her mother had lived together for many years and the bond between them was very strong. Esther loved her big house with its comfortable furnishings, most of which she would have to leave behind. Twenty-five years in this home filled it with memories — some very sad ones but others which were joyous and inspiring.

When Pardon returned on June 2nd, he was far from well. He had contracted malaria which flared up and subsided. He was enthusiastic about the Illinois country where he thought life would be simpler. He had felt a greater sense of freedom there — people were busy with their property rather than politics and competitive churches. On days when he was well enough, he inventoried his belongings, deciding what things could profitably be moved and which should be sold. On some days chills and fever rendered him quite helpless and very rebellious.

On July 19th, 1838 Pardon died. This was a great shock to his family and a fatal blow to Clarissa who had borne her sixth baby on July 8th. On the 20th, while preparing her children for the funeral of their grandfather, she died leaving Hezekiah with children ranging from 12 days to 12 years of age.

Four times death had visited their family within a year. Prudence, Esther and Hezekiah comforted and helped each other as best they could. Clarissa's young sister, Nancy Cornell came from Black Hill to care for Hezekiah's children. His eldest daughter Mary was an able little girl who was accustomed to caring for little ones. Prudence divided her time between helping her mother and giving what attention she could to Hezekiah's family.

There was no thought now of moving West. Contacts were made to restore the Illinois property to its former owner or another person who had expressed an interest in it. There was no immediate result from these efforts. The lists which Pardon had made in deciding what to take west now became the inventory of his estate.

It seemed certain that Prudence and her family would remain in Canterbury. Calvin agreed to occupy the pulpit of the Packerville Church for the month of August. He preached at other times throughout the year, but continued to make frequent trips away from home. Sometimes these were in connection with church work; at other times he would wander off rather aimlessly to look at a piece of property or to try to transact some financial deal. Prudence had accepted his restlessness and since his health was better she did not question either his intention or his destination.

Elizabeth and Prudence were readmitted to the Packerville Church by letter. Young Calvin had refused all attempts to get him to join the church. This was interpreted by his father as purile stubbornness but Prudence recognized it as a defiance of his father's authority because of his resentment of the severity of his discipline. In quiet talks with the boy Prudence found that he seemed to have a basically sound philosophy.

In April 1839, young Calvin qualified as an able seaman. This was done against his father's wishes and while his father was away. Prudence too was disturbed at this since Calvin was not quite 17 and was almost too small for the rigorous life of a sailor being only 5'4" and weighing only about 100 pounds.

Now the family in the Crandall home was made up of four women — the oldest and the youngest very ill. The fields and pastures were rented to neighboring farmers on a sharing plan. Calvin came home so seldom that he seemed more like a guest than a member of the family. The marriage of five years had long since become an impersonal relationship.

On Sept. 4, 1839 Hezekiah married his second wife. He and the widow Burgess — Almira Clapp Burgess — were married in the Westminister Church by Rev. Charles J. Warren. This was a merger of large families. Almira's five children were Clarissa, Philetus, Harriet, Joseph and Albert. Hezekiah's youngest child had been placed with a neighbor to be nursed after her mother died and she was left there a while longer. Two of Almira's older children stayed with her parents, Seth and Charlotte Clapp.

This left eight children in Hezekiah's home. His daughter Mary went to work in his cotton mill where she became very adept at the work and could soon handle four spools. His sons Reuben and Obediah helped with the chores both at home and around the mill. They went with their father into the bogs to dig the peat which was used for fuel in the mill. They cleared up and packed the waste. Esther was her step-mother's helper in the house. Prudence was no longer needed as a worker or counselor in this home but she made frequent visits there as she was very fond of each of the children and they were devoted to her.

In 1840, Calvin decided to try to settle down. He bought a 100 acre farm from George Cady. Prudence was pleased to have a home of her own again but it became a lonely home when in June, arrangements were made to send Elizabeth to her Uncle Boneparte so that she could have constant medical care. Prudence was hopeful that the peaceful home of her uncle would be better for her. Tension and discord was inevitable in the Philleo home. The traits in Calvin which Prudence had found disagreeable when they lived in Boonville now seemed to be many times multiplied. He was frequently in a row of some sort with neighbors. Arrogant and argumentative, he dominated the household. Frequently forgetful, continuously confused, he refused to accept even the gentlest reminder or kindest suggestion. Prudence finally decided that she could no longer cope with such an intolerable situation. While her step-children were with her, she felt impelled to care for them and found real joy in lavishing affection on them. Now young Calvin was away at sea, and there was no hope for Elizabeth's recovery. Elizabeth died in August, 1841.

Curious and concerned about the land his father had left in Illinois, Hezekiah took a trip west. He took an ox team with him and carried a load of kitchen utensils, yard goods and seeds which he knew would be salable in the western area. He was very favorably impressed with the fertile, level land. People he met while traveling and the few who had settled in Troy Grove Township were very optimistic about the future. Chicago, eighty miles away, was a rapidly growing city. Traffic on the Mississippi a hundred miles farther west, was increasing rapidly as new towns developed along the banks of the river.

Hezekiah was sure that the land should be kept in the family but he could not see his way clear to settle there. It would be too expensive to build a house large enough for all his children and step-children. There were no schools nearby and his wife was unwilling to leave her parents and her two married children who lived near Canterbury.

When Prudence confided that she must find an escape from her distressing domestic situation, Hezekiah urged her to go to Illinois. In this her mother concurred. Esther sympathized with her feelings about Calvin. Although she was practiced in patience and imbued with the conviction that women were supposed to be submissive, Esther saw in the behavior of her son-in-law eccentricities and humiliations from which she felt her beloved Prudence should be relieved. Such encouragement from her mother and brother was all Prudence needed. She made her plans carefully and quietly.

CHAPTER ELEVEN
ILLINOIS

EARLY in 1842 Prudence set out for the Western lands with her nephew Obediah, who was 13. After traveling across New York State on the Erie Canal, they took a steam boat over the Great Lakes and went from Chicago to Troy Grove Township, Illinois, a distance of 80 miles, by ox cart.

There was no rise or hillock in sight in any direction from their house, built by Pardon in 1838. Flat, level, rich land spread out all around them. A large section of their property was a veritable forest. There were very few houses in Troy Grove Township, only those of the Setchells and Roots were within sight of their home. Prudence made their crude little cottage as comfortable as possible. She and Obediah planned together about the development of the farm. She bought a horse, a cow and a pair of oxen. Obediah was an energetic, conscientious boy, devoted to his aunt and eager to please her. He plowed 50 acres in which he sowed wheat. A small plot was planted with potatoes. Prudence made a kitchen garden from which she dried and preserved vegetables for the winter. As she worked she planned the large house which she would build in the future where she would have a school. Her resources were small but her hopes were high! Her mother had supplied the money for their trip and for their living expenses until they could pay their way from farm crops.

A letter from Hezekiah reveals the accomplishments of Prudence and Obediah during their first few months as pioneers.

Nov. 29, 1842

"Dear Sister —

I received your letter about 10 days ago...when you write again say if you received the stove, a box of cards and two batts of batting. Your letter and Obediah's were very satisfactory. From the estimate I judge you have 50 acres of wheat in. I want you to say if the fence is up and if the wheat is secure from the cattle. Say if there are rails enough out to finish the fence, if so we shant want any other lots this coming year as there is enough in the wheat field and pasture for breaking and then we can sow it in the fall. Get Turner to sled and if you can go with two teams to get out stakes and rails be sure to get rails enough to keep the cattle out of your wheat and corn. You and O. have done wonders for the time. Just look back and see what has been done since you left Canterbury — 1500 miles to travel — done a large haying — got in 50 acres of wheat, made many repairs, etc. This proves what you can do. I hope you got the wheat of Turner at cash price. Look carefully over the papers and letters I sent and the book and enquire of mr. Kelcy and you will find out whether you had to pay anything twice over.

The move of the cow and the horse was a good one but you ought not to have told Philleo as he will be out and claim the whole lot. You may depend on his coming. He has rented his farm for some years and is in York State this winter. Calvin is at home and entered the study of law. Mother's health is first rate. She is set on coming out next spring. Briggs is coming out in May . . . Tell me if your rail road has made any more this winter or last summer. Mr. Kelcy said in one of his letters he paid C. Webster $5 towards the corn house. This I want you to get up if possible. Get a few logs to the mill by some means and have them sawed staves or some way and have the corn house sot on 4 or 6" tall blocks to prevent the rats. If rats pass up and down they are exposed to cats in open ground. I know how the oxen are situated and I am satisfied. I hope you kept the Briggs oxen at home as I fear the others would not be so kind for Obediah. It is best to sow half the ground left with oats and have them in as early as possible in order to have them out of the way before the wheat harvest. Mow them pretty early and stack them for fodder . . . And now a few words to dear Obediah. The children are all well. Mother and babe and my health is very good. Situated as you are with the chance of study and books and slates you will make the best use I know. When you ride or go to meeting take your great coat. Even, moderate exercise is best. Horse dung will keep potatoes from freezing the best of anything and preserve the grass and vegetation in the bottom of the heap. Early planted potatoes do best as they get set, and grown some before the drouth. When you write see that you spell your words right. Have you seen a deer or wolf or caught a prairie chicken or quails? Have you seen the great flock of sheep? See what the price of sheep is and let me know. If you get a dog, get the best kind — sheppard dog. They were to get some at the sheep fold.

Yours with great respect
H. Crandall"

Prudence was very glad to report in her next letter that the stove had arrived. With this set up in her little house, she and Obediah managed to be warm and snug. Snow drifted across the prairie and frequently high winds threatened to overturn their house. They were very isolated. The Roots and Setchells, their nearest neighbors, were nearly a mile away. The winter days were spent doing the chores — chopping wood, bringing in the water, caring for the cow and other animals. They had time for a good deal of reading and followed Hezekiah's advice — making extensive use of the scriptures. They had long talks about their loved ones who had died during that one tragic year. They recalled the cheerful Clarissa and her many wise admonitions to Obediah and her other children. They talked of the lovely, gentle Hannah Almyra. Hers was the first death of a person close to Obediah. He had grieved at her passing and his mother told him she had become an angel — his guardian angel. It was thus that he thought of her and at times he thought he heard her voice. Prudence, too, felt a nearness to her sister and sister-in-law and she found her thoughts frequently turning to her father and brother Reuben. They were so different in their philosophy — her father always a doubter, daring anyone to induce him to accept the religious concepts of his day. Reuben, trained and knowledgeable in science was a devoted and firm believer. How he had labored with his father urging him to "repent and be saved." Prudence smiled sadly as she recalled the attitudes Reuben held about what was womanly — she must not pray or speak out in any public place. He had urged humility and submission on her at the time of the school controversy — not because he thought the school was wrong but because he considered it unladylike of her to go contrary to the wishes of her opponents who were men and therefore superior! She wondered what he would think if he had lived to see "women's rights" upheld by Garrison and other anti-slavery supporters whom he had admired.

This quiet little house was indeed different from the big home filled with noisy children where Obediah had grown up. He missed his family, especially his brother Reuben, but he enjoyed his aunt's company, proud that she treated him as though he were a grown man. From the standpoint of practical knowledge and responsible behavior she thought he merited the respect due an adult.

He hunted prairie fowl and small animals for food. At times Obediah would get up at night, and taking a lantern check the outbuildings to make sure the animals were safe from prairie wolves whose howls sounded quite near. Toward spring Obediah went into the woodlot and marked the trees which were big enough to fell for lumber for the new house Prudence was determined to build.

Occasionally an itinerant preacher would come through the area and a meeting would be arranged in one of the homes. For the most part worship was an individual or family matter during the early years in the west. There were no other meetings to which Prudence could go during that cold winter. She drew comfort and inspiration from the familiar, favorite books she had brought with her and from her memories and meditations. Mail was infrequent and expensive. It cost 25¢ to send a letter back to Connecticut and getting one to a post office was a real problem.

With the coming of spring there was great activity on the Crandall place. With the help of a neighbor, Mr. Turner, Obediah logged many trees which were taken to the nearest sawmill. The boards were drawn to the spot where the house was to be built and stacked with air spaces between them to allow them to dry. This work was done while the ground was still frozen. As soon as the ground had thawed and dried the plowing was started. Obediah worked steadily during the daylight hours. Prudence prepared the most nourishing meals she could concoct for him with the limited foods at hand. She fretted over him, fearing that he was working too hard for a growing boy. His complacent temperament and well-ordered pace of working seemed to keep him from getting thoroughly exhausted. On days when it rained, he busied himself with repairing tools or whittling or carving some decorative or useful item. He frequently sang as he worked, tapping time with his foot. Regardless of weather or the pressures of work to be done, Prudence insisted that only the most necessary chores be done on Sunday so that he should have one day of rest. When Mr. Briggs came out in May, he brought messages and several packages from friends and relatives. He also brought cuttings from fruit trees. As a very special gift, Esther had included cuttings from her yellow rose bush. These Prudence planted and tended very carefully near where her house would be built.

She planned to start the house as soon as the crops were harvested in September and have it framed and enclosed before snow fell. She had talked with Mr. Turner and he agreed to seek out two or three men who could help with this project. Panes of glass had been brought from Chicago by a neighbor who had gone there on business. These were carefully wrapped and stored under cover. Handmade bricks were secured for the chimney. Native stone would be used for the foundation.

The only grave worry with which Prudence was struggling concerned her husband. She still felt bound to him by the marriage sacrament and drawn to him by pity, but she was sure her physical and mental health, to say nothing of her financial security, was improved by being independent of him.

She learned from letters from young Calvin and her mother that he had problems with the Packerville Church. A variety of rumors about him, relating primarily to unpaid bills and questionable business dealings, were rampant in Canterbury and Plainfield. A church committee was formed to examine the stories and determine if he deserved to continue in Christian fellowship. He met with the committee and answered questions to their satisfaction.

Early in the summer Calvin appeared in Troy Grove. Just as Hezekiah had predicted, he tried to take over the property and dictate about the farming. Fortunately Esther still held title so he could only fume and fret. He purchased a small tract of land from Benoran Briggs on July 20th and subsequently departed from the area.

Prudence's step daughter, Emmaline and her friends, especially Rev. May, kept her informed of cultural and religious developments. Both sent her books, papers and newsy letters from time to time. She continued to follow with great interest the efforts for freeing the slaves, as reported in the *Liberator.* There were no Blacks in this section of Illinois. Prudence heard occasionally from some of the colored students from her former school. They never failed to emphasize their appreciation of the training they had received in 15 months in the Canterbury school. Prudence found this most gratifying. The success of a few of her pupils justified her support of them during those troubled times. She never ceased to regret that she had to forsake her school. But she had little time to dwell on the past.

The second year on the farm was more successful than the first had been. More land was fenced in. More acreage was planted to wheat and corn. A second cow, pigs, sheep and chickens were added to the farm yard. Time to become acquainted with the woodlands led Obediah to where he could gather wild grapes, elderberries and nuts, and honey from a "bee tree." These foods made a very important change from the starchy, monotonous fare of the previous year.

In November they moved into their new house. It was only partially finished on the inside but the work could be done on winter days. By spring Prudence hoped that her mother would join her. Esther was now alone in Canterbury. She had changed her mind about leaving her home now that her mother had died. Prudence's letters about their flourishing farm and the adventures and experiences she was having intrigued Esther. She wanted to see the place and be reunited with her daughter. Late in May, Esther with her granddaughters Esther and Clarissa arrived. Prudence and Obediah were delighted to have their relatives with them.

News from the East in letters from Emmaline and young Calvin indicated that their father was wandering about and leaving a trail of unpaid bills. His children decided to have a conservator placed over him and they petitioned the Probate Court for this purpose.

> *"To the Honorable Court of Probate for the district of Canterbury to be holden at the Probate office in and for said district in said Canterbury in the County of Windham on the 17th day of June 1844 at 2 O'clock P.M. The petition of C. W. Philleo and E. C. Goodwin of Canterbury in said county respectfully represents that they are children of Calvin Philleo of said Canterbury, that said Calvin is the owner of certain valuable estate both real and personal in said Canterbury, and that said Calvin Philleo is now an insane person: and by reason thereof is wholly incompetent to*

manage said estate and is unable of taking care of himself. The petitioners therefore pray the Court aforesaid to inquire into the condition of said Philleo and on finding the foregoing allegations to be true to appoint some proper person to be the conservator of said Philleo, agreeably to the provisions of the statute in such case made and provided.

signed C. W. Philleo
E. C. Goodwin"

Young Calvin and Roswell Ensworth, a selectman, were appointed conservators.

Prudence found herself in agreement with the action taken but was grieved and worried to learn that her husband's where-abouts were unknown to his children, his brothers and his friends.

After several months, Calvin returned to Boonville and corresponded with his son.

"Thursday,-10th-Oct-1844

Booneville
My dear son I would inform you that on due reflection I think not best to leave this region and go to Illinois. I think it best for your Mother to return immediately — best for our mutual happiness — best for our interest — best for our credit — best in every point of view. If I ever leave it will be till my matters are all adjusted — Mr. Pardon Bennet will hire my farm next season Your Mother will open a boarding school on the premises — Mr. Bennet will board and lodge she will return and will go out that is certain. The farm is fast improving in productiveness — by standing by it and hold on things will come right. In order to have any credit I must be settled — your Mother must be home. I shall remain here till tomorrow to finish up here. — Cleveland says I must — I shall then go to Pawtucket — I may go to Boston — this is barely probable — I appreciate your kind offer and the interest you take — when I return we will consult together on all things.......My wife will now come home without delay — no mistake — her coming is the only proof of the fallacy of reports that she has forsaken her husband. This report is in the church at Packerville as I suppose from your Mother's letter to me. I am determined to stand my ground and live down and out the whole of this bundle. Stand with me in the battle. Be careful of your health — exercise exercise — don't fail to do this. I must close — with best wishes for your usefullness and happiness.

Calvin Philleo"

Calvin W. Philleo
Pawtucket, R.I. Oct. 22nd, 1844

My dear child I came into this place last week — I found a warm and friendly reception among all the people. I preached last Sabboth in the first church. There were more than a thousand people present. I am holding meetings this week in different places. I called at our old place where we were once together as a family. Oh how solemn the place where your dear Mother breathed her last. I could not remember her charge to me respecting you. I went to the grave to weep and pray. I did resolve while there that I would live more for eternity and less for time. I promised there and then while standing by the head of her grave that would write you stating my feelings. I hope you will without delay the eternal interest of your soul. I have felt for sometime to earnestly beseech God to have mercy on your undying spirit. People are very anxious I should stay awhile. I think I shall go to Boston. I talk of going to FallRiver before I return. They made a collection at Pawtucket last Sabboth for me of $24. I have found Abenesy Merchant kind as ever. Business with him will be arranged without trouble or costs. A gentleman from Rhode Island a machinest will go to Boonville in a few days to see that place to ascertain whether the cotton business might be started there and if so he wishes to commence there in some way.

I may if there should be an opening engage in my appropriate business perhaps at Fall River. They are destitute of a pastor. The minister in Pawtucket has written to them. I expect a reply this week. There is a church there if seven hundred members. All this however uncertain. I am in good demand here perhaps it is all for the best that I came this way at this time. I shall return after election and see you if the Lord will and make all needful arrangements, — I expect your Mother at Canterbury soon and hope to meet her there. After I left you on more reflection it seemed to me most advisable that she should return to stop the talk of her leaving me and also to inspire confidence in the public mind. I could have no credit while she is West and I looking and going by that way. I am determined to go through my matters and pay for that place and then if best sell it. I mentioned to you that I thought of hiring the farm to Pardon Bennett and opening a school there in the spring. Mr. Bennett Board. I would do this if no other door should open better. We must act in concert — we will consult together when your Mother returns. Be careful of your health — do exercise more. There are two Baptist churches in this place (Pawtucket) and another will be organized this evening in Central Falls. I am requested to be present and assist. The people inquire after you and send love. Mr. Charles Ripley died a short time since. I must close — I am making calls — Mr. Babbett's people are well. Mr. Princeton's also — I saw Dorcas Hadman formerly from Suffield — Pawtucket Central and Valley Falls are one continued village. Dorr is yet in prison — politics rages high. Polk is the man among the Dorrites. If Polk is elected Dorr they think will honorable discharge. — If Clay by force. This is talked — I feel better than I did — I am in my best clothes — new boots and hat and gloves only think of this. Who knows but I may yet be a man. My health is good my mind is more at rest though this suit dont suit me. But I see daylight never mind. I called to see Dyer found good natured. I told him he would not lose by me, but must be patient. I will never give up — I will stand firm to the helm till the storm abates. I never yet knew a storm but was followed by a calm. Hold on then I mean to God helping — he has helped and will help. If you should see Mother before I return give her my best regards and tell her every man to his past. Keep the pump going and beef the Mainsail. Look well the soundings and make up the ....and then the needle moves well we shall get into port and then says I don't put out to sea without getting insured. Bought wit is good if it don't cost too much. You ought by this time be pretty well versed in the danger of the sea. I guess we will go in the same ship. I mean to take all the comfort I can in this excursion and leave my troubles till I return and have some help to bear them. With due respect your anxious and affectionate Father

Calvin Philleo"

Calvin W. Philleo

CHAPTER TWELVE
NEW VENTURES IN NEW ENGLAND

HIS letters were rambling but his expectations proved valid for his son soon received a welcome note from Prudence, written in Canterbury at their farm home. With members of the family in control in Illinois, Prudence felt duty bound to check on Calvin.

North Society Nov. 16th, 1844

"Dear C. I arrived here last night. If you know where your father is I wish you would inform him that I am in the homestead south chamber with a good warm fire waiting to see him or you or any other good friends that may please to call.

Yours in very great haste
P. C. Philleo"

Prudence and Calvin stayed on their farm for a few months and then went to Providence. There Prudence organized classes of colored adults to teach them to read using the "phonotypic" method. This was taught from a book and chart. The chart contained 42 characters, which represented each of the sounds of the spoken language.

In May 1846, Prudence wrote to Mr. Garrison that she was conducting an adult class in Boston. Her letter was printed in the *Liberator* of May 1, 1846.

Liberator 5/1/1846

PHONOTYPIC SCHOOL

Boston, April 22, 1846

Wm. L. Garrison:

Dear Friend — I presume it will be a pleasure to you, and to the friends of the writing and printing reformation, to know that I have in this city, in successful progress, an adult class in Phonotypy, consisting of nearly thirty colored persons, some of whom cannot read in the old way. Among the number who are unable to read are several of our Southern friends, and a woman about sixty years old, who was once a slave in the State of New York. Her freedom was purchased by her husband for the sum of $400, after paying the same amount for himself, and $20 for their infant son, in his mother's arms!! The class will meet the remainder of this month in a room occupied on the Sabbath for worship in Belknap Place. We meet at the hours of 6 and 7 in the morning and at 3 o'clock in the afternoon. Some citizens and a few persons from *abroad have favored us with a call. If others are disposed to do so, we shall be happy to see them.*

Mr. Hiram Wilson gave us a call before breakfast, and seemed not a little interested. I hope he will soon be able to introduce the system among the fugitive slaves, or, rather, freed men of Upper Canada.

I view this reform as a great lever, by which the condition of the human family is to be morally and intellectually raised. If, at the time of British emancipation, this new method of reading and writing had been introduced among the stricken and smitten inhabitants of those verdant islands, what heart cheerings would it now have been the result! No withering blast of discouragement would then have succeeded the full glowing hope of high intellectual attainments, in any of those untutored minds that have since given up in despair under the ponderous load of English Orthography. The advocates of language reform may toil, and anxiously lament the apathy of an enlightened people, but they are destined at no distant period to receive the heartfelt gratitude of the wise and the good.

I also have a class of colored gentlemen and ladies in Phonography, and shall commence another on Thursday evening next, for beginners, and on Saturday next I shall begin with a class of colored children in the same study.

The colored people in Providence seem quite interested, and have formed a Phonographic Society.

Yours for reform,
PRUDENCE C. PHILLEO

(Mrs. Philleo, it may not be known to all our readers was formerly the celebrated Miss Prudence Crandall of Canterbury, Connecticut whose trials and persecutions in her noble efforts to give instruction to young colored females in that state will ever constitute a prominent feature in the eventful history of the colored population of the United States, and command for her the gratitude and admiration of posterity. The novel experiment which she is now making in this city in Phonotypy, with her characteristic zeal and assiduity, is deserving of special encouragement; and we trust she will have many friendly visitors in her school.)

Ed. Lib.

These years were evidently not very happy ones for Prudence as we gather from a letter of Emma Goodwin's.

2/24/1847 — Emma Goodwin to her brother Calvin,
writing from Concord, Mass.

(She states that "Father is preaching at a Methodist Church" and that he is up to his old tricks in renting his farm in Canterbury . . .)

"I have not heard from mother until recently. She left Providence at the time Father came here. Mary & John went to Providence a few weeks ago, and on calling at the house where mother had lived found her absent and learned that mother had been obliged to give up her house as the only way of getting rid of father. This woman spoke of father with the greatest dislike and said his abuse of mother was beyond conception. Mother was teaching a class in Phonography when she wrote to me. I have heard from another source that she has some idea of taking the Graham House. I think she would succeed there very well. She has great tact I think at getting along."

A few months later Prudence decided to go west to her family. She was in desperate financial circumstances according to a letter from Emmaline to her brother, dated July 18th.

". . . Mother left Boston a fortnight since for Illinois. She had not money enough to go on entirely but intended when her funds failed to pledge her clothes! She wrote to father accepting now the offer he made in the spring, to go on at his expense with him and present themselves to the Crandalls. If they met a cordial reception to live with her together if not to take to the prairies together, father has called it off wanting an immediate reunion with mother and he wrote her about definite plan about going West. She wrote me she should pass within nine miles of father's place but could not for want of funds go to see him. I have had frequent letters from father lately, one which I sent to mother a day or two before she left Boston had a plan to make a fortune by making a sort of fence with turned wooden posts. He had written to Washington about a patent. He merely mentioned by way of incidental remark that if I did wish to enter into partnership on the fence account to just advance 30 dollars. I didn't do it. . . ."

Calvin also wrote to his son about Prudence's departure for Illinois.

"Your Mother has gone west — wrote to me from Boston — as she expressed — I invite you to go with me with all my heart whether friends appeared not — I wrote her I could (not) leave — I next heard from her on a canal boat bound to Buffalo — So (as) things are — I must stick close to my matters at present — I shall do the best I can."

Prudence had a few months of respite in which she planned for her school to open in the Fall. Peace and quiet with her family did not last long since Calvin soon arrived on the scene. He left again in the Fall and wrote to his son from Princeton, Illinois in November:

"When I last was at Troy Grove your mother and all were well. . . . I feel displeased with myself that I should have come out here. I shall never crouch to the Crandal. I shall never submit to banishment and sink into a shell of a house — on mere sufferage. I have no complaint to make of your Mother. She is willing to do right. Rest assured of this — that I love and regard you with deepest interest . . . Remember me to Emmeline . . . I and your Mother shall, if the Lord will, leave early in the Spring for the east."

This time his expectations were not fulfilled. Prudence decided to continue in Troy Grove, surrounded by her family, conducting her little school. She had some girls as resident students and boys and girls who came in during the day from nearby farms.

CHAPTER THIRTEEN
ROOTS IN ILLINOIS

PRUDENCE and her family were overjoyed when in the summer of 1849 a letter from Hezekiah told them that Reuben was on his way to Troy Grove. Reuben had wished for a long time to join his brother and sisters and be re-united with his aunt and grandmother. His sister Huldah went out in 1846. He had finally persuaded his father to permit him to leave. By custom he could have been held at home two years longer until he was 21, to help support the family. Although he was a valuable helper, his father knew that the work of providing for six people in Illinois put quite a burden on Obediah. Prudence had frequently commented on this in letters to Hezekiah, lending her support to Reuben's pleas.

Late on a Saturday afternoon, Reuben arrived at his grandmother's house. A fluttering female contingent supplied him with food as they plied him with questions. His quietly beaming brother scarcely entered the conversation, content to listen.

Reuben had much to tell about his trip from Canterbury. He had started out with $47 which his father had given him. He had walked most of the 1500 miles. Food and lodging had taken only $20 of his hoard. Alert to opportunity, accustomed to hard work, he had secured boat and wagon passage for a few miles here and there in exchange for labor. The way had never been lonely since all roads west were crowded with people flocking to California in search of gold.

The day following his arrival in Troy Grove was one for feasting, visiting and thanksgiving. His family and their neighbors, the Roots and Turners, gathered at Prudence's house for a bountiful dinner. No fatted calf but the plumpest hens were roasted.

Reuben told his eager audience of the many changes which had taken place in Connecticut. Rail lines had been extended. It was now possible to go from Central Village to Worcester by the cars so the stage was no longer operating. Railroads through the Thames and Connecticut valleys had replaced cargo boats to a large extent. Packer's woolen mill had been greatly enlarged and was very busy, and cotton mills such as Hezekiah's were flourishing. He told, too, of the spreading interest in spiritualism in Windham County. Prudence listened with great interest, resolving to question him more on this subject when they were alone.

Another matter of genuine interest to Prudence was his report of the abolition of slavery in Connecticut during the previous year. There had been very few slaves in the state in recent years but Prudence felt that the official banning of slavery indicated a stand on principle. She considered this a tribute to the efforts of her friends — the Bensons, Garrison, Arthur Tappan and others — whose support had meant so much to her 15 years before.

In the late afternoon the Roots and Turners left. After the young men had finished the evening chores, the family lingered over their supper, still finding much to talk about. Prudence and her mother asked anxious questions about Mary. Her letters of recent months indicated that she was quite unhappy. Reuben explained that she was required to work very hard. Their stepmother, Almira, had not been well since the birth of her youngest child — George — three years ago. With little George and Nancy, Hezekiah and Sarah, aged three, five, seven and eight, to care for Almira left most of the heavy housework for Mary to do when her work in the mill was finished. In addition to the seven members of the family still at home there were four millhands who boarded there. Three of these people were recent immigrants from Ireland — Charles Pattern, Ellen Smith and Bridget Volabru.

Reuben amused his young sisters with imitations of the brogue of these three people, but he was emphatic in his praise of them as workers. He resented the animosity toward these newcomers which was expressed in mean behavior and meaner words by many of his former townsmen. Prudence smiled quietly; she understood his feelings. Here was another Crandall affronted by unkindness to disadvantaged people! Was this a family characteristic or a result of Quaker training, she wondered.

After the family retired, Prudence sat down to write a long letter to Hezekiah. She told of the safe arrival of Reuben and his whole-hearted welcome. She urged Hezekiah to consider sending Mary to them if he could possibly arrange to get along without her. This would bring all of Clarissa's children together until they were ready to go their separate ways. Prudence gave a very encouraging account of the farm. Obediah had improved and extended the acreage under cultivation each year. A substantial quantity of food had been preserved by Esther with the help of her three granddaughters, giving assurance that the family would be well fed during the winter months. Prudence also told her brother of the growing importance of her little school. As more families settled in the area, more day pupils were brought to her. She wrote enthusiastically of the growth of the state — Chicago was growing rapidly and there were rumors that the railroads would be extending quite close to Troy Grove. In the past ten years the value of land in the area had doubled as some was now being sold for $2.50 per acre. Prudence hoped that good news of his family in the West would comfort and encourage Hezekiah who evidently had cause for concern and worry about both his financial affairs and his wife's health.

After finishing her letter, Prudence brooded for a while about her brother. He had always worked so hard and been so devoted to his family but he seemed to be on a treadmill with no expectation of anything other than bare necessities. Nothing, that is, except his fine children of whom Prudence was so fond. How proud Clarissa would have been if she had lived to see her sturdy sons grown to manhood — serious and able workers — and her happy, pretty daughters. At least the three in Illinois were happy and perhaps they would soon draw Mary into their family circle.

In hearing about Canterbury from Reuben, Prudence thought wistfully of her home and hopes of earlier years. How exciting it would be to go to Worcester and on to Boston by train and visit with Emmaline and Mr. Garrison or to New York and visit with Mr. Tappan and her other friends. Or just to stay in Canterbury and go to a church attended by 50 people — but this was not to be and she would rejoice in the freedom of the wide-spread West and her personal independence.

Reuben spent his first few days resting and surveying his new surroundings. Obediah took great pride in showing him the boundaries of their 600 acres. Six times as large as their grandfather Crandall's farm in Canterbury and perfectly flat; the fields spread out around them, broken here and there by a few trees. The southwest section, the woodland acres, showed promise of future wealth. Reuben was eager to be the working partner of his brother. He invested his $27 in a mare. The horse was available at this comparatively low price because she had a bad reputation for balking and not being useable in a team. Her owner wanted to be rid of her. Reuben was confident that he could work her. She was young and healthy. (Over a period of years she bore several colts which were sold for a total of $1500.)

Whenever they had a few free minutes, Prudence and Reuben would chat. Prudence was interested to hear his views on political and religious matters. She had read with great interest of the experiences and experiments of the Fox sisters in Hydesville, New York and the developments known as materialization-responses from the departed through rappings. Reuben told her of similar reports from Danielsonville, Hartford and Ledyard. There were several people who claimed to have had messages from deceased relatives and friends. Prudence found that some of the things Reuben told her confirmed some of her thoughts. Several times, especially during the long quiet days of her first two winters in Illinois, she had sensed a nearness to her sister Hannah Almyra and her brother Reuben. On two occasions Obediah was with her and he, too, had a very strong consciousness of Hanna Almyra. More recently, busy with her school and with her mother and nieces for company, Prudence had

had little time for meditation. She resolved to ask her eastern friends — Rev. May and Mr. Garrison — to keep her informed of any articles or books on the subject.

In reporting on the folks back home, Reuben could supply little information about Prudence's husband. He could add little to the information Prudence had received from young Calvin and Emmaline. They were loyal and devoted to their "Mother Prudence" and wrote frequently. Widowed Emmaline was teaching blind children at the Perkins Institution in Massachusetts to support her three sons and her daughter. Prudence was greatly impressed with Emmaline's accounts of her work with the blind, especially Laura Bridgman who was deaf as well as blind. Young Calvin was practising law. He was living in Suffield and planning to marry Elizabeth Norton of that town in November. Prudence wished that she might go East to see her young man married. She was proud of the reputation he had made as a lawyer and writer and that he had been the clerk of the Connecticut Legislature. Through him she learned of her husband's most recent activities. He had been spending much of his time in the Boonville area. He had bought land there again and was pressing a law suit since the Government tried to secure part of his property for the Black River Canal. He reportedly hovered about the State Capitol in Albany and fancied himself quite a negotiator. His opinion of his financial acumen was not shared by his son. Young Calvin spent money, time and energy trying to keep his father clear of entanglements. He had succeeded in clearing up his Canterbury debts and preventing him from getting into mischief in Connecticut by being named his conservator but this did not deter Calvin from getting involved in New York deals. Young Calvin had to go to Boonville to resolve the suits and counter suits in which his father was enmeshed. Calvin eluded him, fearful because of a former threat to have him confined. (Several of his letters to his son proclaimed Calvin's conviction that he was not insane. However, these very letters and his actions as described in them gave rise to serious doubts of his judgment.)

A letter early in 1850, which young Calvin forwarded to Prudence, read in part "I intended to have gone West before this but God who in sickness holds me here gives special indications of his Providence and outpouring of his spirit . . ."

This letter aroused Prudence's pity and she wrote to her husband, assuring him of a welcome and care in her home. This was all he needed to bring him to Illinois. Prudence had cause to regret her compassionate impulse. She was shocked to see the change in him. He had aged more than the years would seem to warrant. He was gaunt and shaky, querulous and garrulous. He tried to impress his views on farm management, financial planning and religion on all members of the family. Poor

Prudence had to arbitrate the quarrels he provoked and soothe the hurt feelings which he caused.

He claimed ownership of everything she had as his right as her husband. Fortunately he could not dispose of her property since in giving it to her, her mother had entered into a legal agreement that provided for lifetime control of it. This precaution on Esther's part probably was taken with forethought because of Calvin's previous actions. Obediah and Reuben had land to farm and had agreed to provide a home for their sisters until the girls married. These plans had worked out well for all members of the family and amiable, harmonious relations made their lives satisfying and pleasant. When Calvin found he could not take over or control this fine farm or dictate to the family, he managed to make himself obnoxious. At the most inopportune times, he would summon the family to prayer. His prayers were interminable and impertinent since he frequently beseeched the Lord to deal appropriately with the "stiff-necked Crandalls." Prudence sometimes slipped away to tend to some worldly work, always managing to be back on her knees before the final Amen! Out of respect for Prudence the rest of the family put up with him.

Out of pity for him and respect for her marriage vows, Prudence determined to cope with his eccentricities. It was impossible to avoid argument, especially when he tried to get greedy hands on her small reserves or to interfere with her school. Even if he had demonstrated competence in money matters, she felt she would be reluctant to surrender every vestige of independence. Since his record was one of failure, she felt justified in sharing her resources with him but retaining her control. Her personal experience strengthened her convictions that women should have equal rights with men in financial and political matters. She resolved to use any influence she might have to further women's rights. She read avidly all reports which came her way regarding suffrage.

Calvin wrote fretful complaining letters to his children, but their sympathies were with their step-mother. Emmaline wrote indignantly to her brother "Father has no more rights out there than any squatter. It is a wonder our poor mother does not go crazy!"

When his health permitted, Calvin took to roaming and bargaining again. He bought a farm in Nauvoo where good farms were available at low prices after the Mormons were driven out. He went further up the Mississippi and bought land at Cordova, not far from Galena where one of his nephews had settled. No one could understand how he could buy with little or no money, but he seemed to be able to talk people into unbelievably shaky deals. As he had done earlier in Connecticut, he lived as a guest in his wife's home, coming and going at will, accepting her hospitality as his right; making no contributions except unwelcome advice and unwarranted criticism.

It was with mixed feelings that Prudence bade good-bye to Obediah late in 1851 when he left for a visit of several months in Canterbury. She wished that she, too, might see Hezekiah and her other relatives and friends in the East. She knew the winter months would be lonely without her dependable, delightful Obediah, but she was glad that he could have the trip for which he had been planning and saving for many months.

Almira had died and Obediah thought his father would be lonely at this time. He wanted to see his Grandmother Cornell and other relatives including the half-brothers and sisters with whom he was acquainted only by hearsay. He hoped also to see Mary although she was no longer living at home. She was working and boarding in Fishkill. Her letters dwelt at length on her longing for the hereafter where she would be with her mother whom she still missed after thirteen years. Obediah thought a woman of 25 ought to be looking forward to some joy in life. He felt that if he could persuade Mary to return to Troy Grove with him she might develop a brighter outlook.

Soon after he arrived, Obediah wrote to his Aunt Prudence that his father was less lonely than expected. In fact he was courting Mrs. Patience LaValley and expected to marry her in the spring. Mrs. LaValley lived in a pleasant farm house a short distance up Mud Hole Road from Hezekiah's home and mill. Her children were grown — her daughter already married.

Neither Prudence nor Obediah questioned the appropriateness of Hezekiah's marrying since he certainly needed a wife to look after him and his four small children. Nancy was at her Aunt Sweet's and Sarah was with Mary Burgess. Hezekiah hoped to have his brood together again and planned to live in Mrs. LaValley's home. He could then either rent or sell his big house. Practicality was a prevailing principle of life.

Prudence relived the scenes in her home place as she read Obediah's letters. He told of the singing school which met twice a week at the town hall. In one letter he gave an account of an evening of entertainment by a Negro which all the boys attended. It was held at Captain Woods and lasted until 10 o'clock. Other social activities which Obediah recounted included sleighing parties — one drew 60 couples to Canterbury Green from Norwich. In more serious vein he told of attending church meetings and a temperance lecture by the "Great Humbug — P.T. Barnum."

Prudence could give little time to thinking about her relatives in the East. Those near at hand were keeping her busy. Reuben was anxious to marry Amanda Smith, the lovely young daughter of a neighbor. He wrote for his father's approval which was conveyed to him in a letter penned by Obediah. The wedding took place on March 4th, 1852.

From her personal experience, Prudence had little reason to hold marriage in high esteem. Calvin was at home and was being especially difficult. He criticized every move of each member of the family. He argued loud and long and prayed louder and longer. His crotchety behavior was especially disturbing to Esther who was staying in Prudence's house for the winter. Huldah and Clarissa were keeping house for Reuben. Prudence was sufficiently inured to Calvin's peculiarities to cope with them, but she lost patience and scolded him when he badgered her mother or the rest of the family. She fervently hoped that he would go back to Nauvoo or some equally distant place in the spring. His constant wrangling about money matters was unbearable. To relieve him of any thought that she was imposing on him, or that he had a hold on her because he was "supporting her" she arranged for his food to be paid by him. Her food and that provided for her pupils was paid out of school funds and cooked and served separately. He usually consented to sit at the table with the others. However, the students were rather afraid of him. Their gaiety and spontaneity were very subdued in his presence. Those who lived in her house could not escape him entirely. Sensing their feelings, Prudence urged him to stay out of the classroom during lesson periods. He resented this and referred to it as a further indication that she was unreasonable and obstinate.

The winter seemed endless to Prudence. She was happy to welcome spring and Obediah quite simultaneously. Her joy was complete when Calvin departed. She expected to see him in a month or two but it was nearly a year before he returned.

In 1854 crops in the central part of Illinois were severely damaged by a plague of the 17 year locusts. Grasshoppers were large and common in the area but no one had ever seen such devastating hoards of insects as came over the land in cloud-like formation. Crops were devoured by them within a matter of minutes. Reuben and Obediah heard of their approach and with the help of all the members of the family hurried to put as much food and fodder as they could gather under cover. They made a hedge row fire across much of their land to destroy the creatures. Apples and potatoes were buried in a ditch and covered with soil to keep them from the invaders. In spite of their precautions their losses were heavy.

In addition to pestilential insects, nature also provided beautiful ones. Prudence looked forward each year to the days in early September when the monarch butterflies would be migrating. Trunks of trees and sides of buildings would suddenly shine with the deep gold, fluttering blanket of these winged beauties. They came to rest on every flower and seemingly each blade of grass treasured one at least momentarily. Within a few days they would all disappear — heading for some distant southern point.

CHAPTER FOURTEEN
MENDOTA

WITH what seemed to Prudence like miraculously swift change a small city came into being two or three miles north-west of Troy Grove Township. As railroads from East to West and North and South were built they formed a junction. A town was laid out at this point which was platted in 1853 and called Mendota. The name was borrowed from an Indian word which literally translated means "junction of waters." Only one house and one store were standing within the town boundaries in 1853 but within three years there were churches, a hotel, stores, a printing office which published a newspaper, homes and schools. Prudence and the others at Troy Grove watched with amazement this change in their neighborhood. Prudence visited each church as it was formed — Methodist, Baptist and Unitarian. She met and talked with new people whenever her responsibilities permitted her to have a little time away from home. There were occasional lectures and other meetings which took her attention and made her feel that she was part of the wider world.

She was quick to respond to the opportunity when she read an announcement of the Mendota Fremont Club on September 4, 1856. It stated: "The Mendota Fremont Club will meet tomorrow (Friday) evening at the old school house. Let everybody turn out. We are particularly requested to invite the LADIES. This is not a Bachelor party. "Jessie" bears a part in this campaign." The Republican Ticket carried

for President John C. Fremont of California,
for Vice Pres. Willian L. Dayton of New Jersey,
Electors at Large — A. Lincoln of Sagamon County
Frederick Hecker of St. Clair County.

Prudence persuaded Obediah to take her. It was seldom that LADIES were invited to such affairs.

The same issue of the paper carried advertisements which gave evidence of the growth of the community.

"Mendota Bank — Hastings, Phillips and Scott. Buy and sell Exchange, Gold and silver, Land warrants, Uncurrent money, receive money on deposit and make collections on all parts of the country."

"D.T.F. Woodbride — Surgical and Mechanical Dentist — Office over Reed's Land Office, Main St." and

"Iced Soda Water at Kaysbier Drug Store."

"Millinery: Mrs. A. M. Pearce would respectfully inform the public that on Saturday the 21st inst., she will open in the 2nd story of her residence on Washington Street, 2ND DOOR EAST OF Hasting & Phillips Banking House a new and splendid stock of millinery just from New York. She will sell them at Eastern Prices!"

Advertisements for —

"Ill. Central R.R. James Clark Supt. of N. Division
3 trains going north — 3 going south daily."
"C B & Q — C.G. Hammond, Supt. 4 trains going west —
5 going east daily."

A spirit of progress and hope pervaded the area. Everyone was busy and there were many plans which gave promise of more work. The Board of Trustees adopted an ordinance providing that — "There shall be two Public wells sunk in said Town . . . The said wells shall be made of sufficient depth to afford an ample supply of water at all times. They shall be walled up with stone at least one foot thick, six feet thereof on the top shall be laid cement and said wells shall be six feet wide inside, wall to wall in diameter and shall be covered over with plank. A suitable pump shall be set in said wells and the whole shall be done at the expense of said Town, the digging and making thereof to be done by contract."

At a later meeting the trustees announced "Sealed proposals solicited for laying down Plank side walk across east fronts of Blocks 47, 46, 31 and 32 in West's addition to Mendota."

Access to tools and machinery made the farm work easier for Reuben and Obediah. The new populace meant a large market for produce near at hand and an even larger one accessible through rail transportation.

The flourishing conditions in the West were not prevalent in the East. Emmaline wrote at length to her step-mother about the problems her sons were having finding work. She had finally agreed to permit LeBarron, 18, to ship out on a merchant vessel on which one of his uncles — John Goodwin — was the mate. When his uncle left the ship at Melbourne, LeBarron was promoted to second mate. Months away from home and the rough life at sea did not appeal to LeBarron as a career and when Prudence wrote urging him to come West, he lost no time in getting there. His grandfather had paid a visit to Emma in September of 1857. The account of prosperity in Illinois made LeBarron and his mother think it wise to see what success he might have there.

Not content to have just this grandson with her, Prudence wrote letters to her step-son urging him and his wife to come West for good or at least for six months. Calvin W. was in failing health with an obviously progressive case of consumption. Prudence assured him that the climate in Illinois would be very beneficial for him. She expressed her pleasure in having LeBarron with her saying:

> *"I am very pleased with LeBarron. He reminds me of you often. I think he will do well. There were raised on this place this year 870 bushels of wheat and 246 bushels of oats besides some which is*

not yet harvested. We have in the garden 60 — 70 bushels of potatoes, fat hogs in the pen and plenty of chickens so you see we have enough to eat. I wish you could spend a year with us; we are not out of the world, we can speak to New York or Boston as quick as you can or any other place . . ."

With all the progress, cash was evidently hard to get. LeBarron wrote his Uncle Calvin for a loan. He was to farm his grandmother's land on a sharing basis. In his words. . .

"On this farm there were no horses and to plough will require two or a yoke of oxen. Oxen are so slow and almost useless for other work and we concluded to get a span of horses, Grandmother one and I the other. She paid for both and I am to pay her as soon as possible. Now times wasn't hard when this bargain was made but now they are like adament. I owe her $150 and she owes some $200 on which she is paying 25% interest. I wrote to you and John (his brother) for $75 each to pay her for she would, had it not been for this, have paid her installment of $150 toward getting rid of this 'shame on the face of the earth' as she calls interest. Also I want seed wheat which is hard to obtain without cash . . . Grandfather P. is at Watertown I believe or thereabouts on business. I was at work with Obediah Crandall today. He says he remembers hearing you spin yarns when you came home from the sea."

This was soon followed by a letter dated Dec. 10, 1857 from Calvin which sheds a little more light on the Troy Grove picture and reveals his feelings.

. . . . ."I have been to Watertown. All right there as to money matters. I was sorry LeBarron should have written you such a letter. I offered to purchase a team and necessary tools and, of course, own them and thus manage the farm jointly and have a part of the crop. But this did not take. 'She is wiser than seven men who can render a reason!' How she will make out remains to be seen. He is as much attached to his bed in the morning as you used to be. Your mother is gone to Mendota — 2½ miles — I am seated at a west window, 2nd story. LeBarron is below keeled upon bed with boots upon the white spread reading Shakespeare. Your mother rode upon her white mare, It is 4 o'clock P.M. and I am looking now for her return when we shall hear an account of the preaching."

On her white mare, Prudence rode slowly through the darkening hours, wrapped in a knee length coat to protect her from the cold. She had found the church service thought-provoking and her brief respite from her husband was rewarding. She thought about the countryside — homes, churches and schools where such a few short years before there had been only wilderness. Wilderness and wild creatures and the good Shabbona and his fellow Indians. They still came into Troy Grove occasionally but they spent most of their time further west where there were fewer people to hamper their hunting. She thought, too of the circumstances which led her to leave her native New England. Few children came to her for training now that there were district schools which most of them could go to easily. Nevertheless her days were full. She took an active part in the running of her 100 acre farm. With her mother to help her in the house, she found some time for reading — keeping abreast of the anti-slavery efforts of her friends in the East, following the reports of the woman suffrage leaders, Mrs. Stanton and the newcomer — Susan B. Anthony.

Obediah had married Myra Bowers a year ago and was living in a large house he had built across the field west of Prudence's home.

Prudence enjoyed the company of LeBarron. Like her step-son he loved to read and could converse interestingly on many topics — if his grandfather was not around to monopolize the conversation. They had all read young Calvin's book — "Twice Married." They followed his Granger letters in the New York Tribune. Prudence wished fervently that his health would improve and that he could continue writing. But she feared that his time was short — she knew only too well the inexorable course of consumption. Although she had never seen him, she felt a sense of kinship with Emma's second husband — Charles K. Whipple. LeBarron spoke kindly of him. The fact that he was Garrison's assistant and edited the *Liberator* when Garrison was away, made Prudence very proud. In the twenty-three years since her Canterbury trials the controversy over slavery and the problems of free Negroes had intensified to a truly frightening degree. Rumors of possible violence between the states were circulating. This surely was an exaggerated notion!

In Mendota the panic of 1857 was known as the "pressure." Prudence and the others at Troy Grove felt the pressure for cash as prices and interest rates soared. Want in the presence of plenty was difficult to comprehend. Prudence thought that another man-made evil similar and perhaps related to the evil of slavery, in a land dedicated to freedom!

It seemed to her that she was catapulted into the fray when the Dred Scott Decision was issued. Chief Justice Taney, in formulating the decision used the argument, which Judge Daggett had used at her trial, that Negroes were not citizens. Taney carried this premise further declaring that Scott or any Negro "whose ancestors. . . were sold as slaves" was not entitled to rights as a Federal citizen and had no recourse to the court. In the same decision the Missouri Compromise was declared to be unconstitutional. It seemed to Prudence that since Judge Daggett's decision had been overruled by a higher court in Connecticut it should not be given credence in a Federal Court. During the intervening years free Negroes had proved their ability in so many ways!

Her pupil, Julia Williams had married a brilliant young clergyman, Henry Garnet. He was one of the Negro students whose education was interrupted when a school conducted by William Scales in Canaan, New Hampshire had been set upon by townspeople and the building dragged off by dozens of oxen and dumped into a swamp. This young couple had settled in Troy, New York in 1841 and spent several years teaching in a school for colored children and preaching at the Liberty Street Presbyterian Church. They had subsequently left for Jamaica B.W.I. where they were missionaries.

Certainly a fine man like Frederick Douglass who had secured his freedom, educated himself and was an outstanding orator and editor was worthy to be considered a citizen. But then, women were excluded from full citizenship along with "Indians, idiots, paupers, insane and criminals." Men who had the intelligence to conceive and create steam power for boats and trains, machines for factory and farm and all the wonders of the past fifty years were certainly slow to grasp the ideas of freedom for all people, and peaceable solutions to problems.

Prudence and her neighbors were much interested in the development of the new political party. They followed the reports of the speeches and debates in which Mr. Lincoln of Springfield made a stand against the extension of slavery into the territories and the Dred Scott decision. Prudence was disappointed, as were her abolitionist friends, that he did not speak out forcefully for the immediate abolition of slavery. He did favor eliminating it gradually, in the District of Columbia which showed that he was willing to incur the enmity of pro-slavery people. The speech he made on June 16th was widely publicized throughout the country. In it he stated that "a house divided against itself cannot stand. I believe this govenment cannot endure permanently half slave and half free." Prudence saw this statement as applicable to the national situation; she also saw its application to domestic situations. It was fodder for her women's rights talks.

She found occasion to speak to groups of people in her immediate area. The many newcomers welcomed any opportunity to attend gatherings where they could meet their neighbors. Before she secured her white mare, Prudence had walked to these meetings which were held in the little district schoolhouses. One of her nieces would accompany her, carrying a lantern. Prudence did not wait for invitations but spoke up wherever there were a few people about. At Obediah's she perched on a high stool and talked to the hired hands who were helping him harvest the wheat. They laughed at her, good naturedly jeering at the notion of women voters and possibly lady officials, but they heard her views!

Within the family changes were taking place. LeBarron had become discouraged with farming and lonesome for his mother, other relatives and friends in Boston. He left for home early in 1858. Prudence moved to the second floor of her house, since she no longer had boarding students. A young man named Henry Keith and his mother rented the lower rooms and Henry took over the farm work.

On February 7th, Henry Keith was married to Clarissa Crandall. It seemed unbelievable to Prudence and her mother that this girl was old enough to marry. Never rugged physically, Clarissa had been the child of all the family. Her sisters and brothers had been married for some years. She had spent much time in her brothers' homes. Seeing their young families had given her an idealistic concept of married life.

Amanda was an excellent cook. She and Reuben worked most harmoniously in their home and farm tasks. Obe and Myra had been married for a shorter time but they, too, had a home in which Clarissa felt unusual warmth and contentment.

Clarissa and Henry were married on the first Sunday in February. The wedding was attended by Clarissa's sisters, their husbands and children, her brothers and their families as well as Esther and Prudence and their neighbors and friends. The occasion was as gay as was appropriate for a Sunday gathering. The newlyweds made their home with Henry's mother in the first floor rooms.

Prudence had hoped that her step-son and his wife would come to see her in the spring but this could not be. He had gradually lost his fight against consumption. On June 30th he died. Prudence wrote to his widow a letter of consolation.

"Dear Elizabeth:

I have intended to write but have been waiting my husband's return, I have long wished to see you but since the death of your dear dear Calvin, I have been doubly anxious to make your acquaintance. That dear child died too soon. Alas too soon! But why do we say died? He is not dead, neither do I say he has put on immortality for from the commencement of his existence he was already immortal. Neither, my dear Elizabeth, do I say he has gone to eternity; he with us, was always in eternity but I do say his spirit has shuffled off this mortal coil and entered on a higher state of existence where he will be enabled to learn the lessons of love, truth and purity in the school of our Heavenly Father. When you visit the mound that covers his perishing remains do you never feel the presence of that precious jewel whose dust crumbles at your feet, comforting your sad heart? I do not doubt his Spirit presence is with you and that you could with certainty realize it, if you only knew how to answer it Spirit to Spirit in your own soul. Perhaps you do already and can anticipate more than I say. When I married, Calvin was a little boy. I loved him dearly and always did. I lament his untimely change. I have many little rememberences in store when you come to see us which I hope will be during the coming summer. I wish to induce if possible our dear Emma and her husband to visit with us. How happy I should be if you and they could come together. What a noble soul she is — an ornament to our sex — and her dear husband writes with a masterly pen. God bless him now and forever. Mrs. Whipple is the dearest step-daughter that any one ever had.

Prudence C. Philleo

Calvin returned around the middle of August and learned from Prudence of his son's death. They had had many differences throughout his son's life. He was glad that their last meeting in September of '57 had been amiable and mutually enjoyable. They had stayed in Boston and had travelled to the Standish triangle at Duxbury with Emma. The two men had a long conversation about many things, not omitting Theology. Calvin was satisfied that although his son had not conformed to the formal aspects of the Baptists that his thinking was reasonably sound. He announced to Prudence that he would forgive his son for "interfering" in his affairs. Prudence wisely kept her thoughts to herself but she would like to suggest that he should not only forgive but should be grateful since without the patient "interference" and good judgment of his son, her husband would undoubtedly have landed in jail! He stayed at home for a few weeks and then went off again.

Time passed swiftly for Prudence. She had many interests. In spite of the "pressure," Mendota continued to grow in population and to encounter problems associated with cities. It was reported in February of 1859 that "It is said there is more suffering in town at this time among the unemployed than there has been in any previous session during the pressure. Those who are willing and able should see to it that those who would do if they could are provided for.."

Some of the problems were solved rather forthrightly according to one paragraph in the Mendota paper:

"Saturday night last some of the people of Mendota who have been outraged by the conduct of a family named Goodine, consisting of the father, mother and three grown daughters, proceeded

in a body to the shanty occupied by them on the East side and tore down the tenement, leaving the inmates shelterless. The house has been a resort for our most vicious young men and although such violent remedies are generally to be deprecated, it is to be hoped that the nuisance is abated!"

Prudence felt deep pity for the hapless family. She knew the horror of having a house battered in!

Another item states:

"Mendota a gambling Hole. It has been apparent to observing people for some months past that Mendota has been a rendezvous for gamblers and thimble riggers."

Several saloons and a brewery were soon operating in the town. Prudence added Temperance to the topics on which she was willing and eager to lecture. As she often did, she penned a few lines on the subject using the pen name "Hope."

The Temperance Cause

We celebrate as worthy of all honor
To stop the stains of sin and shame
And mitigate our sorrows
We pity those who can't refuse
The use of wine and brandy
When asked to drink by some old friend
Who keeps a bottle handy

Come Youth and children, one and all
And make a resolution
That you will never sip the cup
That leads to desolation.

Good resolutions made and kept
Are dying consolations
And as we pass our life along
Help purify the nations.

Hope

As the town grew a music hall and an auditorium known as Hastings Hall were built. A variety of meetings were held in these buildings. There were dances and festivals by a great variety of groups. Numbers of German people came from Pennsylvania and directly from Germany. There were soon two German churches — Lutheran and Catholic. An Irish Catholic Church was also established as the Irish faction increased.

To accommodate travelling men and men who came without families, several hotels were built. The largest of these was the Passenger House near the depot. "Aunt Em" who cooked there was acclaimed in the press as about the best cook anywhere. In the advertisement for Mrs. Brown's hotel the fact that it was *clean* was emphasized.

During the first week of May 1859 the brother of Charles Dickens, A.N. Dickens was in Mendota to lecture on Shakespeare. On May 13th Horace Greeley passed through on the C B & Q Railroad on his way to the West.

The description of the Fourth of July parade plan indicated a great show. "Order of Procession on the Fourth: 9 A.M. Congregational Church. 1st Band; (2) 4-horse conveyances; (3) 2-horse; (4) cavalry procession down Jefferson to Main, Main to Washington, down Washington to Michigan, down Michigan to Monroe. . . Tables will be prepared in the Grove."

An item on July 15th states: "Old Abe Lincoln, Judge Logan and several other distinguished gentlemen came up from the south (of Illinois) on a special train and dined at the Passenger House today. The object of the journey seems to be simply to take a leisurely view of the state from the Illinois Central."

Mendota had much excitement during the election year of 1860. The staunchly Republican town watched with pride and enthusiasm the progress of Illinois' native son candidate. On Oct. 15th "Mendota was the scene of one of the most successful and enthusiastic meetings of the campaign. The people assembled by the thousands to hear the eloquent Senator Hale. One of the most interesting features was the delegation of ladies from LaMoille, dressed in national colors who marched in procession day and evening."

Prudence viewed this as an indication that women were recognized to a degree but not as she considered they should be as participating equals. Progress was so painfully slow in all the causes for which she felt concern — in suffrage and the anti-slavery movements gains were being made, but it seemed that temperance was losing ground and the threats to peace grew daily more ominous.

Prudence rejoiced with all of Mendota over the election of "Old Abe." His election gave a real lift to the Anti-slavery Convention which was held at the Music Hall on Nov. 10th and 11th.

Parker Pillsbury came to Mendota for this convention. Pillsbury was one of the more radical of the Anti-slavery orators. His actions and speeches had even drawn cautioning comments from Garrison. During his visit to Troy Grove he gave Prudence much information and many anecdotes about her old friends — Garrison, Charles Burleigh, Samuel May, Mrs. Childs and others whom Prudence had not seen for so many years. Pillsbury was one of those who was bitter about the role of the church in the struggle against slavery. He and a co-worker, Stephen S. Foster, entered churches in the East and attempted to address congregations. They were ousted on several occasions by less than gentle hands. At an anti-slavery meeting in Boston they had succeeded in including in a resolution the appellation of "Brotherhood of Thieves" to those clergymen who were not in favor of the abolition of slavery.

Calvin was at home during his visit and was in a good humor. He was in agreement on the anti-slavery issue but against Pillsbury's attitude toward the church and clergy. Prudence found Pillsbury's visit and the seriousness of the local anti-slavery group inspiring.

Prudence's high spirits were soon brought low as she realized the intensification of hostility between the states. The local paper reported the threat of secession — "Dec. 12 thirty millions of American Freemen have elected a President and therefore because they have done so the people of South Carolina, Georgia and other cotton growing states openly and loudly declare they will withdraw from the Union."

CHAPTER FIFTEEN
CIVIL WAR

THE fateful day came when the newspaper — the Mendota Reporter — of April 12, 1861 announced:

"War has begun. The rebels of South Carolina opened their batteries upon Fort Sumter on Friday morning last.

"Union men of Mendota met in Music Hall. The reports that the war had begun created the most intense feeling and without distinction of party our citizens came together with cheeks burning with shame that our national flag had been insulted and the insult still unredressed. We rejoice to know that we have no traitors or rebel sympathizers in Mendota."

Within a few days they found one to deal with. Rev. or Parson Fisk had been in and out of the newspaper business in Mendota for several years. He had chosen late in 1859 to establish the "Mendota Times" — a pro-slavery paper. The rival "Mendota Observer" carried the information that on April 20th "Our citizens forced two union speeches from the last one suspected of any predilection for the disloyal party." A company of men complete with drums had waited on the Rev. Fisk and "suggested" that he make a public statement against slavery and for the Union. He left the area soon after this episode.

Within a week after war was declared Mendota had organized a full company of men to "fight manfully the good fight." It was reported the "Germans are turning out largely" and "A reserve corps is to be immediately formed of the aged citizens. Large sums of money are to be raised as soon as possible for the support of the families left behind."

Prudence followed with interest the activities of the local young men. From Emma she learned of the whereabouts of her grandsons. John, who had visited his grand-parents briefly on two occasions, was working in the office of the Secretary of War. LeBarron was in the Navy and Frank, whom Prudence did not know, was with the 55th Regiment.

Emma was raising money to secure the promotion to lieutenant of a colored man who was a sergeant. She had received money from Wendell Phillips and several other prominent Bostonians. Prudence wished that she could send money to some of those needing help. She wrote Emma saying it was her dearest dream that she might do something for the colored women and children. How she would like to have a home and school for needy colored children!

In commenting on this in a letter to Elizabeth, Emma wrote that she "would enjoy seeing her able to carry out her plan of making a home for destitute children of color and others. It lighted up my day to have a glimpse into a loving heart like hers."

Supervising her farm and helping members of her family in a variety of ways took all of Prudence's time during the early months of the war. She again urged Elizabeth to visit. Her invitation was cordial and revealing:

"We wish you to come when you best can — it will make no difference to us as to the time. We live 2½ miles East of Mendota so when you arrive there you will have to take a carriage at the livery stables to bring you here. Please write and say when you will come and my husband will be sure to be home. I promise myself a great deal of comfort in your contemplated visit. How I wish our dear Mrs. Whipple could be with us. I believe that Calvin's spirit is sometimes near to me — that is saying a great deal but really do not doubt it. Leave your time to return indefinite so that you can stay here as long as you can leave your friends and be happy. You must expect to find very plain folks and surroundings so you must not be disappointed."

In correspondence about the trip Emma also stressed the limitations of the Philleo home saying:

"While I am sure you will love mother, I fear you will not have a very pleasant time, you will find few of the comforts by which you are surrounded, but you will confer great happiness on mother.

"I am glad it is convenient for you to carry a little present to mother, and what you suggest, a mouseline de laine is a very good thing. If I were going to choose for our mother Prudence, I should get a grey sort of dress. She is light and has blue eyes and a grey dress is always becoming and useful . . .

"I fear you will find it very uncivilized, but mother is a royal queen of women, let her surroundings be what they may. I wish I could believe that great heart of mother Prudence ever had any joy except what comes from the sense of duties faithfully done!"

Elizabeth had advice from another member of the family, too. John Goodwin had visited Mendota in the past. Never a very steady worker, he had incurred his grandfather's ire by trying to borrow money and refusing to take work on one of the farms. He had raised a number of rather impertinent questions about the Philleo resources and realized that he had not endeared himself to his grandparents. He wrote to his "Aunt Lizzie":

"I think a visit by you to Mendota might do much good. Your influence might go a good way toward inducing Mr. Philleo to

arrange his business matters so that a business man could, when need come, make some head or tail of his affairs. If there is anything, and there must be considerable property to be finally disposed of, it would be a pity to have it appropriated to those who have no claim on it. It would be useless for me to speak of such things to him or attempt to find out how matters stand but I think you could get an idea of the condition of affairs. I know that you will not find the undertaking to your taste but when you consider that you would be doing a good work for mother you will be urged to do it."

Elizabeth went to Mendota in July of 1861. The train trip through the prairie was extemely hot. There were delays because train schedules were disrupted by troop movements. She was greatly surprised by the activity around the station at Mendota. It seemed as though all of the town's 2000 inhabitants must be in the business center! She left the station in a livery carriage and was soon riding through vast fields of corn and wheat. Oak and hickory trees shaded the road as they passed an occasional house. On a slight rise in the fields was Prudence's house. The yellow roses were beginning to fall but other flowers were evidently well tended. She had a sense of "home coming" when she met the mother-in-law about whom she had heard so much. During the ensuing weeks the two women came to know each other well. She wrote long reports of her visit to her sister-in-law and from Emma's reply we know a little about her reactions.

Emma wrote:

"Many thanks, dear sister, for your letter and all the details of your visit with Mother Prudence and Father. I was sure you would love her. Who could resist one like her? I accept it as a high compliment that mother reminded you of myself.

"Do not for a moment doubt that Father expressed his sincere feeling for you. No man ever loved his children better than he has sometimes done, and no person was ever more demonstrative in his feeling than he. If he was always up to his best moments life would have been a very different thing to some who have suffered from his eccentricities and characteristics. I am glad to have this revival of all the tenderest and best in his nature come to his old age.

"I have often asked father to sit down in these evening hours of his life and write out all he can remember of his own life, never with a view of publication, however, and never with any reference to dear Calvin. Father would be the last man to give a true idea of

poor Cal. I trust Father will now find time to use for this purpose tho' I have often thought he might make a very interesting autobiography. His experiences have been very varied and he could give many pictures from different stand-points but Heaven save the mark if he should attempt to write the life of the child whom his injudicious management so much imperilled. His emotions are as changeful as a child's. I am so glad to hear that he once more rides a buggy instead of walking."

In the Spring of 1862, Prudence was again involved in anti-slavery work. The *Liberator* of May 23 carried an account of her work and comments.

TRACT DISTRIBUTION

Dear Mr. Garrison, — You will be glad to hear that your old friend, Prudence Crandall Philleo, is still active in Anti-Slavery work. I lately sent her a box of tracts, books and papers for distribution, and have just received a first report of the use made of them of which the following is an extract:—

"Mendota, La Salle Co, Ill. May 10, 1862.

"The box and its contents arrived safely on Thursday the 7th, and since that time I have been busily engaged in distribution. You said, 'send them broadcast and give them to soldiers.' This I am endeavoring to do. I got liberty to set the box into the front room of a shoemaker's shop (as we live 2½ miles from town) and I think you would laugh to see me perform the duty of giving. I go into the streets and ask the women I meet (and also some of the men) if they live in the country: if they say yes, I am sure to give them some, as that will scatter them far apart. The owner of the shop is Mr. James Pilkington, an Englishman who has helped off many a slave to Canada, and the present occupant, Mr. W.H. Ashton, was engaged in the Chartist agitation in England in 1848, and was a delegate to the Chartist Convention, and was one of the sixty who volunteered from Illinois, and joined John Brown, Jr. in Kansas. They both have hearts as great as Big Thunder. Mr. Pilkington left yesterday for another part of Illinois, and took a lot to distribute on the cars, and at his place of destination. Captain John Phillips, Co. A. 57th Reg. Ill, came in yesterday, and I gave him a lot to take to

the soldiers. He said reading matter was scarce with them. Inclosed I send you a note which I received to-day."

This note was as follows: —

Mendota, May 8, 1862

Mrs. Philleo — I am very much obliged to you for having placed in my way this little book, "The Right way the Safe Way," as it has disproved what I have been forced to take for granted as true, regarding British emancipation in the West India Islands having been a failure. In all my reading, I have never happened on anything that so plainly contradicts the assertions of the enemies of emancipation as this little work, and I have taken the greatest pleasure in reading it. Yours truly,

Chas. M. Higgins

No doubt many of the Western papers have kept repeating, like our Post and Currier, and the New York Observer and Journal of Commerce, the stale falsehood of "the utter failure of West Indian Emancipation." People who take these papers, and who do not see the books and articles that have demonstrated the thorough success and the immense advantages of West Indian Emancipation, will of course be deceived. For these persons, nothing can be better than Mrs. Child's excellent little work, above referred to; since it not only gives, in moderate space, the important facts respecting the working of freedom in the British West Indies but refers those who have time for further investigation to the fuller original documents.

The note of Mrs. Philleo's correspondent shows the effect of "The Right Way and Safe Way" upon a candid mind. Many more of them ought to be circulated here; and those who are disposed to aid in this work can be supplied at the Anti-Slavery Office; and funds to print more, left at the same place, will greatly help this very important department of anti-slavery labor.

— C.K.W. (Charles K. Whipple)

Prudence had noted in recent months that her husband seemed to have mellowed. He was still unsettled but he seemed under less pressure. He approved of a plan she had considered for some time to rent the farm and take a house in town. There were now 2400 people living in Mendota.

They rented a large, square house just east of the depot. The house was next to the Presbyterian Church. As soon as possible Prudence found some tenants who took half the rooms. One of the tenants was a young teacher who had her little sisters and brothers living with her. Prudence found it exciting to be living in a town again after twenty years on her farm.

At this time Prudence was wearing trousers — partly to show her support of the women's rights movement and partly for comfort and convenience. She wore black pants under a coat-like dress which came to her knees. She was willing to lay aside this outfit for social occasions. To go to a church wedding she solved her "nothing to wear" problem by taking down her white curtains and fashioning a dress from them.

Other women in the town were much more fashion conscious. Those who could afford to made annual shopping trips to Chicago. During almost any pleasant afternoon little groups of women could be seen at the depot where they had a hasty view of what ladies travelling from New York or other eastern cities were wearing as they jouneyed west on the C.B. & Q. Interest in style was not limited to the female population. One advertisement indicated that "Fred Shafer, the barber has just opened a new shop on the East Side where he is ready to do hair cutting, shaving, shampooing and *beard coloring* in the best style of the art."

The barber was given small encouragement for his "hair cutting" and "shaving" from the phrenologists who were still considered authorities. An article on beards states:

> *"If amputating the beard were merely a harmless, fashionable whim, we would not notice it. But as watchmen — self-appointed perhaps — upon the walls of health of body and vigor of mind, it becomes us to sound public and general alarm respecting whatever impairs either. Thus we conceive shaving and frequent hair-cutting does: and for the following reasons:*
>
> *"First Electricity is the grand motive instrumentality of all forms of life and mind. If abundant, the life-power is abundant, if diminished, all those functions and powers — mental included — it carries forward are weakened.*
>
> *"Secondly, Hair is one of the very best conductors of electricity that exists. This all electrical experiments conclusively prove. The head requires more electricity than any other part because of the organ of the mind. To collect this stimulant of the mind from the atmosphere, and transmit it to the brain, the head is surrounded by hair and the face by beard. Amputating them prevents the coming in of as much air or gathering up as much electricity as by being left long and flowing. Long beard and hair, then promote mental power and brilliancy. Heartily we say, let them be worn.*

"What proof can be more conclusive than that a most intimate inter-relation exists between the beard and the manly element itself? The masculinity of every man corresponds with, measures and attests the amount of this virility. To men, then, it becomes both a sign and promoter of masculine power and beauty. Its amputation then must be attended with both injury and deformity.

"But we are persuaded that men shave and barber mainly to please women. Yet only sickly feminine taste — or rather want of taste — still require it.

"Women too, especially those whose hair can be trained to curl gracefully, will do well to wear their hair in flowing ringlets, rather than to tie it up closely, for they will thereby collect and furnish a larger amount of that electricity which alone can impart that glow of health called beauty, that warmth and fervor of feeling called soul, that buoyant, happy hilarious ecstasy which forms a chief attraction of women, and that sprightliness and clearness of mind so desirable to every human being."

"Shades of Samson" thought Prudence as she read this. She continued to wear her hair short and brushed back from her forehead. Although she was 60 her hair had not turned grey. She had little interest in style and no use for the science of phrenology. She remembered with distaste the role and the words of the phrenologist used to support Connecticut's Black Law. As if to prove how wrong his assessment of the Negro had been, she received word from Emma about a visit with that first Negro pupil — Sarah Harris Fairweather. Emma wrote:

"At one of the meetings of the anti-slavery Society, a colored woman of very pleasing manner and appearance came to me and asked me if my name before I married was Elizabeth Philleo. I told her that was my sister's name and inquired if she had known my sister. She told me she was the first colored scholar who attended your school in Canterbury and that she knew my sister and brother there. I invited her to come and pass the afternoon with me which she did yesterday and I wish you could have been here to hear her talk of the persecution in Canterbury . . . I don't know when I have enjoyed an afternoon better than this woman's society. She is very intelligent and lady like."

Of course she was intelligent and lady-like, thought Prudence. All of those girls were both and so lovable! How she wished she might gather in those Blacks who were now being displaced from their former homes! So far Emancipation meant the end of legal slavery but the fate of the emancipated was far from clear. Many were migrating into areas where they were not welcome. Others were continuing to live on the properties of their former master. They were the victims of this dreadful war. When it ended they would find freedom and a place in the scheme of things, she knew.

As always Prudence had people close at hand who needed her concern and consideration. Clarissa, who had moved to Iowa with her family, came back to Prudence when she expected her second child. By the time she was well enough to return to her own home, Prudence decided she must give up her pleasant living arrangements in Mendota. Calvin was too old to continue commuting several times a year to Cordova. Since he refused to dispose of his property there, Prudence thought it wise to move to Cordova. To him this was another shrewd business proposition as is clear from a letter Calvin wrote to his daughter-in-law.

> *"I have sold my farm (in Cordova) to my wife and her mother for $2000. She will build a nice house on it this season. I sold her much lower than to anyone else. Mrs. P. sold her house and lot . . . She will not build a large house but a comfortable one. The place is a perfect beauty on the Mississippi."*

CHAPTER SIXTEEN
POST WAR YEARS

ON August 28, 1864 Calvin wrote again:

> *"We have at length got settled down in a most delightful spot. Our house is sufficiently large, fronting on the main travelled road. We have a most interesting view of the river and boats passing. The town is dotted with buldings amid the most beautiful groves, valleys and rising grounds. The place is quiet — moral — I may say a religious community . . . on the whole we are a quiet, happy family."*

Throughout the country there were efforts being made to improve the lot of the Negro. The Freedman's Bureau in Washington set up a school and undertook a variety of projects in their behalf. Prudence was pleased when she learned in 1868 that Connecticut had passed a law making it mandatory for the towns to educate all children over six years of age regardless of color or race.

Perhaps it was the publicity about this law which caused a renewed interest in the story of Prudence's school in Canterbury. She was surprised and flattered when she received a letter from Ellen Larned of Thompson, Connecticut asking for the information to use in a series of articles. Prudence related the story in a letter written on May 15, 1869. In addition to the well-known facts she wrote:

> *"I wish to say that the jailer was very polite to me and to my friend, Miss Benson, sister of Mrs. William Lloyd Garrison who very kindly volunteered to remain with me during my imprisonment be the term long or short . . . I think you must possess much patience and great perseverance to perform the labor you have undertaken.*
>
> *Sincerely yours in the cause of the right"*

A second letter was written ten months later. In this Prudence suggested some changes in articles Miss Larned sent her saying:

> *"Your undertaking the arduous task of writing the "History of Windham County" has vastly brightened my estimation of your energetic character. I hope you will be liberally rewarded. I hope you are an advocate of the Woman Suffrage question. In your well-written articles you sent, for which I thank you, there are a few*

discrepancies as could possibly be expected when written by a stranger to the immediate circumstances and at this late period. There is one error only that I care much about and that is in relation to Mr. Olney. You say that his case never came to trial and that friends from Norwich sent up money to release him . . . Mr. Olney was tried before the county court and honorably acquitted . . . By whom the fire was set is still a mystery . . .

"I should be very happy to see you in Illinois and if I ever visit Canterbury again, I shall certainly do myself the pleasure to call at your home . . . "

Prudence wondered wistfully if she would ever get back to Connecticut. She would dearly love to see Hezekiah and her many Carpenter and Crandall cousins as well as the green hills and fine homes. She tried to imagine what her life might have been had she spent it all in Canterbury. Much hardship would have been avoided but she would have missed the challenge of change and the excitement of seeing this new part of the country grow and develop. She liked to think that through her teaching and lecturing she had contributed to it.

Through the years the farms prospered. Prudence left its management to her husband as she became increasingly busy with the care of her mother. By 1869 her mother's condition was such that she could no longer care for her without help. Esther was lonely for her other loved ones and it was decided that the Cordova family would move into part of Obe's house at Troy Grove.

Here on the edge of Mendota they lived for the next two years. These were exciting years! On June 24th a great fire in Mendota destroyed twelve business houses with a loss of $40,000. These were all frame buildings. Since this happened on a windless night, incendiarism was suspected.

Prudence was pleased to receive letters from Sarah Harris Fairweather and her replies give an account of some of her activities.

Mendota, LaSalle County, Ill.
Dec. 2, 1869

"My dear Mrs. Fayerweather,

Your very kind letter came to hand in due time. I have been waiting this long long time to get settled so that I could give you my post office address which is as above. You do not know how much I thank you for your kind remembrance and how much my cup of joy would run over if I could see you face to face if it was but one *hour. I had not heard of the death of your dear husband till your letter came. I feel that you are not without consolation in the midst of your berevement. your dear children are coming up so nobly to fill honorable positions in life. They must be a great comfort to you. I did want to get a letter to you before your daughter left for the South but I thought you could send her my best cheerings when you wrote to her. I trust you will do so. May her mission, health and life be precious in the Divine sight. I must give you some of the reasons for the long delay since the reception of your letter. I have been selling off my stock-cows, calves, hogs, etc and my farm also that was beautifully situated on the Mississippi River. My stock I sold for a little over $500. My farm sold very cheap for the sum of $3,500. I have been so much unwell this fall that I could not take care of the farm or stock and besides my mother has become very helpless, rarely ever moves a step without help. She has had several shocks of palsey — her speech is much affected and she does not always know all the members of the family, often thinks she is not at home. I send you a lock of her hair as requested. She is a good soul and was glad to hear from and did remember you. We have moved back to the place we came to when we came to Illinois — Troy Grove. You doubtless remember Obediah B. Crandall, my brother's oldest son. He is a noble man and had lately built a large brick house and we occupy a part of his house. Mr. Philleo, my mother and myself constitute our family. We are very comfortably and happily situated. I am now 65 years old and I joy and rejoice to see this day. I thank God that Garrison has lived to see the schackles fall from the slave — and oh the glorious future that will be the result of the Labors of God's noble ones both colored and white that are now active laborers in the vineyard of the Lord and that vineyard is the whole human family. Do write again soon. Give my best to your family and friends and keep lots for yourself.*

P.C. Philleo

In June Prudence arranged to have other members of her family care for her mother while she attended a woman's Suffrage Convention. Susan B. Anthony and Parker Pillsbury were speakers. Miss Anthony also gave a temperance lecture in the Baptist Church. This was indeed a mental feast for Prudence.

The 1870 Census showed that Mendota had a population of 3547. Some of the newcomers were Germans who came directly from Germany. There was also a colored population in the area. A news item about one of their social functions reads:

"Last week a grand colored Ball was given at Pool's Hall in the city at which all the 15th Amendment Citizens of this and adjoining towns participated. Delegation of City Aldermen intimated to a faithful colored janitor at the outside door that they would be pleased to look in and participate. Were informed that with "no tickets, no admittance." This spirit of insubordination in our colored brethren we take to be highly reprehensible."

In the fall a letter from Elizabeth Norton Philleo brought an invitation to Prudence and Calvin to attend the bicentiennial celebration to be held at Suffield on Oct. 12th. All former clergy of the several churches were being invited. Calvin wrote a long reply setting forth some of his views on national, international and metaphysical issues:

Oct. 1, 1870

"Your welcome letter dated Sept. 26 was duly received for which I thank you and those extending a kind invitation to me and my wife to attend the celebration of the 12th of Oct. in Suffield. You ask my sentiments in regard to such occasions. I reply my mind is occupied with scenes of the future state of my being. I am in the 84th year of my age. My hope in God is unshaken amid all the revolutions and changes in a protracted life. We live in an era of great interest and surprising changes. The next great event in the unfolding purposes of God, I think, will be the restoration of the Jews to the land of their fathers. Russia, from indications plainly manifest, will be employed as the favored instrument to the obstacles in the way of their return.

"Russia may have no higher motive than her own aggrandizement in the enlargement of her own vast empire. The Jews, wherever located, though possessed of great wealth, are not the owners of real estate; consequently they stand ready at the providential signal to march in rank and file under the banner of the Great Shepherd of Israel to possess the land promised their fathers . . .

"I like to have forgotten Suffield in my flight of thought. But I still remember her and feel happy to know that I am kindly remembered. I well remember after being in an extensive revival of religion in the State of New York, I took a journey eastward and called on Elder Cushman in Hartford, to visit and hear preaching. He urged me to go to Suffield . . . I complied with his urgent request. I found the people without a pastor and somewhat divided . . . I stayed in Suffield and enjoyed a second glorious revival . . . I

never found a kinder people than the people of Suffield. I preached twice on the Sabbath and then in the evening to Boston Neck, then to Christian Street at Simon Kendall's school house, Sikes school house to complete the circle at Sheldon school house. The meetings were always well attended . . . The church believed in opening the doors after preaching to give time and opportunity to any one who might feel it their duty to drop a word of exhortation warm from the heart. Captain Appollos Phelps sometimes would burst like a bomb shell upon the congregation, which made that old meeting house crack again, and the church felt warmed, awakened and comforted under such a powerful explosion coming from a heart filled with the love of God. Sister Gunn, Deacon Gunn's wife, would rise to speak, stand erect in the door full six feet tall, would pour out a warm exhortation full of good sense and comfort. She was a strong woman physically and mentally. To carry out her views of the rights of women, she went into the mowing and harvest fields and performed the work of men and received men's wages, though she was independent in her circumstances . . .

Your affectionate father and friend:

Prudence added a few lines to his letter:

"Although I was never a resident of Suffield, anything done in the State of Connecticut where I long resided becomes to me very interesting. It is my estimation, a noble act to celebrate in after time great and noble deeds. I presume on this occasion you will have a grand mental exhibition of the vast improvements that have been made in the administration of government of the American people since the days of British rule. I should be glad to be with you and listen to the glowing eloquence that will doubtless be displayed on the occasion.

"I hope the ladies will be remembered during this bicentennial and some suitable credit given to them for the many heroic and philanthropic deeds they have performed during the growth of our national republic.

Affectionately yours,"

Prudence let no opportunity slip by for getting in a plug for women and their rights! She also wrote about peace and ardently wished that there need never be another war.

In 1871, she wrote a "Peace Song."

Philosopher, savant, saint or sage
Brave heroes of the present age
So hold the lamp of truth divine
That on our path the light may shine.

Chorus

Help on the glorious jubilee
That peace may reign from sea to sea.
Let us where plants of peace can grow
Where purest waters ever flow
Lift up the banner of the Lord
With motto love and sweet accord.

With gems of truth and richest love
Heal the wounded, sick and sore
The feeble lay upon Your breast
And give the nations peace and rest.

Calm all rough passion of the soul
And teach the art of self control
Learn though injured to forgive
An enemy and let him live.

Then send the joy from shore to shore
That nations fight and kill no more
But in wise deliberation
Seek all redress in arbitration

Then millenial light shall dawn
Nations in a day be born
With grateful heart refuse to sin
And take the King of Glory in.

"Hope"

Since war was not of national concern at this time, it is probable that these lines were inspired by the war between France and Germany. The local German population was very active in raising funds for the

Prussians and had great celebrations when word was received of Prussian victories.

The year, 1871 started off with a troubled period and there were a number of catastrophes before it ended. In January there was a three-day snow storm which marooned trains and destroyed telegraph wires. The spring months were very dry. June saw a return of the 17-year locusts but they wrought less havoc than in 1854. The news account of them shows that the farmers were prepared to cope with them: "17-year locusts have made their appearance in this section. Same 'varmints' that paid us a visit in 1854. In that year they made themselves disagreeably familiar. Farmers went out with their shot guns and large numbers of them slain. A good many were driven into hog pens at night and eaten."

The drought continued. Obe had to carry water in barrels from the creek. He faced the water shortage as he had always faced problems — complacently. Prudence admired him and found much pleasure in being with him and his family. His son, Mark, now nine years old was a fine little fellow in whom Prudence took great pride. He was considerate of his ailing Grandmother and a willing runner of errands.

In July Prudence replied to a letter from Sarah Fairweather giving information about her activities and thoughts.

> *"As I take the Standard I had the sad news of our dear friend Samuel J. May's death. The account I have seen in several other papers besides. He was one of the best persons I ever knew, and he has gone to that Heaven where soul responds to soul, and love and affection never dies — where the welcome plaudit will ever be "well done good and faithful servant enter thou into the joy of our Lord," I have no doubt.*
>
> *The debt of gratitude I owe to him I can never pay, as well as to many other precious souls that came to me when I was cast out as evil by those who professed to be the followers of the meek and lowly Jesus —*
>
> *My old Mother enjoys for an old person, very good health in body save in the effects of palsy. She can talk so well that I can understand the most that she says, and she can feed herself when the victuals is cut, and put on a waiter before her with her eating apron under chin just like a child. She can not take one step alone and is drawn in a rocking chair from one room to another. Sometimes her mind seems much more shattered than at other times. Yesterday for a long time she did not know me and said "her heart was bursting for her Prude was drowned." She often gets such strange impressions. I asked her if she remembered you and*

she said she did and to test her I asked her what color you was and she replied that you was almost white. Then I gave her the kiss and told her who sent it to her and she seemed very much pleased — My husband was 84 years old the fourth day of this month — his health is not very strong — he feels the effects of age and wishes to be kindly remembered to you. I am so glad to hear about your children. I think you must be a happy mother to have your daughter trying to do good to others — I am glad you went to Boston. Did you see Mrs. Whipple? North that writes the Boston letters is C.K. Whipple, Emma's husband — I think he has laboured late and long in the Anti-slavery cause and I believe he is in every other good reform with his whole soul. Mr. Garrison was at Mr. May's funeral and was the only one that said any thing in relation to the active part Mr. May had taken in the female suffrage question. Bless his dear old soul he has a long piece in the Independant in relation to the San Domingo question.

My health is good. Do write often and tell me all you can . . . I had the impression that Ann Hammond was dead — glad to hear she is going to England. I do want you to come out here very much.

Truly yours,
P.C. Philleo."

In the middle of October, Mendota and all of the area round about was shocked by the great fire in Chicago. The local paper was limited to one sheet because the paper supply was cut off by the fire which was the chief news. The district burned was two miles wide and seven long — 18,000 out of 60,000 houses were burned. Mendota sent a carload of provisions to the stricken city.

In November there was a second big fire in Mendota. This one was caused by a can of varnish falling on a hot stove. More business establishments were destroyed. Brick buildings — some "elaborate and elegant" were built to replace those which had been destroyed.

Had he been a little more vigorous, Calvin would have interpreted these disasters as a cause for a revival. Since he was not strong enough for such an undertaking, he had to be content with haranguing his wife and her family with his prophesies and predictions. Prudence humored him and the rest of the family followed her example.

The main concern of all the family was the care and comfort of Esther. She usually retained her mental clarity, her pleasant disposition and a touch of humor but she was entirely helpless physically. Prudence fed her as she would a baby and was constantly at her bed side to anticipate her needs.

Early in the morning of February 13, 1872 Esther died at age 87. Her philosophy of life encompassed an acceptance of death. Prudence knew she would miss the fine woman who had been her dearest friend as well as her adored mother. They had shared nearly 70 years. Esther was buried in the family burying ground, which was on the edge of Obediah's land. Her grandson Reuben was already buried there.

After a few days of rest Prudence returned to Cordova. Evidently the sale of the farm had not worked out. They lived in the upper rooms and rented the farm land and lower part of the house. Calvin had suffered a stroke and spent most of his days indoors wrapped in a dressing gown.

That Prudence was in good spirits is evident from a letter she wrote to her nephew:

Cordova Sept. 9, 1872

"My Dear Nephew O.B.

"I think you must wish to preserve my likeness to be willing to pay as much for it ($2) . . . There is no artist now in Cordova — They keep their rooms on wheels and move on the river from village to village. As for the tomb stone I have no suggestions to make. I think your judgment would be better than mine. Not long since I saw my dear mother's face shining with light — and I said 'My precious mother' and as soon as I could say it she was gone. — You will doubtless call it illusion, a phantom but to me it is reality and I enjoy it. I saw her with my spiritual eyes not with the physical eyes for I have both as well as every other human being.

"The rye crop is good, corn is very good, buckwheat filling nicely. My team is excellent, my plow-boy not to be beat but he has been having ague and much hindered — Early in July only a little after the fourth Charlie cut the rye and has kept it standing in shock till two weeks ago today before he could plow one stroke in the rye stubble. — I am as happy as a clam in salt water . . ."

Charlie was Charles Phillips who lived in the first floor rooms. He worked the farm on shares.

Through the summer months people came out from Cordova center and Port Byron to picnic in a beautiful grove next to the Philleo farm. A wooden platform had been built and on this picnickers danced to the music of violin or accordian. This activity and gaiety was pleasing to Prudence but a source of annoyance to her husband.

Almost before Prudence had time to get rested from her long years of nursing her mother she had new responsibilities. Clarissa brought three of her small children and came to live with Prudence. Her husband Henry wanted to try prospecting in Colorado. Clarissa had lived in Iowa and Missouri but did not feel up to going into the rougher west.

Prudence loved having little children about again, but Calvin was irritable. He continued his practice of long prayers. Often he chose to kneel in the doorway between the kitchen and dining room after a meal. The girl who was helping them would have to go out onto the porch and around to the kitchen to get her work done. After one altercation with his wife he prayed pointing out to the Lord that she was "an old squash head." Prudence knew she must tolerate this temper with the same patience as might be needed in caring for a fractious child.

During the last year of his life, Prudence had to hire a man to help her care for her husband. He was bed-ridden and severely paralyzed from a stroke. He passed away Jan. 5 in 1874. His funeral was held at the Baptist Church.

Prudence, Clarissa and Clarissa's children Lucy, Lorena and Willie continued to live on the farm for another year. A different family — the Lamberts had taken the place of the Phillips family.

A letter to her niece Esther Worsley gives a picture of her busy life:

Cordova May 21st 1875

"Dear Esther

I have not heard from any one of our dear friends in your region in a long time and I think I have not written you since the death of Mary Crandall Bass, Hezekiah's oldest daughter. Huldah, Myra and Josephine all wrote us about her sickness and death and I answered their letters; but I think none of us have written since . . . I do wish that you and Joseph could come out here together . . . I shall ever remember with gratitude that you and Joseph always treated Mr. Philleo with kindness. Why can not you and Huldah come out here together this summer and how glad we should be to have Magie come with you. I think some day George Webster may come out here just for the fun of shooting ducks and ketching fish —

Lucy Jane and Lorena go to school and are getting along very well. Mary, Clarissa's oldest daughter is in Nebraska attending a high school fitting herself for a teacher — She is making great improvement — I think she bids fair to be a very good scholar — Clarissa enjoys much better health than she did when she first came here. She is very busy doing housework and making and mending for the children. Lucy Jane and I do the chores. We have twelve little calves to feed every night and morning. LeBarron Goodwin and family are now on the farm where Wm Worsley was located. They have only two children, both girls, one ten and the other seven years old. We have a Sunday School held one Sunday here and the next Sunday at Goodwins — He has a very nice wife she is indeed a lovely woman. We read a sermon preached in Boston and published weekly by the Rev. Freeman Clark. The children read pieces in a little book prepared for children, and commit to memory something to repeat besides, and we try to sing some of the good old tunes such as Hebern, Old Hundred, Greenville etc. etc.

June 7th. You see by this date that I have been a long time writing this letter — I am so busy that I cannot get time to do half I want to do. When the garden gets out of the way, and my calves get a little older, I intend to visit you all — I want to see you very much — I intend to stay with each family two or three days apiece . . . C. is very busy sends love and says you must write. Our wheat looks well our corn in the field is coming fast since the weather has got warm. Our garden bids fair to do well — We have seen only two potato bugs in our garden yet. Cut worms are doing great damage in some places, but our garden has not suffered very much yet.

Do you keep up with Beecher?

We like the family who live in the house with us very much — Their name is Lambert . . .

I think Mr. Lambert is a good farmer; and he certainly is a very kind man and his wife is as kind as he is. We get along in much harmony — They are members of the Methodist Church.

Love to yourself and family and to Huldah & Myra and all the friends & tell them that we are all enjoying excellent health this spring — write when you can —

Your affectionate aunt
P.C. Philleo

After she was "rid of" the garden, Prudence sold her farm and bought a house in the town. She bought a large rambling house. There was a substantial two story school near by for the children.

She now was back in her element, with many opportunities to speak on the subjects of interest to her. Her house was a gathering place for many in the area who liked to hold discussions of religion. Prudence could present the Unitarian views of Rev. May as she understood them from her long association with him, through correspondence in these later years. She was a close follower of the sermons of Henry Ward Beecher which appeared frequently in papers to which she subscribed. Among these papers was a Spiritualist publication called "The Banner of Light."

There was great patriotic fervor at this time as the centennial year of the nation approached. Prudence spoke on patriotic themes, never failing to stress the contributions which women had made to the country's progress.

She read with much interest the plans for celebrations in Philadelphia. How she would like to go east to see the exhibits and hear the orations! She knew this was a vain hope. She was glad to learn that Obe and Myra were going. From them she could count on first hand reports.

Obe and Myra went to Canterbury before going to Philadelphia. They arrived there to find that Patience, Hezekiah's wife had just died. Hezekiah at 76 was at a loss to know how to spend his remaining days. Obe helped him settle his business affairs and persuaded him to go west and be near his children.

Hezekiah agreed to this. He visited his daughters and stayed with Obediah for several weeks and then accepted his sister's invitation to settle with her in Cordova.

Rumors about the climate and prospects in Kansas circulated in the town. "Sister and brother" Glassek went from the Baptist church in Cordova to Elk Falls in Kansas. Prudence was impressed with stories of progressive social attitudes in the new state. She was an easy customer for a man who came from Elk Falls and offered to swap a farm there for her Cordova residence. The deeds were drawn and plans were made for going South in the spring of 1877.

HEZEKIAH CRANDALL, 1876

This table delineating the descendants of Prudence's brother Hezekiah and his first wife Clarissa Cornell is provided to identify his children and grandchildren who lived with Prudence and corresponded with her. Their correspondence, diaries and memoirs are essential to the story of Prudence's life.

(1)

HEZEKIAH CRANDALL MARRIED (1800-1881) CLARISSA CORNELL 4/14/1825 (1800-1838)

Mary	Esther	Obediah	Reuben	Huldah	Clarissa
m	m	m	m	m	m
Henry Bass	Joseph Worsley	Myra Bowers	Amanda Smith	Geo. Webster	Henry Keith
Arvian	Frederick	John Rand	Eula	Samantha	Mary
Maudana	Addison	Jane	Eleanor	Charles	Lucy
Leander	Mary	Jessie	Josephine	Ann	Lorena (Rena K. Clisby)
Orrin	Margaret	Mark	Montford	Frank	Geo, Willard (Willie)

(2)

HEZEKIAH MARRIED MYRA CLAPP BURGESS 1839

Mrs. Burgess was a widow who had five children. Four children were born to Hezekiah and Myra.

Hezekiah	Nancy	Sarah	George

(3)

HEZEKIAH MARRIED WIDOW LEVALLEY 1852

CHAPTER SEVENTEEN
KANSAS

THEY went by train across Missouri. It was necessary to travel the last 35 miles by stage. "The roads were new and rough, and many times we swayed perilously while Grandfather (Hezekiah) shouted 'By George, we're gone!' His speech was so decidedly 'down east' his ability to sound his r's in such words as horse and barley so pronounced, that I heard the driver say, 'They date from way back east.'" according to Rena Keith Clisby, Clarissa's daughter. They arrived at Elk Falls, traveling the last mile out to the farm in a livery wagon. Here they found a little shabby three room house. Prudence bedded everyone down for the night on the floor.

The next morning they surveyed their surroundings. — 160 acres of dry soil, half of which had been cultivated.

A team of oxen was hired to plow and corn and sugar cane planted. Living was very plain for the family during the first few months. Gradually livestock, chickens and peach trees were added to provide a living for the six members of the family.

Elk Falls was a town of 565 people in Elk County eight miles from Howard the county seat. There was a flourishing central village near a waterfall on the Elk River. Spread out around this center were farms which had been laid out as 160-acre homestead plots. There was more roll and rise to the land than there was in Illinois. The soil was rocky in spots and not nearly as rich as that in Illinois. There were so many stones that Prudence decided to have a regular New England stone fence put around her property. For this she paid $500 in advance. The fence was started but never finished.

Before many months had passed Prudence had made known in the area her interest in teaching and lecturing. She gathered about her children from neighboring farms as her pupils. Grateful parents brought her such produce as they could spare from their farms.

Blacks in great numbers were coming into Kansas. Prudence's reputation was known among them and frequently they came by to see her. She could give them little other than encouragement. Her three little rooms were more than crowded with three adults and three small children. The first few months were some of the most difficult of her life. She frequently had only molasses and corn bread, potatoes and milk to feed her family.

By fall, she was doing well according to a letter to her niece:

Elk Falls, Kansas
Nov. 1st 1877

"Dear Huldah

If I remember correctly it was 7 yrs. ago the 30th day of Oct. that my dear mother with O.B. & myself arrived at O.B.'s. How many changes we have passed thru since that time. Who ever dreamed that at that time I with my dear brother would be living in Kansas. We are delighted with our new home. I know if we are industrious and careful we soon shall have a very pleasant home. I intend to give this farm to Clarissa to make her independent in her old age when I am dead and gone. We have all enjoyed excellent health ever since we have been here. The weather this fall is very fine. Our corn is harvested our sorghum made up 18 gals. the best I ever saw, our potatoes are dug, pumpkins gathered & our turnips are growing so finely we shall not pull them up just yet. The turnips are very sweet . . . It is a settled fact that we are soon to have a railroad thru Elk Falls then you can come by rail; now we have to come to Independence and then take a stage 30 miles to this place . . .

We have had no grasshoppers except the native hopper and they have done no harm. I never spent a more pleasant summer than this has been in all the 74 years of my life. I suppose we are more than 200 miles further south than you are but the heat is no more oppressive than with you. We have all of 200 peach trees on the place. We think they will bear next year. One little tree bore 13 peaches this year. We dried 3 wagon loads of peaches — I mean our little wagon. Dear Esther fears we shall starve here in Kansas. But do assure her there is no sort of danger yet.

Goodbye
Aunt P C P

Correspondence and vists from her nieces and nephews brightened her days. John Rand Crandall, son of her nephew Obediah, came from Clay Center, Kansas for a visit. Prudence tried to persuade him to come to the Elk Falls area.

Sarah Harris Fairweather came for a visit of several weeks with her old teacher. She was a fine looking woman with white hair. Her complexion was so light that she passed for white when traveling to avoid any unpleasant "Jim Crow" treatment. From her Prudence heard many inside stories of the anti-slavery work in New England and the part that many Blacks had in this work.

As they talked, Prudence realized that she was one of just a few of the old guard abolitionists left. Rev. May, Arthur and Lewis Tappan and Sarah Grimke had all passed away. All had lived to see the cause to which they had devoted their energies succeed.

Life was difficult in many ways on their little farm. The house was too small for their family of six. The soil was poor in comparison to that in Illinois.

When she was not too busy with duties and chores, Prudence wrote letters and poetry. Some of her poems were published in area newspapers. In a Scrapbook, which is cherished by a member of the family, several of her poems have been preserved.

"Elk Falls, Kansas Mrs. P.C. Philleo, of this township, furnished a piece of poetry for this week's paper. Mrs. Philleo is 77 years old. In her younger years she was a school teacher. Read the poem," the newspaper clipping reads,

Questions by "Hope"

Say, what is science, ye that know,
Is it the voice of God below?
Do all things preach, do all things pray?
And why all the general display
That seems to mark a full control,
If everything has not a soul?
Say, scientists, if you can
When first intelligence began,
Why do the trees know how to grow,
If not by intellect they know
To fix their basis by the rule
That's taught in mathematic school?
If no intelligence is there,
How ply the compass and the square?
Why in the forest grow so tall
If they never pray at all?
Does the tender little vine
Pray around the tree to climb?
Or by mutual friendship does it climb
To topmost bough on which to twine?
Do rocks and stones grow while asleep?
And what for them their vigils keep?
Is it the stars that ever shine
Without a change of place or time?
Why all the grandeur of display
Mid rolling orbs by night and day
If no intelligence is there
To hold the balance-wheel in air?
Why does a tiny drop of dew
Become so beautiful to view,
If there's no object in the sight

But to divide the rays of light?
Is not benevolence displayed
By every ray of light and shade?
What of the thousand little flowers
Which so adorn this world of ours
Do they not live and grow and feel?
Are they not stamps on beauty's seal
Why pour their fragrance on the air
If no benevolence is there?
Have they no justice in their state?
Have they no law of give and take?
And why do plants resist control
If they possess no inner soul?
The sensitive plant from touch will shrink
Has it not power to feel and think?
The waving plant of India, why never still
If it has no power to think, no power to will?
Say what is music and why man control
If in itself it has no living soul?
Has its body just eight notes and nothing more
To repeat itself times o'er and o'er?
Does it not fill the immensity of space —
Our Heavenly Father's dwelling place?
Can a stick have one end and not two?
Is there anything God cannot do?
Can he annihilate both time and space
And of Himself leave not a trace?
Is eternity a thing that's made
Is it a thing of which to be afraid?
Were all things of nothing made?
Where is the proof of such a trade?
What is the element of fire?
And electricity? Can they expire?
Can self existence ever die?
Should gravitation cease its aims to ply?
Would it leave this little world of pi
Or would it to some larger planet fly?
What is attraction but the power of love
Seen in the vast universe, below, above?
Can there be an action without a will
If matter has no soul would it stand still?
Why is it an axiom that twice two makes four

Is it because its nothing less nor more?
Are axioms self-existing or are they made
Like passing shadows or a shade?
Does man know anything he has not learned?
Can he justly own a thing he has not earned?

. . .   .

Early Love of Friends
A parody of lines "He Doeth All Things Well.

I remember how I loved them
While a young confiding child
When for little acts of kindness
They looked on me and smiled.
My cup of happiness was full
My joys no words could tell
As I blest the Glorious Giver
He Doeth All Things Well.

Months passed, their love and friendship
Was unfolding every hour
I thought that earth had never smiled
Upon such noble ones.
So lovingly they well might grace
The bowers where angels dwell
And waft their fragrance to his throne
Who Doeth All Things Well.

Years fled on, those gifted ones
Were as dear as life to me
And waked in my confiding heart
A love of liberty
They worshipped at no earthly shrine
Lured by some magic spell
Forgetful of the praise of Him
Who Doeth All Things Well.

They were as the lovely day star
Which 'round my pathway shone
Amid this vale of tears
Through which I journeyed on.

Their radiance was reflected light
Which 'round God's throne doth dwell
They wandered not away from Him
Who Doeth All Things Well.

Those stars went down in sorrow
Yet they're shining sweetly now
In the bright and dazzling coronet
That decks the Savior's brow.
They fell by the destroyer
Whose shafts none may repell
But we know for God told us
He Doeth All Things Well.

I remember well my sorrow
As I stood beside their bed
And the deep and heart felt anguish
When men told me they were dead.
And oh, that cup of bitterness
Let not my heart rebel
God gave, He took, He will restore
He Doeth All Things Well.

... ...

Hope's Soliloqouy

The daily work will give thee pleasure,
If thy duty is but done;
Look within my soul for beauty,
'Tis seen with Spirit eyes alone.
Give to Thy kind and heavenly Father
All thy heart and anxious fears,
Learn the lesson of forgiveness
And 'twill dry thy bitter tears.
Life is just what thou wilt make it,
Pleasure, profit, peace or pain,
And thy home a little heaven,
If the right is all thy aim.
From thy common occupations
Thou must draw thy filtered joys,
Riches, poverty, health and sickness

Sad hearts, glad hearts, give employ,
When thy duty is thy pleasure
You will find a living joy.
Come ye bitter cups of sorrow
Ye can never my peace destroy
I'm on a voyage of endless pleasure
And will banish angry strife
On times current I am floating
Ever budding into life.

(This poem was in Prudence's hand writing, no indication of date or whether it was published.)

... ...

In March of 1879 a daughter of Sarah Harris Fairweather wrote that her mother had died. Prudence wrote back expressing her sympathy and urging Mary Fairweather to continue writing to her.

She also wrote to Wm. Lloyd Garrison.

3/20/1879 Wm. L. Garrison

Elk Falls, Elk Co., Kansas
March 20th, 1879

"As Samuel J. May would say "My dear Garrison." I thank God that you still live, and have the ability to hold up the standard of justice as in former days. I thank you very much for the American Traveller. Your criticism of Bain I read with so much interest. And whenever any paper falls in my way containing anything from yourself I always listen for I am expecting something good for humanity is uttered.

I wish to ask you if the George W. Benson who so intimately associated with Miss Francher the Brooklyn wonder is your brother-in-law. I am not aware that he has a W. in his name. I suppose him to be yet in the form as I have not heard of his death. (If it proves to be my old friend George I want very much to write him.) In a frame under glass I have a group of dear friends (I mean their pictures) and among them is Benjamin Lundy, Wendell Phillips, and your noble self. I would cut the picture of your dear Helen from the book you sent, were it not for injuring the book so sadly.

It is two years this spring since I purchased a farm of 160 acres near the village of Elk Falls and moved from Cordova in Illinois to this place.

I paid fourteen hundred dollar for the farm. My brother Hezekiah manages the farm; his wife died about three years ago. We like the situation very much. The climate seems to be very congenial to us, for we have enjoyed excellent health since we came here. Within a few weeks I have heard of the death of Mrs. Fayerweather. She that was Sarah Harris my first colored pupil. So we pass on!

Surveyors are out to locate a rail road from Independence to this place — so we shall be connected by rail to the large cities again as we were at Cordova. Yours for justice and truth.

Prudence C. Philleo

. . . .

To Wm. L. Garrison

Elk Falls, Elk Co., Kansas
April 20th, 1879

Dear Friend Wm. Lloyd Garrison

Today is Sunday; I commenced to re-read your Beautiful Memorial to your precious Helen; and when I read the letter you presented her on her fiftieth birthday my tears of joy fell copiously and I determined not to group those noble countenances with others however much I may love them, for it would be too much like allowing my unholy hands to touch you.

I have devoted a frame to those pictures alone, in memory of that holy union that existed between you. I think that there are but few more perfect unions this side the Eternal World. Joseph Dugdale (you know him if you never saw him) said at my house, that he and his wife were married in time of flowers and they had lived in flowers ever since. Precious union! I need not thank you for those photographs for you know that I appreciate them.

My little grand niece nine year old Lorena B. Keith is committing that printed sheet to memory and will speak it in school.

You do not say when you spoke of grand children whether they lived with, or near you. However that may be, they, and the coming generation "will rise up and call you blessed." I have not written to your brother George, for I thought I would ask you if he was married and whether his sister's husband was living for I hardly know how to address them. Will you have the kindness to tell if Wendell Phillips' lecture on the Lost Arts has ever been published?

If so, I have never heard of it, and I thought it would be very interesting if it could be obtained. How many many of your early co-workers have gone to the higher life — C.C. Burleigh, Geo. Thompson and a multitude of others. I know it is impossible for you not to be interested in the woman suffrage question for it comes under your ban of Liberty for all. I am interested in your Boston lady workers particularly in Mrs. Howe, She is such an advocate of the peace question. Perhaps I am taxing your valuable time too much to ask you to answer this, but if you can conveniently at some leisure moment I would be much obliged. I saw in some paper that a company of colored persons are about to make a settlement in the Indian Territory west of Kansas.

I almost wish I could go with them. My health is very good and if I should continue to enjoy the same till they get settled I am sure that I shall visit them some time. Indians often camp in a grove on the stream called the Wild Cat, in sight of our door. We are 25 to 30 miles only north of the Indian Territory.

Truly yours, and may the white dove of peace rest upon you is the prayer of your admiring friend Prudence C. Philleo.

May 10th, 1879

Since the first date of this sheet I have heard that the colored people from the south are by scores coming into Kansas — but I have heard of none near us — but quite a number have been sent to Topeka.

It was with some misgiving that Prudence saw her niece Clarissa married to Mr. Hannant. Clarissa had been divorced from Henry Keith for several years and had lived with Prudence since joining her in Cordova in 1873. Prudence knew she would miss Lucy, Willie and Rena. The Hannants continued to live in Elk Falls so the children visited their Aunt and Grandfather every week.

That she was still active and concerned with public affairs is obvious from a letter she wrote to her great niece Josephine in Mendota.

Sunday P.M. Elk Falls
July 25, 1880

"My dear Josephine:

I this morning received your very welcome letter for which I sincerely thank you. How I wish you could come and make us a long visit. We should enjoy the visit so much. We have excellent *health in this climate. I like this part of Kansas very much indeed. Kansas is 400 and 200 broad and it bids fair to be one of the most noble states in the Union. There seems to be a thought in the hearts of the people for the best interests in humanity. I think the governor of this state with other officials have shown themselves to be noble men in relation to the Exodus. There are but few colored persons who have come near here as yet. I understand there is a family not far from us and Aunt Clarissa and I have agreed to go to see them before long. Grandpa, Aunt C. and myself went to see a milk factory last Thursday about 3 or 4 miles north of us where they milk 84 cows. I will assure you it was no small sight. Their cheese brings them $12 per day — they sell for 10¢ a pound — they were loading a wagon at the door to go to market. The name of the family is Chafee and to our utter astonishment we found that the father of the firm was a grandson of my mother's brother Daniel Carpenter. He was the eldest son of my grandfather by his first wife and my mother the youngest daughter of his last wife. Uncle Dan loved my mother very much. She played with his children and his last wife was my Grandmother's sister Thankful so you see that Father and son married sisters. The state normal school is now in session at Howard, our county seat eight miles away, and next Tuesday if the day is pleasant Grandpa will take Lucy Jane and me to spend the day at the school. The last year the school was in Elk Falls.*

There is a nice Hotel built at the Depot where four trains a day stop to take meals. It is quite surprising to see the amount of cattle that are passed though here on the trains together with every type of train you can mention. With this I mail the Elk Falls Signal for Montie. I wish you would write to me. Markie wrote me a long time ago and I answered very soon after and I was very glad to do so. I never shall forget how kind he was to me when I was there with my dear old mother, together with all the rest of you.

I think you have all remembered us here in Kansas with many specialties; I think of you every day when I put that nice brown bonnet on my head and that splendid brown apron I wear every forenoon. It is the most valuable apron I ever had. I cut one just like it for afternoon.

My old clock keeps excellent time and I generally get my work done by the time the 8 o'clock train comes in so I have a pretty easy time with no one to wait upon but Grandpa and myself. Willie and Rena are here today. They were here last Sunday and Sunday before. Rena is coming soon to make her a scrap book of the stories that she has been reading for a long time in the Windham County Transcript. She has read them with great interest ever since we have been in Kansas. Your cousins Keith are all smart children I will assure you they will make their mark in this little world of ours some day. I think such folks that are industrious are good and the world will be better for their living in it . . .

Lucy Jane is learning fast, cuts and makes anything for herself and all the family.

Peaches have been in the market a long time and are said to be plenty through the country but our trees were killed with the frost last year and why they do not bear this year I do not know unless they stand too near together. We have had a fine season so far. Our land is rented to wall in what is plowed and it will be finished according to agreement. Our cattle are doing well. We have had 9 head and will have two young calves in the course of a month so we shall have butter as we did last winter. It will pay for making in the winter and it will bring cash.

William Smith has gone to Colorado. He says wages from 80¢ to $2 per day and board from $6 to $10 per week but he cooks his own grub and it costs $2 per week. I am glad Anna Smith has written you. I wish she could come here and open a school. I think she would find it a fine place.

Wed. July 28

We went yesterday to Howard and had a grand time among the professors. I wanted to stay the balance of the school but had to come home to attend to the cares of the body. I expect to enjoy life when I get to the spirit world and leave this body behind which is made up of what I eat and drink. I saw a beautiful colored girl at the school. Her name was Calla Swindle. She said she rode into town on horse back every day and took her dinner at the hotel . . .

Any one having a large self esteem as I have likes to be appreciated. I thank you for your opinion that some of my compositions are worthy of a place in your scrap book. At this time I cannot write or copy anything for you with conveneince but some time I will give you all you can preserve. I look forward to the time when Markie is coming to Kansas as he wrote me. How I wish you and Josie could come with him. I wish John's land was as far south as we are. I do like this climate so much . . .

Yesterday while we were gone to Howard the freight train gave a big smash on cattle and among the number was one of the oxen we sold to Mr. Bennet for making the Wall so the wall will have to wait a while. The wall is made on the south west and north and partly on the east side so I think it will be done in due time. I have a swamp of morning glories — red, white and blue in our flower beds. Some zinneas, some marigolds, hollyhocks, asparagus. In the yard we have many wild flowers all summer through . . .

Among Rena's scrap book items were several poems one which was set to music by someone named Williston.

Jonathan's Vision

I on my couch recumbent lay
And by the moonbeam's pearly ray
I saw my loved one glide along
As with a sweet enchanting song,
She smiled on me or as it seemed
Oh, tell me not it was a dream.

For soft the evening zephyrs played
In robes of light she was arrayed
Pure love was beaming from her eye
She bid me ne'er the truth deny
Then smiled on me or so it seemed
Oh, tell me not it was a dream.

She sang the glorious time to come
When all shall say 'Thy will be done'
The prisoner leaps to break his chain
And parted loved ones meet again.

Say what is wealth or talents rare,
Or what can with my love compare.
Her glowing radiance so divine
Has calmed this fearful soul of mine.

... ...

In an earlier spring she had revealed a more wistful mood.

A Lover's Wish

I wish I was a courting
My heart is full of love

I wish I had a lover
I'm longing to be loved.

The happy birds are mating
The mother builds the nest
She makes a pretty circle
For her darling ones to rest.

I wish I was a courting
I love a home so well
I wish I had a lover
To come with me to dwell.
The cage I have is ready
The bird is not in store
How long shall I be waiting
To be loved and to adore.

All nature looks so smiling
So beautiful and gay
I wish I had a lover
To smooth life's thorny way.

I wish I was a courting
I'd never more be sad
To be loved and to be loving
Would always make me glad."

... ...

Contacts with the East were resumed from time to time. In December of 1880 she had a letter from Suffield:

"Respected Madam,

I am preparing a history of the 2nd Baptist Church in this place and of its ministers. Your deceased husband accepted a call to preach here in August 1825 and continued until the close of the year 1829. He was often a welcome visitor at the home of my Father and Grandfather during that period and I think visited them once after his marriage with yourself, in company with you. He also came here once after he met with an accident by burning. Mr. Philleo was very successful here, was a good extempera speaker, a fine singer and drew crowds of hearers. He had some

Eccentricities — was keen, shrewd, witty and aggressive, but kind and generous. He was then about 40 years of age — in manhood's full prime. —

"I remember his very features, expression and form as though it were yesterday. I was but 10 years old, but the subjects of some of his sermons I still remember.

"My father who was about his age was an intimate friend. Of Elder Philleo's history since he left Suffield I can learn but little. May I ask of you the favor to supply for me an abstract or sketch of his life since that time; with dates, etc. May I also ask the favor of some questions pertaining to your own history.

H.S. Sheldon

Prudence wrote to Emma sending her Mr. Sheldon's letter and saying:

"I send you Mr. Sheldon's letter of inquiry . . . I have in moving around in this little world of ours lost my marriage certificate and do not know the day of the month. You will recollect the time I brought you the bouquet of flowers — you may have some date that you can refer to. Do, Dear E. answer him, you can do it so much better than I can. The first time I ever saw your father he came to my school as a friend of the colored people."

It was a source of satisfaction to Prudence to know that her husband was still remembered after all these years. She found, too that she was also remembered. A clipping was sent her of a letter to the Mendota paper from one of her former students.

1-14-1881
Ophir, Ill.

"I saw in your paper of the 14th, some lines composed by Mrs. Prudence C. Philleo. Few, if any, know that lady better than myself. Fifty years ago, she taught me my ABC's. I learned then to love and respect her. Those feelings never ceased. She is of the noblest of women . . . In my opinion she did more to break the shackles of slavery than all the Presidents of the United States put together; for what she did she did from choice; what they did 'twas of necessity. When she throws off the mortal coil, wherever it may be there should be a granite slab erected, that time cannot deface, and there upon should be inscribed "Here lies the casket that once

contained the mother of American Liberty for the slave.

Yours respectfully
Dan Carr"

(Dan Carr lived in Plainfield, Connecticut as a child.)

Prudence read with interest but thought it seemed a pretty exaggerated view of her efforts! It was good to be remembered and well thought of and her work with the colored girls did have far-reaching effects. She had recently heard from Mary Harris, now Mrs. Williams who was teaching colored people, young and old, in Greenburg, Louisiana. Her husband was also teaching and one of her sons had supervision of six schools in New Orleans.

Changes in her home situation took Prudence's attention. Her 80 year old brother was taken sick and died on March 22nd. The letters she wrote to his sons and daughters record his last days and her anxious care of him.

Elk Falls, Kansas — March 15, 1881
12 o'clock at night

Dear O.B.

Grandpa is quite sick with numonia fever. — though we think him better than he was — He was taken sick last Friday morning — He went out to do the feeding as usual, came in to breakfast, but did not eat but a little. He soon wanted to lie down and I discovered that he seemed to be trembling very much — I thought perhaps he had taken with an ague chill; but he said he was not cold . . . Sunday we sent for Dr. Olney he sounded his lungs, but he said the air did not pass freely in the left lobe of the lung . . . The Dr. said it was a case of real numonia fever and if he was a young person nothing alarming but how it would terminate with him he could not say — Monday Dr. came again and said he thought him better, but he must be closely watched . . . Dr. Olney is a regular M.D. and a man of much experience; he will be here this forenoon and seems to understand his case exactly and will not leave him till he is out of danger. Father says tell O.B. that if he gets well enough he wants during the summer to go to your house and on his way to visit John and his wife and see their farm — for he can never do chores another winter and if he does not get well then he will die here. I am glad if he has found out that he ought to keep quiet in the winter — I have watched him all the winter as you would a babe begged him not to be out in the night but if he must do the chores to get them done before the chill of the night came on but all I could say to him made little or no difference to him — If I said a word against his working plans it made him very unhappy — A few days ago he wanted to go digging stone — I told him he was no more fit to dig stone than a baby — Later part of the winter I would not let him cut the wood at the door I got Mr. Bennett to cut it — the man that engaged to make the wall. I have Mr. Henry Fraley to take the plow land and rent the cattle on shares as William rents to Mr. Hannet — He has a wife and baby — They have moved into the house with us, so we are not alone. Will write often

Aunt P.C. Philleo

12 o'clock at noon Grandpa sat on the side of the bed drank tea and eat some boiled rice with sauce on it. He was quite tired when he lay down he seems to tremble a good deal. He takes medicine just as the Dr. directs I leave nothing out of his bill of comforts. He has lemons, rice cracker, Brandy, Etc., Etc. . . .

. . . .

Elk Falls Elk Co. Kansas April 12, 1881

"Dear Ester and Huldah

I presume Obediah has given you the particulars in relation to the sickness and death of your father which occurred so suddenly . . . Sunday I sent for the doctor and he pronounced his case Pneumonia fever. He had been tanning some hides and I think he put his hands into cold water is the way he took such a sudden cold, but I do not certainly know it — he tanned one hide with the hair on and he washed that in cold water I know. When he had been sick the fourth day I told him I was writing to O.B. that he was sick. He said to tell Obediah that if I get well next summer I want to come to his place and on my way to stop and see John and Magie and their farm but if I do not get well I shall die here — Whenever he was unwell his voice would always grow weak and as soon as he was better his voice would be strong again. Now his voice kept growing weaker till it was difficult to understand what he said.

Some Baptist friends with whom he was acquainted came to see him and he wanted the Hymn sung that was sung to Mr. Garrison by his children when he was dying. The hymn was sung

— it commenced "Ye Tribes of Adam Join" and the hymn "Nearer My God to Thee" was then sung also. He wanted them to pray with him and Mr. George Brigham knelt down near the bed and made a prayer — His voice was so weak he could not talk much but I understood what he said and told them — The dear man's anxiety for the iniquities of this world is done and I have no doubt of his happiness in the world to which we all hasten — especially myself. He is eighty years and six months old the 22 day of March the day he died.

The bed that brother had without pillows or sheets I gave to Clarissa. He had one bed quilt which I presume your own dear mother pieced — and a blue yarn coverlet which I know was your mother's. When convenient I will send them to you. Your father said two or three years ago that Huldah wanted that coverlet and he wanted that she should have it. He had one other quilt but it is so worn that it is not worth sending to you — it has been worn on his bed for so long — He brought no sheets from Connecticut with him. I would be very glad to have letters often from you all . . .

A family moved in with us a few days before your father was taken sick otherwise I should have been alone.

Your affectionate aunt
P.C. Philleo

Obediah and his sons, Mark and John Crandall called on Prudence soon after Hezekiah's death. They were worried about their aging aunt and would have been happy to take her back to Illinois. It seemed wrong for her to be alone among strangers, but she was still very independent and wanted to stay in her own home. She felt that she had made a place for herself in this community. They had asked her to read the Declaration of Independence on the Fourth of July. The Bennet boy and some others came to her for lessons. Clarissa and her chidren were frequent visitors.

Reluctantly her nephews left her and returned to their own homes, little thinking that this dear old soul would again gain nation wide attention.

She still dreamed of being useful to the colored people. The author of a genealogy of the Philleo family, David Van Hoosear, wrote to her for information about Calvin and added a foot note from her reply: "I have great hope yet — may I live to see it — a college built on my farm for all classes and colors, particularly the chidren of colored wanderers. I want professorships of the highest order."

The wanderers were many. By 1880 there were 43,107 colored people in Kansas. Some 20,000 of them had been lured there by false promises. One man was largely responsible for inducing some 7,000 to settle in three colonies — Dunlop, Singleton and Nicodemus. Property was available because first settlers had left the state after serious drought. They had gone to the more lush lands in Oklahoma. The Blacks came as share croppers but the soil was so poor that they were hard pressed to earn even a very poor living. In spite of the obstacles they faced the 1880 census had shown that there were 15,834 colored teachers and 16,800 schools for colored children in the country.

Benefactors had come forth to help them. Prudence was greatly impressed to learn that John F. Slater, an industrialist of Norwich, Connecticut had given a million dollars for the Christian education of the lately emancipated people and their descendents in southern states.

In the many years since the Emancipation Proclamation, Blacks throughout the country had faced many hardships and it was evident that their problems would be serious for many years. At least legal chattel slavery had been wiped out.

Some of the other causes with which Prudence had long been concerned were also meeting with a measure of success — at least in Kansas. A prohibition act had been passed in 1881; more recently a Woman's Suffrage Society had been organized.

On Sept. 2, 1884, a reporter named Mariana T. Folson interviewed her and wrote: "Prudence Crandall today is as vigorous an advocate of Woman Suffrage and temperance as of anti-slavery in the olden time. She has instituted a Temperance Festival among the people of her neighborhood. This Festival uses bread and honey with water for the body and intellectual exercises for the brain. The first meetings were held in her own home but last year the company had outgrown a private dwelling and adjourned to the school house where the fourth annual meeting will be held in February 1885."

Not only could she organize meetings but she could speak forcefully. On the Fourth of July in 1884 she had addressed the largest audience she had ever faced. Published reports indicate that there were 2,000 people who had gathered at the fair grounds from throughout Elk County. From the bandstand she had spoken to them of the glories of the country and the strivings for freedom which made it great. They had listened to her for nearly an hour.

Exhausted but exhilirated she had been accompanied by Abraham Williams back to her house. Mr. Williams was a young man who had come to Elk Falls for the Government to study and report on the weather. He had lived at Prudence's farm, taking care of the property and doing the chores since the Hannet family had left soon after Hezekiah's death. Better educated than most of her neighbors and with a knowledge of science, Prudence found him an interesting person to have around. He stayed on after Clarissa left her second husband and came back to her aunt. Her children had left Elk Falls and were living with their father in Sheldon, Missouri.

Prudence missed the children. Their visits had brightened her days. She still had little George Bennet who came by frequently. One day several children from the village school were brought to pay her a visit. As they went up the path each child tried to avoid being first. Hearing them she hurried to open the door before anyone quite reached it. She had just come into her house and was still wearing her large brimmed, low crowned black hat which tied under her chin. In a very few minutes the children were clustered about her, listening to her stories of long ago. When they left she sat quietly for a while reflecting on the story she had told them, wondering how long they would remember it and wondering too, if any one would remember it for many more years.

Prudence continued to write poems and relate them to her broad philosophical interests. Here is a clipping from an unidentified newspaper, name and date not attached, found in a family scrap book.

"Mrs. Prudence C. Philleo Heard from Again

I am 81 years old and am greatly interested in the success of Women's Suffrage and the National Liberty League, the object of which is to settle difficulties by arbitration. The following is my prayer.

God bless the Liberty League forever,
Let the champions of the field
Boast a glorious work accomplished
And the contest never yield —
'Till the world redeemed from bloodshed
The brotherhood of man shall own,
AND THE ORPHANS AND THE WIDOWS
Cease with tears to sigh and mourn.
Let arbitrators pass in honor
Through the battlefields of strife,
And the milk of human kindness
Show the sacredness of life.
Deal in justice with the erring,
Never hide a fault they see
But in love and truth confiding
Help the erring bend the knee
Help the nations rule in justice,

No more tyrants to betray,
No more lift the hilted sword,
And in wrath a brother slay,
Trust in God and help the nations
Universal peace proclaim
Then by no revengeful anger
Shall the enemy be slain.

... ...

The Flag of My Country

The flag of my country
With firmness I hold
I am proud of my country
They are fearless and bold,

In glory and honor
May this flag be unfurled
'Till justice and freedom
Shall encompass the world.

(Hand written, no date or indication that it was published.)

PRUDENCE CRANDALL PHILLEO, 1874

CHAPTER EIGHTEEN
ACTIVE TO THE LAST

ASSURANCE came unexpectedly that her story would not die out very soon. The September 1885 issue of "The Century Illustrated" carried a reproduction of her portrait and a long article about her by Wendall Garrison, the son of William Lloyd Garrison. It was entitled "Connecticut in the Middle Ages."

In this article Prudence read for the first time how her portrait became the property of Cornell University and that the story of her school in Connecticut was known to a noted German scholar and author.

"President White kindly furnishes the following: I first knew the portrait, as perhaps you did, when it hung in the parlor of Mr. May's house at the top of James Street Hill in Syracuse. He had a special affection for it and told me the story of it, I being then in my boyhood . . . On the last afternoon of Mr. May's life I called on him. He was very cheerful, insisting that he had but a short time to live, that he was very glad of it, that he had seen slavery abolished, that his work was done and that he would confess to some curiosity as to the beyond! I insisted that we could not spare him for 10 years yet and in a jocose way he asked me if I could not compromise on three to five years. He then called his daughter and pointing to the picture above him, told her that when he was gone that picture must be sent to me at Cornell. The next morning to my great surprise, news came that he was no longer living . . ."

"When Professor Von Holst, of the University of Freiburg, the author of the well-known history of the United States was in this country, I invited some gentlemen to meet him at dinner in New York and next to him sat the Hon. Lafayette S. Foster, formerly president of the U.S. Senate! . . . A man as you will remember, very much respected throughout the country for his character and ability. In the course of our conversation he said something about Windham in Connecticut, whereupon I asked him if he had ever known anything about the Prudence Crandall case. He smiled as he answered that he was her junior counsel and gave me interesting details regarding the matter. Thereupon I turned to Von Holst and said 'There is one point in American History which I dare say you never heard of' when to my great surprise he showed that he knew the whole case thoroughly in its details and bearings. I never realized until then how minute the knowledge of a German Professor in his chosen department could be made."

For Prudence the publication of this article started a chain of events which changed her circumstances in many ways. Her fame rippled over the country again. Professor James H. Canfield at the University of Kansas submitted to the "Topeka Daily Capital" (10-18-85) an account of an interview with her of some of his students and excerpts from some letters:

". . . I have received reports from some of my students who have paid her most sincere homage at her own home. The last, something over a year ago speaks of her as keen-eyed, quick in her movements with some reserve when speaking of herself and her past but with exceptional conversational powers, full of energy and zealous in all good works. She feels sadly alone in the world and calls herself 'The Last Leaf on the tree' . . .

"It is quite possible that your readers may be interested in these facts. I beg leave to add a few quotations from some of Mrs. Philleo's somewhat recent letters . . . How natural it is that such a woman with such a history and with the old fire still in her veins should be spending her declining years in this tempest-born-freedom-loving state!

" 'Born and bred abolitionists can never feel as strangers to each other, though they never have the pleasure of personal acquaintance' she wrote . . .

" 'My house though comfortably warm is made of rough boards on the outside and planed over on the inside.'

". . . 'I am earnestly engaged in the temperance cause, Women's rights question and indeed every reform for the good of the human race. I like Kansas very much, my humble dwelling is one of the most beautiful spots on earth . . . I feel like one alone in the world but I have great hopes of the future good that I may do before I die in the way of schools for the poor and needy and shall do what I can to have my farm made useful in that way. The aspirations of my soul to benefit the colored race were never greater than at the present time. I hope to live long enough to see a college built on this farm into which can be admitted all classes of the human family, without regard to sex or color' . . .

"Your readers (concludes Professor Canfield) ought really to take a second look at the excellent Cornell picture of the young heroine."

At about this time Prudence had a visitor from Canterbury. Mr. John S. Smith who had heard of her experiences from older relatives and neighbors, was aghast at the contrast between her poor Kansas home and the house she had had to leave in Canterbury. While visiting with her he suggested that he would see what might be done by Canterbury or Connecticut people to make up for her troubles.

Prudence carried on an active correspondence with him for several months. Her first letter was written when she was eighty two.

Elk Falls Co. Kansas Nov. 3 1885

"Dear Friend Mr. J. S. Smith

Now about that petition to the Conn. Legislature. What would you advise me to do? Take the case exactly as your own. I shall never plead poverty — for with industry and the economy that I daily practice I have enough to lay me honorably in the grave — I would be glad to enjoy a few of the luxuries of life such as taking the cars occasionally, visiting old friends and the colored people scattered in many parts of this state whose cause has ever been dear to my heart. It would be a great pleasure to visit the colored people in the cities where I have been some what acquainted in former times — some of my former pupils still live and when I hear from any of them I am always highly gratified.

My plea will be for justice. When a state has falsely imprisoned an innocent citizen and passed unconstitutional laws by which they are harassed and property destroyed it's right they should compensate the abused. I wish to make no exorbitant demands I would willingly leave the amount of compensation to their honor and I would be content. I feel that it is a duty I owe myself and also to the State to ask for redress for such slander and abuse as I have received at their hands. In case you think favorably of the petition what is the course to be pursued? . . .

I am sorry to trouble you in the least and if you can say to me what to do I will do as you say. Where does your Legislature meet this year? New Haven is not as good a place as Hartford. I do not know your smart lawyers. I suppose the case must be spoken to by somebody — I could do it my self if I were there — I cannot pay a big price to some one to speak for me — I presume somebody can be found to speak for me on consideration and if they get nothing let that end the matter. If you say go ahead then I will write a petition and send it to you for inspection and if it is not all right, correct it and send it back and I will copy, sign and return —

I suppose I have no time to delay to have all things right and done in good time.

Yours truly
Prudence C. Philleo

Consult some of your wise friends and see what they will say in relation to the petition.

A second letter followed very soon.

Elk Falls Elk County Dec. 2nd 1885

"My very dear Friend

I thank you so much for every kind suggestion and I feel sorry to have you sacrifice so much time and care and thought for me. You shall be amply rewarded for all, if there is anything obtained.

What I demand is on the score of justice. Of want in the sense of charity I do not plead. Of the $70 you were so kind as to loan me to put a fence around land on which I have to pay taxes without getting profit from it I have $25 I can pay any time and the remainder will surely come.

Beef is very low and pork too. But I think with care and economy that is my pleasure to practice I shall never be in want for bread. Some of the luxuries such as owning a horse and buggy to take me where I wish to go, and not walk or be dependent on some good friend to take me is what I much desire.

I deliver lectures on Woman's Sufferage, Temperance Spiritualism and the National Arbitration League — and a conveyance of my own would be solid comfort. I do not want anyone to give me one single cent, but I pray that revenge may never rest in my soul. That book I presume you will receive, for it was not mailed with the letter . . .

The petition is all right. Please give my best regards to Mr. C. Burleigh and thank him for writing that petition and any interest he may take in my behalf.

Love to you all
P.C. Philleo

The people of Canterbury were very busy during the week preceding the meeting of the General Assembly. Descendants of her former persecutors were chief among the signers and circulators of a petition urging that Prudence Crandall Philleo be given a pension to recompense her in part for the loss of her livelihood.

The Petition read as follows:

"We, the undersigned citizens of this State and of the town of Canterbury, mindful of the dark blot that rests upon our fair fame and name for the cruel outrages inflicted upon a former citizen of our Commonwealth, a noble Christian woman (Miss Prudence Crandall, now Mrs. Philleo) at present in straightened circumstances and far advanced in years, respectfully pray your Honorable Body to make such late reparation for the wrong done her as your united wisdom, your love of justice and an honorable pride in the good name of our noble state, shall dictate.

"It will be remembered that she stands in the Records of the Court as a convicted criminal for the offense of teaching colored girls to read and suffered unnumbered outrages in person and property for a benevolent work that now to its great honor the general government is enjoined in.

"We respectfully suggest that you make a fair appropriation in her behalf which shall at once relieve her from any anxiety for the future and from the official stigma that rests upon her name and purge our own record from its last remaining stain in connection with the colored race.

"And your petitioners will ever pray. Signed

Thomas J. Clark" (and many others)

(Thomas J. Clark was a nephew of Andrew T. Judson.)

Again the newspapers took up the Prudence Crandall story. The Hartford Daily Courant of Jan. 21, 1886 told at some length the history of the school and trials and brought it up to date by saying . . . "And now the citizens of Canterbury are petitioning the General Assembly to make some late and inadequate reparation for the wrongs done by Canterbury citizens partly with the aid of the Legislature to this noble heroic woman.

"For Humanity Sweeps onward,
Where today the martyr stands
On the morrow crouches Judas with
The silver in his hands
For in front the cross stands ready
And the crackling faggots burn

While the hooting mob of yesterday
In silent awe return
To glean up scattered ashes into
History's golden urn."

In spite of public sentiment in favor of the petition it did not have clear sailing. The "Hartford Courant," the "Hartford Times" and the "Hartford Post" all supported the petition with editorials as did the "New Haven Palladium" and out of the state papers including "The New York Sun," the "Springfield Union" and "Boston Transcript" all took up the cry when the matter was tabled.

When it looked for a few days as though the legislature might not act favorably on the pension, a news item in the "Courant" carried the information that a leading citizen had proposed that her former house be made available to Mrs. Philleo and that she be urged to return to Connecticut for her remaining years. The "Hartford Courant" of March 5 carried the story . . . "There are several philanthropic gentlemen who were interested in the case, who thought it would be poetic justice to purchase the old home of Miss Crandall where was her school and where she so bravely contended with her persecutors for nearly two years. The building still stands and on the changed feeling of the good people of Canterbury, it was thought it might be pleasant for her to return there and spend her few remaining years. A suggestion to this effect was made . . . A gentleman (Samuel Coit) afterward wrote to Mrs. Philleo on the subject. We publish her reply herewith because it shows that age has not dimmed her mental faculties or weakened her pluck and it also incidentally presents a vivid picture of the Connecticut school ma'am of 1833, now a widow of 83 years, patiently and cheerfully accepting her fate and preferring to make her own way than to be an object of charity. She writes:

" 'Dear Sir:

I thank you for your kind letter and your thoughtful remarks before the committee on appropriations in your State Legislature. The climate of Kansas, my adopted place of abode, is very congenial to my health which is very good for one of my age.

" 'I am very happy in my little pioneer box house of 3 rooms, situated in the side of a hill about a mile west of the little city of Elk Falls of which I have a view.

" 'The most of my farm is what is called second bottom laid open to the common last spring.

"Then I sent east to my kind friend Mr. Smith living a little distance from the village of Canterbury and obtained $75 to assist

me in putting a post and wire fence around the remainder of the farm for which I gave him my note, which is not yet paid. Whether I live or die that money will be paid for I have part of the money ready.

" 'I do not consider I am an Object of Charity. I do not want any person to give me one cent — but I do ask the Connecticut Legislature to pay me a little part of a just debt that I feel they are in duty and honor bound to pay. When my hopes and prospects were destroyed by an unjust and unconstitutional law I wrote to a dear friend Rev. Joslyn who was pastor of a colored church in New Haven that for me to beg I thought there would be no necessity.

Yours sincerely
Prudence C. Philleo' "

The "Hartford Courant" continues: "There is the Prudence Crandall of today. She is no beggar. She simply asks Connecticut for a 'little part of a just debt.' She is past four score years and can live but a few years at best. What should be done is to vote her a little annuity — not less that $500 and not grudgingly or as if it were a gratuity but as payment of a just debt. To plead the statute of limitations in such a case or to avoid doing justice on any pretext is beneath the dignity of the state and to neglect a golden opportunity to wipe out a foul blot on its record."

There were many prominent citizens who gave support to the effort for the pension. Samuel Coit, who had been one of her pupils in Plainfield, worked tirelessly. Rev. John C. Kimball printed a pamphlet called "Connecticut's Canterbury Tale" which he distributed to members of the Legislature. Rev. Twitchell of Hartford spoke and wrote in favor of the pension. Senator Marvin of Saybrook spoke very eloquenly, saying: "As the death of the martyrs was the seed of the church so truly was this oppression the seed of the anti-slavery movement." . . . Stephen A. Hubbard, publisher of the "Hartford Courant" led the press with editorial comments, news from the Legislature and reprints from newspapers throughout the country urging passage of the pension.

After having voted against the measure, the appropriation committee found the pressure from the public so great that they reconsidered. After a delay of several weeks during which this bill gained much publicity, the committee brought out the bill and it was approved. The amount was settled at $400 a year. The date of the first payment to be on April 1st. The bill was approved on March 31st.

She was notified by telegram and wrote a letter of thanks saying:

"What an amount of obligation I am under to the press generally and above all to those notable progressive persons who got up the petition at the first to be presented to their Legislature in my behalf.

"I wish to express my gratitude and thankfulness to that worthy body for their appropriation with which I am more than satisfied. In 1833 when the law was passed by which my life prospects were destroyed, it was celebrated by ringing the bell in the church into which we were not allowed to enter. And by firing a cannon 13 times, placed upon an elevation a few rods from my door: and today when your telegram arrived the only jubilant display I wished to make was to have a private nook where my tears of gratitude and joy could flow unobserved for the change that has been wrought in the views and feelings of the mass of the people."

After the legislature had acted favorably on the pension, the Hartford Courant (on April 3rd) revealed that Samuel Clemens was the man who had offered to lease her home and have Prudence return to Canterbury. Upon hearing this Prudence penned a letter of gratitude to him.

Elk Falls Elk Co. Kansas April 14th 1886

"Mark Twain

My very Dear Friend

God bless your dear heart is my prayer for you.

It is only lately that I ascertained that you were the person that offered to reinstate me in my home that I bought in the long ago in the town of Canterbury, Conn. It is a matter of great surprise that anyone could be so kind to an old woman like me whose days are almost done in the physical form. My admiration of your own dear self has not now just arisen but I have often thought of you ever since the city of New York paid to you their sincere compliments. I once borrowed of a friend Innocense Abroad and could keep it only long enough to read it partly through.

Would it be too much for me to ask you to give me a volume of the same, that I may be able to finish the book and loan it to others who are not able to purchase it that they too may learn from you, to describe the most trivial thing in such beautiful language as they can find.

I greatly desire your photograph to place under glass with dear friends but I must not ask too much.

Yours with very great respect
Mrs. P.C. Philleo

Elk Falls Elk Co. Kansas May 19th 1886

Mark Twain
Dear Friend

Excuse me for not thanking you before this date for your photographed countenance. You are not aware how greatly interested everyone is to whom I show the picture.

Mr. Samuel Coit, Major Kinney & Mr. Burnham of the Hartford Courant have sent each their photograph to me and now I am waiting to get one from G. C. Gimble and then I shall place you all in a group under glass that I can at any time look at the picture of those who have said and done so much for me during the last session of your State Legislature.

Mrs. P. C. Philleo with great
respect
Yours truly

Although she had written that her little farm was one of the beauty spots of the world, Prudence decided to leave it for a large house at 127 Osage Street in Elk Falls. She paid $850 for this house on April 9, 1887. The house was centrally located so that she could get out to stores or meetings.

She realized that she could never bring into being a school for colored young people. Clarissa was penniless and Prudence decided to leave her town property to her. On April 9 in 1888 some young men came by to witness her will and a deed by which she gave her farm to Abraham Williams whom she called her adopted son. These papers were witnessed by George Fain, M.F. Arnall and J.V. Blake.

Eulogies in the press continued. A Mr. J.C. Hebbard wrote in the "Capital Sunday Times:"

"In no one of the 100 counties of the great Commonwealth of Kansas is there a more precious human spirit than Mrs. Prudence C. Philleo, a venerable widow whose residence is a short distance west of the little city of Elk Falls — a place of 565 by the 1885 census . . .

"It may be said that John Brown who came to Ohio from Connecticut and from Ohio to Kansas as the most conspicuous man related to Kansas, among the defenders of the rights of human nature especially of those so long denied to the black man. May it not also be said that Prudence Crandall of Connecticut coming to Illinois as the wife of Calvin Philleo and from there to the prairies of

Kansas, most righteously deserves to have said of her by the people of Kansas 'many daughters have done virtuously but thou excellest them all.' "

"The Lantern" of Jan. 15, 1887 reported that:

"Recently this grand old heroine of Liberty was asked if she had ample means for her comfort to which she replied, "Oh, dear yes! I have a good farm just on the edge of town and it is well stocked. I have all the reading matter I want and all my faculties, except, you see I am a little deaf. I am comfortable and happy. My whole family has preceded me to the home beyond but I have an adopted son (Mr. Williams) of whom I am very fond and a niece living with me so you see I have nothing of which to complain.' . . .

Mr. Hebbard continues: "Now that this dear, old soul looks back upon her life work and her face lights up, she says that of all the acts or pleasures of her life she has the greatest satisfaction with one act of standing firmly before the mob of stones and tongues on behalf of principle as she has lived to see a triumph and be popular all over the nation. In her time the shackles have been torn from off the hands of four million black slaves and the land made one of freedom by constitutional provision, only achieved through a bloody civil war."

"Mrs. Philleo has been a woman of great beauty of person in her time and is still a woman of brilliant mind and a charming conversationalist. Her great desire now is to live to see the emancipation of her sex." . . .

In addition to recognition for her past work, Prudence won acclaim for her writing. A group in Chicago formed a literary club and named it after her. In March 1886, she wrote to its leader Mr. S. Laing Williams:

"Dear Friends:

I yesterday received from your worthy president a letter with information that a company of ladies and gentlemen had denominated their society the above named club . . . I only wish I was more worthy of the honor . . . With this I will mail you two pictures of myself — one taken from an oil painting when I was about 30 years old (paid for by the anti-slavery Society) and the other photograph of me in my old age. It would give me great happiness to meet with you in your associated capacity for it would be the delight of heart.

Yours truly,
Mrs. Prudence Crandall Philleo

Prudence continued to write.

An Address to Farmers
By P. C. Philleo

The meadow lark with song so cheery
And budding leaflets on the spray
Prophesy to every farmer
Of a golden harvest day.

Look ahead ye noble farmers
Fill your mission with delight
On you depends the fate of nations
While they jangle, strive and fight.

'Tis you that holds the nations commerce
Kings only rule by your consent
The proud professor holds his title
By the toils that you have spent.

The crown of princes are dependent
On the laborers' daily toil.
Count your blessings, noble farmers
Plowing up the fertile soil.

The crown of dignity and honor
Rests upon your noble deeds
For the thousands and the millions
That your labor only feeds.

Be not proud of your position
But humbly bow to Nature's nod
Remembering that an honest farmer
Is the noblest work of God.

Hope (1886)

George Thayer, a journalist from Connecticut was travelling by bicycle through the west. He called on Prudence and recorded his visit in a book called "Pedal and Path." . . .

"Mrs. Philleo came in and said cordially: 'I am glad to see any one from good old Connecticut!' As she removed her bonnet, it showed a good growth of sandy gray hair, smoothed back with a common round comb and cut straight around, the ends curling around in under and in front of her ears; medium height but somewhat bent and spare with wide blue eyes and a face very wrinkled and rather long. Her chin was quite prominent and she had a solitary tooth on her upper jaw . . .

"She smiled with her eyes and in a pleasant voice said 'Come, you must be hungry, coming so far' and she urged apple pie, ginger snaps, Johnny cake, potatoes, ham, bread and butter and tea on me in great profusion.

" 'Now come into the other room, I want to show you some pictures.'

"So talking every minute, we went into the sitting room, and drawing up rocking chairs we sat down cozily together. 'I am going to have these photographs of these noble men all put into a frame together. I don't want them in an album for I have to turn and turn the leaves so much. I want them in a frame so I can get the inspiration from them at a glance. This is Samuel Coit who did so much in my behalf last winter and this is S. A. Hubbard of the Courant. This is — Why I see you know these noble souls. Well I want to read you a letter he sent me.' and she slowly picked out the words of the writer who said, among other things that he would be only too glad to load her down with a number of his books and would send her a complete file of them. The letter was signed S. Clemens.

" 'And here is Major Kinney and George Sumner and Rev. Twitchell — you say you have heard him preach! How much I would give to hear that great soul speak' and she handed me Rev. Kimball's photograph and several others, every one of which were more precious to her than gold. In this collection were photographs of W. L. Garrison, Wendell Phillips and several other anti-slavery friends of hers. I noticed several others of Garrison framed and hung about the house. When I expressed the opinion that the amount of pension was too small in proportion to the injury inflicted she said 'Oh, I am so thankful for that. It is so much better than nothing. My whole life has been one of opposition. I never could find any one near me to agree with me. Even my husband

opposed me more than anyone. He would not let me read the books that he himself read, but I did read them. I read all sides and searched for the truth, whether it was in science, religion or humanity.'

"The last thing she said as I left her was, 'If the people of Connecticut only knew how happy and how thankful I am it would make them happy, too.' "

As though to vindicate her efforts in behalf of Women's rights, Elk Falls elected a complete slate of female officials in 1889. The mayor was Mrs. A. L. King. Councilors were Mrs. S. A. Beach, Mrs. Kate Fancher, Mrs. Maggie Hamilton, Mrs. Clara Henderson and Mrs. Anna Welty. The police Judge was likewise a woman, Mrs. Maggie Stout but she did not qualify on technical grounds.

Prudence watched this development with pride but she was too old and feeble to do more than watch. Her heart was tired out and with the complication of asthma she could live no longer. With Clarissa and a neighbor to care for her, she 'slipped out of her mortal coil' on January 28, 1890. Her passing is recorded in the "Howard Courant" of January 31, 1890.

Her grave in Elk Falls is marked by a substantial granite stone provided by her nieces. "Little George Bennet" faithfully decorated her grave each Memorial Day for seventy years, claiming "If it had not been for her teaching in my early youth, I should have grown up a fool."

PRUDENCE IN PERSPECTIVE

The story of Prudence Crandall has been told many times in newspaper and magazine articles and in two books (at the date of this printing). She is listed in all standard encyclopedias. Unfortunately myths and mistakes about her have been perpetuated. She has been referred to as a "fanatical spinster" and a "difficult wife." From her letters and letters of her relatives and friends, from diaries and reminiscences of members of her family we have tried to set Prudence in proper perspective.

If anyone was ever "called" to teach, she was. Wherever and whenever there was some one who needed to learn, she was ready to teach. In addition to the school which made her famous, she taught adults and children in Boston and Providence. She taught neighbor's children in Troy Grove Township, Illinois and Elk Falls, Kansas.

She was selfless in her devotion to her family. Marrying an older widower, she mothered his minor children and helped his grandchildren. For forty years she coped with a husband who was described by his own children as cruel, insane and incompetent. After eight years of dutiful wifehood under trying circumstances, Prudence escaped to Illinois. Periodically, however, she accepted him into her home out of a sense of duty to her marriage vows. Out of pity she contended with his eccentric behavior and wanderings and gave him tender care through his declining years.

The ramifications of Prudence's trials did not end with her demise. The stand that she took in attempting to integrate her school was vindicated 120 years later. Thurgood Marshall, the National Association for the Advancement of Colored People counsel, before the U.S. Supreme Court drew from the briefs of her counsel in 1834. The principles for which she sacrificed so much became the law of the land by the Supreme Court decision of 1954.

[1]See Appendix p. 232

JUDGE DAVID DAGGETT'S CHARGE TO THE JURY OCT. 1833

"You, gentlemen of the jury, have heard the evidence, and as it is your exclusive business to pass upon the facts, you will say whether or not they are true.

"If the facts are not proved to your satisfaction, then you may dismiss the case, for in that event you have no further duty to perform. If, however, you find the facts true, then another duty equally important, devolves upon the jury. It is an undeniable proposition that the jury are judges of both law and fact, in all cases of this nature. It is, however, equally true, that the Court is to state its opinion to the jury upon all questions of law, arising in the trial of a criminal cause, and to submit to their consideration, both law and fact, without any direction how to find their verdict.

"The counsel for the defendant, have rested their defense upon a provision of the Consitution of the United States, claiming that the Statute law of this state, upon which this information is founded, is inconsistant with that provision, and therefore void. This is the great question involved in this case and it should be submitted to your consideration.

"It is admitted that there are no provisions in the constitution of this state, which conflict with this act. It may be remarked here, that the Constitution of the United States, is above all other law — it is emphatically the supreme law of the land. From the highest court to the lowest, even that of a Justice of the Peace, all laws whether made by Congress or state legislatures, are subject to examination and when brought to the test of the Constitution may be declared utterly void. But in order to do this the court should first find the law contrary to the constitution . . .

"The act in question provides that colored persons who are not inhabitants of this state shall not be harbored and boarded for the purposes mentioned without the consent of civil authority and selectmen of the town. We are then brought to the great question — are they citizens, within the provisions of this section of the Constitution? . . .

"The persons contemplated in this act are not citizens within the obvious meaning of that section of the Constitution which I have read. Let me begin by putting this plain question. Are slaves citizens? At the adoption of the Constitution every state was a slave state. We all know that slavery is recognized in the Constitution and it is the duty of this court to take that Constitution as it is,

for we have sworn to support it. Although the term "Slavery" cannot be found in the Constitution yet no one can mistake the object of the 3rd section of the 4th article — "No person held to service of labor in one state, under the laws thereof, escaping into another, shall in consequence of any law or regulation therein, be discharged from such service or labor but shall be delivered upon claim of the party to whom such service or labor may be due.

The 2nd section of the 1st Article reads as follows. "Representatives and direct taxes shall be apportioned among the several states which may be included in this Union, according to their respective numbers, which shall be determined by adding to the whole number of free persons, including those bound to service for a term of years, and excluding Indians not taxed, three-fifths of all other persons.' The 'other persons' are slaves and they become the basis of representation by adding them to the white population in that proportion. Then slaves were not considered citizens by the framers of the Constitution.

"A citizen means a free man. By referring to Dr. Webster, one of the most learned men of this or any other country, we have the following definition of the term — 'Citizen: 1st a native of a city or an inhabitant who enjoys the freedom and privileges of the city in which he resides. 2. a townsman, a man of trade, not a gentleman. 3. An inhabitant, a dweller in any town, city or country. 4. In the United States it means a person, native or naturalized who has the privilege of exercising the elective franchise and of purchasing and holding real estate.' "

"Are free blacks citizens? It has been ingeniously said that vessels may be owned and navigated by free blacks and the American flag will protect them but you will remember that the Statute which makes this provision is an Act of Congress and not the Constitution. Admit if you will that Mr. Cuffee, a respectable merchant, has owned vessels and sailed them under the American Flag, yet this does not prove him to be a citizen as the Constitution contemplates. But that question stands undecided by any legal tribunal within my knowledge. For the purposes of this case it is not necessary to determine that question.

"It has also been urged that as colored persons may commit treason, they must be considered citizens. Treason may be committed by persons who are not entitled to the election franchise. If they reside under the protection of this government it would be treason for them to levy war or aid an enemy, as much as if he were a citizen.

"I think Chancellor Kent, whose authority it gives me pleasure to quote, determines this question by fair implication. Had the author considered free blacks citizens, he had ample opportunity to say so. But what he said excludes that idea." Judge Daggett then read from Kent's Commentaries Vol 2, p. 258:

"In most of the United States there is a distinction in respect to political privileges, between free white persons and free colored persons of African blood; and in no part of the country do the latter in point of fact participate equally with the whites in the exercise of civil and political rights." He then explained:

To my mind, it would be a perversion of terms to say that slaves, free blacks or Indians were citizens, as the term is used in the constitution. God forbid that I should add to the degradation of this race of men, but I am bound by my duty to say they are not citizens.

"I have thus shown you that this law is not contrary to the 2nd section of the 4th Article of the Constitution of the United States, for that embraces only citizens.

"But there is still another consideration. If they are citizens, I am not sure this law would then be unconstitutional. The Legislature may regulate schools. I am free to say that education is a fundamental privilege; but this law does not prohibit schools. It places them under the care of the civil authority and the selectmen and why is not this a very suitable regulation? I am not sure but the Legislature might make a law like this extending to the white inhabitants of other states, who are unquestionably citizens, placing all schools for them under suitable boards of examination for the public good and I can see no objection to the board created by this act.

"The jury has nothing to do with the popularity or unpopularity of this or any other law which may come before them for adjudication. They have nothing to do with its policy or impolicy. Your only enquiry is whether it is constitutional . . .

"You will now take this case into your consideration and not withstanding my opinion of the law, you will return your verdict according to law and evidence. I have done my duty and you will do yours."

ARGUMENTS BEFORE THE SUPREME COURT OF ERRORS JULY 1834

William Ellsworth made his statement. Speaking calmly but eloquently he said:

May it please the court — the statute on which this prosecution is founded prohibits setting up a school for persons of color — not inhabitants of this state, teaching them in any school without first obtaining the consent of the civil authority and the selectmen of the town where the school is situated. The record finds that the pupils in this case were born in the states of Pennsylvania, New York and Rhode Island of free parents and have recently come to Connecticut to attend Miss Crandall's school where they are taught the common and essential branches of knowledge.

The principle asserted in this law and indeed such is its very language that it is a crime for any individual to entertain a person of color not having a legal settlement in any town in this state (though he was born and ever lived in these states) having come here to pursue the acquisition of learning in a manner open, common and lawful to all in our population — white or colored. The condition imposed by the law will be found not to alter the character of the law as I have now asserted it to be. A power to license, implies a power to refuse — what one holds by permission he does not hold by right. And if the Legislature can delegate the power to license, it can exercise it itself, and hence may impose condition tantamount to exclusion or total denial. This statute, stripped of its appendages, makes the place of birth, the criterion of the rights of citizens of these states, it is not a question of color so much as state supremacy; if a state may exclude a colored citizen of another state, it may exclude a white citizen. The defense of Miss Crandall will be rested upon the unconstitutionality of this statute law of Connecticut and may be embodied under these heads.

1. These pupils are citizens of their respective states.

2. As citizens, the Constitution of the United States secures to them the right of residing in Connecticut and pursuing the acquisition of knowledge as people of color may do who are settled here . . .

If color in a citizen of New York is made the ground in Connecticut of political inequality, degradation and deprivation, the principle run out will justify at the pleasure of our assembly a like deprivation among our blacks. If not citizens and protected as such, they are aliens — their property may be confiscated and they may be driven from our borders as Turks or Chinese.

To the first position —

Are these pupils citizens of their states respectively? If they are white it is conceded they would be.

1. A distinction founded in color in fundamental rights is novel, inconvenient and impractical. Hitherto we have seen no such distinction; none in the ancient common law in England which justly boasts of her equal principles; none in that immortal instrument which our republican fathers put forth as the groundwork of all just government — The Declaration of Independence . . . The Constitution of Connecticut too, which this honorable court . . . has sworn to defend declares "all men when they enter into a social compact are equal in rights and that no man or set of men are entitled to exclusive public emoluments or privileges from the community." . . . I trust this distinction of color will not find a judicial sanction in Connecticut . . .

2. Such were not the ideas of our Fathers when the colored soldiers stood in the ranks of that army which achieved for us our liberty, nor when their names were enrolled on the pension list as many of them were, the testimonial that they had a country and bled for it . . .

The distinction of color would be as inconvenient as it is novel. Who can tell the proportions and mixtures of blood? We shall want a scale for the ascertainment of citizenship . . .

3. These pupils are human beings born in these states and owe the same obligation to the state and its government as white citizens.

There is in all the writers of public or municipal law one ancient and universal classification of the people of the country . . . All who are not born within the jurisdiction of a state are aliens. There is not to be found the least trace of any other distinction; no allusion to any existing in fact, none in principle . . . These writers . . . declare the settled law on this subject and the reasons of the law, and color no more than stature or age bears a relation to it. The distinction is not alluded to because it did not exist nor can it exist in the nature of things.

The classification grows out of the doctrine of allegiance, a tie by birth giving rise to rights and duties between the government and individual of the gravest importance and most permanent duration . . . If allegiance is due from our colored population, its correlative is due from the government, viz, protection and equal laws . . . Here, the free man of color may take his position and upon the immutable principles of justice and truth demand his political rights from that government which he is bound to aid and defend; he is not a citizen to obey; and an alien to demand protection. Nor is he an intermediate class. There is no trace of any such thing in the history, the laws or institutions of this country . . . To talk then of a nondescript class of people among us . . . to make a new classification of half-citizen and half alien is equally against reason, justice and policy . . .

We will now pass from the doctrine of natural allegiance which embraces all without distinction of color to the constitutions of the native states of these pupils; for the question is are they citizens of those states? If I am right thus far and we do not find in their constitutions any deprivations of fundamental rights attached to color, we may justly say there is no distinction. The 9th article of the Constitution of Pennsylvania declares, "That all men are born equally free and independent and have certain inherent and indefeasible rights, among which are those of enjoying and defending life and liberty, of acquiring possessing and protecting property and reputation and pursuing their own happiness." No slavery nor distinction of color in fundamental rights exists in the land of Penn . . .

The Constitution of New York contains no general declaration of the rights of the people unless it may be in the first section of Article 7. "No member of this state shall be disenfranchised or deprived of any of the rights and privileges secured to any citizen thereof unless by the law of the land or the judgement of his peers" . . .

The Constitution of Rhode Island is the charter given them by Charles II and embraces "all people that do or hereafter shall inhabit or be within the same." I can see no distinction in the constitutional rights of the people . . .

Again there is nothing in the Constitution of the United States nor in the Legislation of Congress to countenance the distinction of color . . .

When the Constitution of the United States was formed the 4th art. 2nd sec. had these words: "The citizens of each state shall be entitled to all privileges and immunities of citizens in the several states" . . .

Again, by the Constitution of the United States, color is no disqualification or impediment to naturalization. Congress can as well naturalize Asiatics, South Americans, Africans, as Europeans.

There is no constitutional distinction — all — all aliens can be adopted; but if our own colored population are not already citizens, they cannot be made so by Congress, and are worse than foreigners.

Again, all free persons alike constitute the representative mass of the people. The language of the constitution is, 'Representatives and direct taxes shall be apportioned among the several states which may be included in this Union, according to their respective numbers, which shall be determined by adding to the whole number of free persons,' &c., (art. 1 sec. 2) The represented mass is the true source of soveriegnty; to them is due the allegiance and the service of the citizens.

Again, does not the judicial as well as the legislative power of the constitution extend to people of color; among others, the judicial power is declared to extend to 'controversies between a state' and 'citizens of another state: between citizens of different states: between citizens of the same state claiming lands under grants from different states; and between a state or the citizens thereof, and foreign states, citizens or subjects.' Now, I ask if a man of color in New York or Pennsylvania should sue a white citizen in Connecticut in their Federal Court, would it be a good plea in abatement that one of the parties is a man of color? (Art. 3. sec. 2)

So the act of Feb. 21, 1799, granting patents for useful improvements, authorizes the issuing of a patent only to a 'citizen' — Cannot a man of color obtain one? — Such has been done, and he would be a bold officer, who should refuse one, on the ground of color. The act of 1831, on the subject of copy-right, is of the same character.

So the act of December 31, 1792, concerning the registering and recording of ships or vessels. It is enacted, that no vessel shall be considered or treated as an American vessel, unless she is owned and commanded by an "American citizen;' — men of color have owned vessels, and they have always been considered, American vessels.

So the act of Feb. 18, 1793, for enrolling and licensing vessels, for the coasting trade and the fisheries, a like oath must be taken by the owner, before she can be permitted to engage in the same — a 'citizen' only, can do it; but cannot, and have not men of color?

So the militia law uses the words, white male citizens; implying that there are no other citizens besides white ones; for else the word citizens would have been used. It is true colored people are exempt from military duty, but so are all persons under 18 or over 45, and all females; but, yet Congress can call all these into the army or navy, or militia; and none will contend that exemption from military service proves political inferiority.

So the act of May 28, 1796, for the relief and protection of American seamen, declares that any 'citizen' sailor can obtain from the custom house officer a certificate of his citizenship; men of color have often done this, and can again.

So the act of July 20, 1790, for the regulation of seamen in the merchant's service, provides, that every ship or vessel belonging to a 'citizen or citizens' of the United States, of a certain burthen, on a foreign voyage, shall, under a severe penalty, be provided with a medicine chest. Are not men of color bound to comply with this law?

So all the intercourse laws with the Indians, where they forbid any 'citizen' from trading with the Indians, without license, evidently reach people of color.

So it is worthy to remark that all our treaties with foreign nations, use the words citizen of the United States, as touching all our inhabitants, either in the imposition of new duties or the grant of new privileges.

These cases are enough to show that Congress, in its legislation, does not recognize the distinction of color; and I will venture to say that there is no case, where the word 'citizen' is used in the laws of these states, but people of color are included, however penal and severe are its sanctions. Now all this would be inconsistent with the idea that people of color are not citizens, but constitute a new class of human beings, neither one thing nor another.

Again, when Missouri was admitted into the Union, there was a clause in her constitution requiring her legislature to pass a law to prohibit free negroes and mulattoes from coming into the state. Congress required, a condition of her admission, that no law would be passed to keep out of the state any citizens of the United States; this, though not decisive, is strong evidence of the sense of Congress, as to the character of people of color. (Sarg. Con. Law 385.)

Looking, then, to the doctrine of natural allegiance — the Constitution of the United States — the legislative declarations of Congress — the treaties of the nation — the constitutions of the three states, in which these pupils were born, or the general sense of the country as to all free people; there is no reason to believe these pupils are not citizens in their birthplace — and, if citizens *there, then by the constitution of the United States they are entitled to 'all the immunities and privileges of the citizens of Connecticut' . . .*

We will next consider the objections urged against us.

1st, men of color cannot vote in Connecticut, therefore they are not citizens of Connecticut.

Well, they can vote in Pennsylvania and New York; if voting then is the criterion of citizenship, they are citizens there; besides, it appears from the constitutions of the states here before me, that colored people can vote in Maine, Massachusetts, Vermont, New Hampshire, New York, New Jersey, Pennsylvania, Delaware, Maryland, North Carolina and Tennessee . . . Voting is not the criterion of citizenship . . . No female can vote nor any minor but are they not citizens? . . .

On the trial below, the chief Justice drew an argument against our idea of a 'citizen,' from Doctor Webster's dictionary. I do not believe it was the intention of Mr. Webster to use the word in any technical legal sense as is evident from his definitions all taken together. General Jackson, at the battle of New Orleans addressed the blacks as 'fellow citizens;' so the mayor of the city of New York, in his recent proclamation, called upon all the 'citizens' to aid in suppressing the mob . . .

Again it is said Indians are not citizens. These pupils are not Indians. Indians have hitherto been treated as members of national tribes, in allegiance with the U.S. according to treaty stipulations and the intercourse law . . . In New York, before the late change in our Indian affairs, they were there decided to be 'citizens,' by a unanimous opinion of their Supreme Court, on the ground of the State having jurisdiction and the Indian owing allegiance.

Again, it is said, slaves are not citizens. These pupils are not slaves. The reason why slaves are not citizens is because they are held to be property and not men. The reason does not reach these pupils.

It is said in some states we find laws prohibiting the intermarriage of whites and blacks. The law is a wise one; but then it proves nothing: which party does it declare inferior?

Chancellor Kent was cited against us (2 Kent's Com. 39 71.2;) but there is nothing in his books to sanction the objection . . .

I will now consider the second point, viz: That these pupils are by the 4th article of the Constitution of the United States secured in the right for which they are now contending . . . If we may expel these colored citizens of New York today, we may the white youth of New York, in Yale College, tomorrow . . .

All are as it were, members of one government. And now let it not be forgotten, that whatever these immunities and privileges are, they are solemnly secured and guaranteed by the constitution; and let me add, it is the clear duty of this enlightened court to see that they are made so to these pupils, if citizens, as I have contended they are.

It was admitted, by the Court below, that the right to education is a fundamental right, and will it be questioned here? . . . Education is the first and fundamental pillar on which our free institutions rest, and it is the last privilege we will give up. And here let me add, that the restrictions of this law are exceedingly onerous and distressing to the parents of these pupils; shut out as these children are virtually from the schools of white persons, they have retired to a place by themselves, in deference to the prejudice against them — here they have sought out a virtuous and competent teacher to instruct them in the common branches of education, spelling, reading, arithmetic, geography and the like: — Their parents are able to do this — many of them are wealthy, and they feel, that by education their children will be happier and better fitted for usefulness among their depressed fellows, either here or in Liberia. And who, who will rise up to oppose this effort? Let our opponents act openly; let them pass a law to immure in like ignorance the colored population of our own state, and not attempt the same thing, by selecting the blacks of other states, under the pretence that educating them will fill our state with a vicious and pauper population. The moral sentiments of this community will not sanction the idea that a man of color shall not have, like the others, the right to direct, according to his ability, the education of his children. Mr. Wilberforce, aided by several benevolent individuals, established a seminary for colored people at Clapham, a short distance from London. Miss Crandall need not be ashamed to imitate his example. The people of this country forced the ancestors of our colored people from Africa; They have since kept their descendants in bonds and darkness, and now talk of rights, founded in the color and degradation of the Negro, as a justification for continued wrong, and the deprivation, this day attempted, on principle and morality.

Need I tell this honorable Court that we owe a debt to the colored population of this country which we can never pay, — no, never, never, unless we call back oceans of tears, and all the groans and agonies of the middle passage, and the thousands and millions of human beings, who we have sent and are sending, ignorant, debased and undone into eternity.

Chancellor Kent, 2 Kent's Com. 61, says, 'If citizens of one state remove to another, they are entitled to the privileges that persons of the same description are entitled to in the state to which removal is made and to none other. If, therefore, for instance, free persons of color are not entitled to vote in Carolina; free persons of color emigrating there from a northern state, would not be entitled to vote' . . .

But it is asked — may we not keep out of Connecticut, paupers and vagabonds, and have we not such laws of long standing? . . .

As to this ancient statute, my first remark is, that it was enacted before the articles of confederation or the present Constitution of the United States; when this state has a right to exclude the citizens of other states or colonies, for they then stood in no other relation than aliens. I find these provisions in an edition of laws as early as 1750.

My second remark is, that this law is contrary to the constitution of the United States and I am confident that it cannot be sustained. If the 4 art. Sec. 2 means anything, it does secure to a citizen of New York a right to come here, and remain here, if he offends against no general law; He cannot be whipped out nor carried out of the state because he has no legal settlement; he may present the shield of the constitution, and as Paul claimed the immunity of a Roman citizen, he may claim the immunity of an American citizen . . .

While it is urged that the state has power to pass the law now complained of, it should be remembered that it does not propose to keep paupers or colored citizens out of this state: This would have been too bold — hence they come here but they shall have a dangerous and vicious population!

But it is asked, may not the legislature superintend public schools; for they are instituted by the legislature, and sustained by public money? This I do not doubt, nor do I doubt that the legislature may superintend and regulate private schools as it does trades, professions, taverners, merchants and may all the pursuits of the citizens; this must be done on a general and equal law. Mere birth in another state cannot be seized upon as ground of distinction, discrimination and deprivation . . .

The truth is, there is nothing in the settled law of any free state in the Union to countenance the provisions of this obnoxious law.

Enough, however, may be found in the statutes of the slave states. For instance, the legislature of Louisiana have enacted 'that whosoever shall make use of language, in any public place, from the bar, the bench, the pulpit, the stage or in any other place whatsoever, shall make use of language in any private discourses, or shall make use of signs or actions, having a tendency to produce discontent among the colored population, shall suffer imprisonment at hard labor, not less than 3 years, nor more than 21 years, or death at the discretion of the court.' It has also prohibited the instruction of blacks in Sabbath Schools, $500 for the first offense, death for the second. Our law imposes a penalty of $100 for teaching a colored person in a Sabbath School, (having no legal settlement in this state) and $200 for the second offence. In Virginia 'all meetings of free negroes, at any school house or meeting house for teaching them writing or reading' are declared an unlawful assembly. These laws are all kindred in character; they call for universal denunciation, and well may we fear, that a righteous God will not let them pass unheeded or unavenged. And how, let me ask, can excitement be kept down, in the North, while such bloody and cruel laws are enforced against human beings like ourselves, of the same feelings, destiny and hopes. I regret most deeply, that the legislature of Connecticut, so distinguished for her republican feeling, and her attachment to universal education, has been a matter of astonishment and unfeigned sorrow throughout this country: nor has it escaped notice in England. It was an unlucky hour when it was devised and passed . . .

The law is not denied for its impolicy but for its unconstitutionality. Had I been a member of the legislature, I should have raised my voice against it. It is a most wanton and uncalled for attack upon our colored population; it opens wounds not easily healed; it exasperates to madness many who live among us; it strengthens the unreasonable prejudice already pervading the community against blacks; and, in short, it rivets the chains of grinding bondage and makes our State an ally in the unholy cause of slavery itself. Deep, deep are the feelings this moment in the slave states. The moral example of England in her late act of emancipation, — the practical effects of the emancipation of her slaves in the West Indies; the injustice and high offence against heaven of slavery itself, are spreading a gloom over the South, more awful and foreboding than nullification ten times told. Slavery is a volcano, the fires of which cannot be quenched, nor its ravages controlled. We already feel its convulsions; and if we sit idly gazing upon its flames, as they rise higher and higher, our happy republic will be buried in ruin, beneath its overwhelming energies.

Mr. Judson made the argument of the State. With his typical self-condident demeanor he said:

At the trial of this cause, before the Honorable Chief Justice, in the Court below, the facts having been proved, the counsel for the defendant interposed a claim, that the Statute upon which the information was founded, was a violation of the Constitution of the United States. The Chief Justice in his charge did not recognize this claimer, but instructed the jury that the law in question was constitutional. The jury returned their verdict against the defendant, and for this cause, a new trial is sought by the motion in error.

The original claim of the defendant is still maintained by her learned counsel . . . It shall be my humble effort to maintain that the law is constitutional, and the magnitide of the question will assure me of a pertinent hearing. Although this question may be one of vital importance to Canterbury, yet that interest is by no means confined to that town. Should this law be prostrated, this corporation may be prostrated too — the people may be driven away from their homes, and then the evils will but just commence. It is a question in which every town in this state, and every state in this Union, have an equal interest. Let the decision be against this law — let those principles so ingeniously urged by my worthy opponent, be once established by the judiciary, the consequences will inevitably destroy the government itself, and this American nation — this nation of white men, may be taken from us and given to the African race! In this question is involved the honor of the State — the dignity of its people — and the preservation of its name . . .

The objects of this law are plain. The first object of this law is to regulate schools for colored persons coming from other governments, and putting them under a Board of Visitors; and 2nd, if the keepers of such schools will not submit to such regulations, then to exclude them as a dangerous and destructive population . . .

It has ever been the policy of this State, to regulate all its schools, academies and colleges and subject them to strict visitorial power. The seeds of morality and virtue are first sown in our schools, and if neglected, the seeds of vice and immorality would undermine all that we hold dear, even the government itself. If in Connecticut we have any renown, it is because our fathers have watched over the education of youth with becoming solicitude. As early as 1717, a statute was passed by the General Assembly, establishing a Board of Visitors, such as this act contemplates. The act is in these words.

The civil authority, together with the Selectmen, in every town, or the major part of them, shall inspect, and they are hereby empowered and directed as visitors to inspect the state of all such schools as are, by this act, appointed to be kept within said town . . . And if said inspectors or visitors observe any such disorders, or misapplication of money allowed for the support of such schools, as will be likely to defeat the good ends proposed, they shall lay the same before this Assembly that proper orders therein may be given' . . .

The law in question goes back to the early policy of the State and takes the civil authority and Selectmen, as the proper board under this act . . .

There is an additional argument, founded in patriotism and love of country. Are we now called upon to adopt such construction of the constitution as shall render the country purchased by the blood of our fathers, up to another race of men? Then I would appeal to this court — to every American citizen, to say that America is ours — it belongs to a race of white men, the descendants of those who first redeemed the wilderness. The American name and character have been handed down to this generation and it is our duty to preserve that character and perpetuate that name. Let not the determination of this case aid those who are plotting the destruction of our constitution. It rests with the Court to say whether the country shall be preserved or lost and I leave it to them to decide.

Mr. Judson was followed by his colleague, Mr. Cleveland who spoke briefly in support of Judson's arguments.

Mr. Goddard presented the closing arguments for the plaintiff.

"The questions involved in the decision of this case are of immense magnitude and I regret that circumstances make it necessary to discuss them here and particularly at this time. It is singular indeed that occasion has never risen since the existence of our constitution in which the question whether the free, native inhabitants of the United States were citizens and been judicially decided. The circumstances that no such question has arisen, is to my mind high evidence that their rights to the privileges of citizenship are unquestionable; for numerous occasions have arisen in which those privileges have been exercised . . .

> *I do not come to advocate the claims of either of the great parties who are engaged in the business of emancipation, although the plan of educating free colored persons, and planting a colony on the shores of Africa; of sending thither free, intelligent and virtuous instructors to diffuse through a continent the blessings of liberty, science and religion; of commencing the work of renovating that continent, and in some measure repairing the wrongs which its colored inhabitants have suffered from the whites, is a plan which I have always considered grand in all its features; nor is it for me to say whether its execution has been thus far equal to its conception. But whether the views of those who adopt this plan be or be not more correct than the views of those who suppose that the cause of humanity as well as justice will be best promoted by the continuance of these people in the country of their birth, and elevating them to the condition of all other citizens is, for the purpose of this immaterial, as education lies at the foundation of both, and the adoption and execution of such laws as that against which we contend, will forever extinguish the benevolent exertions and hopes of all . . . This statute prohibits their being instructed — it takes away from them the privilege of being taught to read and write — it deprives them of all opportunity to acquire that knowledge and those habits which may render them good citizens, useful to each other and their country . . .*
>
> *It was the intention of those who framed the law to put down the school . . .*

Again, stating that the rights of all citizens were at stake, Goddard completed his argument.

DECEMBER TERM, 1856
DRED SCOTT V. SANDFORD
(OPINION OF THE COURT)

. . . And again, in 1833, Connecticut passed another law, which made it penal to set up or establish any school in that State for the instruction of persons of the African race not inhabitants of the State, or to instruct or teach in any such school or institution, or board or harbor for that purpose, any such person, without the previous consent in writing of the civil authority of the town in which such school or institution might be.

And it appears by the case of Crandall v. The State, reported in 10 Conn. Rep., 340, that upon an information filed against Prudence Crandall for a violation of this law, one of the points raised in the defence was, that the law was a violation of the Constitution of the United States; and that the persons instructed, although of the African race, were citizens of other States, and therefore entitled to the rights and privileges of citizens in the State of Connecticut. But Chief Justice Dagget, before whom the case was tried, held, that persons of that description were not citizens of a State, within the meaning of the word citizen in the Constitution of the United States, and were not therefore entitled to the privileges and immunities of citizens in other States.

The case was carried up to the Supreme Court of Errors of the State, and the question fully argued there. But the case went off upon another point, and no opinion was expressed on this question.

We have made this particular examination into the legislation and judicial action of Connecticut, because, from the early hostility it displayed to the slave trade on the coast of Africa, we may expect to find the laws of that State as lenient and favorable to the subject race as those of any other State in the Union; and if we find that at the time the Constitution was adopted, they were not even there raised to the rank of citizens, but were still held and treated as property, and the laws relating to them passed with reference altogether to the interest and convenience of the white race, we shall hardly find them elevated to a higher rank anywhere else.

SUPREME COURT OF THE UNITED STATES
OCTOBER TERM, 1953

The first comprehensive crystallization of antislavery constitutional theory occured in 1834 in the arguments of W. W. Ellsworth and Calvin Goddard, two of the outstanding lawyers and statesmen of Connecticut, on the appeal of the conviction of Prudence Crandall for violation of an ordinance forbidding the education of non-resident colored persons without the consent of the civil authorities. They reveal this theory as based on broad natural rights premises and on an ethical interpretation of American origins and history. *Four ideals were central and interrelated: the ideal of human equality, the ideal of a general and equal law, the ideal of reciprocal protection and allegiance, and the ideal of reason and substantially* as the true bases for the necessary discriminations and classifications by government. Race as a standard breached every one of these ideals, as did color. What was attacked was denial of human equality and denial of protection of the laws — denials inherent in any racial discrimination backed by public authority. Slavery was the arch evil in this respect, and the primary one, both because of the magnitude of its denials and deprivations and abridgments, and because these necessarily established a whole patten of discrimination based upon race and color alone. It was this pattern of public discrimination that was combatted no less than slavery. It had to be combatted because it was deemed a part of slavery.

Although neither slavery nor segregated schools was the issue in the case, the Ellsworth-Goddard argument is one of the classic statements of the social and ethical case for equality of opportunity irrespective of race. It gave immense impetus to the emerging concept of American nationality and citizenship. Fully reported and widely circulated as a tract, it soon became one of the fountainheads of antislavery constitutional theory. It figured prominently in Abolitionist writings throughout the 'thirties. In the spring of 1835, Judge William Jay, Abolitionist son of the first Chief Justice and one of the founders and vice-presidents of the American Anti-Slavery Society, devoted fifteen pages of his *Inquiry into the Character and Tendency of the Colonization and Anti-Slavery Societies* to a slashing attack on the trial court's decision.

SOURCES

LETTERS

Prudence Crandall's letters and those of her family are widely scattered. Several are owned by members of the Crandall family. Others are in the library at Connecticut College in New London, Ct. A few are in the Larned Collection in the Connecticut State Library. Two letters to Samuel Clemens are in the Mark Twain Collection at the University of California, Berkeley. One letter is in the Suffield Public Library in Suffield, Ct.

The Philleo, Norton, Goodwin-Whipple letters are in the Connecticut Historical Society Library, Hartford, Ct.

William Lloyd Garrison's letters are in the Boston Public Library and the Harvard College Library.

Jocelyn letters are in the New Haven Colony Historical Society and the Cornell University Library.

MANUSCRIPTS AND DOCUMENTS

The Stephen Coit Ledger 1812-1832, is at the Connecticut Historical Society Library. A later segment of it is in the Cheney Library in Manchester, Ct.

The Committee Report on the Brooklyn Jail, 1838 is in the Connecticut State Library. The Committee was chaired by Andrew T. Judson. The jail was found unfit for use.

Some documents concerning the Brig Hope are owned by members of the Crandall family. Others are in the library of the Maritime Museum, Mystic, Ct.

Trial records, warrants, arguments and findings are on file at the Connecticut State Library.

General Assembly records including petitions, passage and repeal of the Black Law (1833 and 1838) and granting a pension to Prudence Crandall (1886) are in the Connecticut State Library.

BOOKS

Carpenter, Amos Bugbee, *A Genealogical History of the Reheboth Branch of the Carpenter Family in America.* Press of Carpenter and Morehouse, Amherst, Ma. 1898.

Crandall, John C. *Elder John Crandall of Rhode Island and His Descendants*, New Woodstock, N.Y. 1949.

Dumond, Dwight L.' *Antislavery, the Crusade for Freedom in America*, University of Michigan Press, Ann Arbor 1961. (This is the source for the quote from Philip Pearl about "tears of blood.")

May, Samuel J., *Some Recollections of the Anti-Slavery Conflict*, Boston, Fields Osgood, 1869.

Thayer, George B., *Pedal and Path, Hartford Evening Post Association*, 1887.

Van Hoosear, David Fellows, *(Philleo, Fillow) Genealogy, Wilton, Ct., 1888.*

NEWSPAPERS

Christian Secretary, Hartford, 1834.

The Connecticut Courant, 1833-34; *The Hartford Courant*, 1838 and 1885, 1886.

Emancipator, New York, N.Y., 1833-34.

Howard (Kansas) Courant, 1889, 1890.

Liberator, Boston, Massachusetts, 1831-1848.

Mendota (Illinois) Reporter, 1853 Centennial Edition.

Norwich (Connecticut) Courier, 1833-34.

The Unionist, Brooklyn (Connecticut), September 5, 1833. American Antiquarian Society in Worcester, Massachusetts has one copy.

Windham County Advertiser, Brooklyn, Ct., 1833 and 1834.